RED AND RAW

Acknowledgements

AUTHOR'S DEDICATION
This book is dedicated to Steve Small, a rabid Red and an old mate from happy days when the merits of Tommy Lawrence and Bobby Charlton seemed like a matter of life and death; with thanks for starting me on a long and enjoyable road, and for the splendidly creative design of *Red And Raw*.

OTHER ACKNOWLEDGEMENTS
A mammoth vote of gratitude goes to Cliff Butler in Manchester and Adrian Killen in Liverpool, without whose help this book would have been a researcher's nightmare, and to Pat, Rosie and Joe Ponting, as ever. Thanks are due also to *(in alphabetical order):* Arthur Albiston, Kyle Barrett, Russell Beardsmore, Ian Callaghan, Phil Chisnall, John Connelly, Andy Cowie and all at Colorsport, Jack Crompton, John Doherty, Bill Foulkes, Jimmy Greenhoff, Steve Hale, David Herd, Gordon Hill, Roger Hunt, David Johnson, Alan Kennedy, Iain McCartney, Hannah MacDonald, Ralph Milne, Brian Pead, David Sadler, Tommy Smith, John Tuckett.

Opposite: Liverpool's Phil Babb
and Paul Scholes of Manchester United
keep the Red flags flying at
Old Trafford in April 1998.

RED AND RAW

A Post-War History of Manchester United v Liverpool

IVAN PONTING

First published in Great Britain in 1999
By Andre Deutsch Limited
76 Dean Street
W1V 5HA
www.vci.co.uk

A catalogue record for this book is available from the British Library.

ISBN 0 233 99369 X

Designed by Steve Small

Printed in the UK by Butler and Tanner, Frome, Somerset and London.

10 9 8 7 6 5 4 3 2 1

Jacket photographs:
© Colorsport: (David Beckham, Denis Law, Tommy Smith and The Shankly Gates);
Action Images: (Michael Owen);
Popperfoto: (The Munich Clock).

Contents

Foreword by Jimmy Greenhoff
(Manchester United 1976 to 1980)

ALTHOUGH every game is a big one when you are playing for Manchester United, none are more momentous than the annual clashes with Liverpool. In recent decades these confrontations have come to mean far more to fans of both clubs than the traditional local derbies against Manchester City and Everton. That became crystal clear to me during 1976/7, my first season as a Red Devil, which I was fortunate enough to round off by scoring the winner in the FA Cup Final at Wembley – against Liverpool.

Okay, I'll admit that my goal was not exactly the product of meticulous planning on the training ground. After all, Lou Macari's shot was going well wide when it bounced off my chest

and skewed over Ray Clemence and into the net. And if Tommy Smith, my fellow contributor to this book, believes I fouled him in the build-up, well, he's entitled to his opinion. Maybe we can discuss it over a pint some time!

The fact is that the goal stood and it was obvious that the joy of our supporters in lifting the trophy was magnified hugely by the fact that we had to beat those fellows from Anfield to lay our hands on it. Similarly, when I headed the winner against Liverpool in the semi-final replay at Goodison Park two years later, the celebrations were all the sweeter because of the identity of our opponents.

It has to be said that the fans' rivalry could get unpleasant at times, and you could feel it on the pitch. The atmosphere became white-hot but it didn't put you off. Rather it made the adrenaline flow more freely, inspiring you with an even greater will to win on behalf of all those people who were shouting for you. Even so, there was never bad feeling between the two sets of players, who were always ready to share a drink afterwards. I hope, and believe, that will never change.

In all honesty, during the four years I spent at United, Liverpool were a truly great side, both on paper and in reality, and we were always striving to get on terms with them. They were the yardstick against which the rest were measured. Everyone wanted to beat the top dogs, to nudge them off their summit, and we were no exception. After all, United had massive ambitions and expectations of their own.

When we played Liverpool we knew we would have to work our socks off to get a good result. We had to harass and pressure them the whole time, otherwise they would keep the ball all day and murder us. Every one of their players could pass the ball beautifully, and their central defensive pairing of Alan Hansen and Mark Lawrenson was as talented as any I have ever seen.

And yet, despite Liverpool's phenomenal record of success on the pitch, United continued to be classed as the top club in terms of glamour and worldwide support. Understandably, that stuck in the craw of the fans from Merseyside and I am sure that it fuelled the rivalry to the extent that any meeting between the two clubs took on the intensity of a cup final.

Since my day the balance of power, in terms of trophies, has shifted but the deep feeling between the two camps has not abated one jot. If anything, it has become even more marked. But we must always remember that it all boils down to a game of football and has to be kept in proportion.

In the long run, if the Liverpool fans who continue to approach me after all these years are anything to go by, there is absolutely no problem. They tell me that they hated me at the time for that lucky deflection at Wembley, but they are ready to hold up their hands and say 'Well done' for the semi-final header. There is no malice and that's the way it should be. For myself, I feel privileged to have played a part in such a long-running and fiercely fought sporting contest. Long may it continue.

Jimmy Greenhoff

Foreword by Tommy Smith
(Liverpool 1960 to 1978)

IT might surprise a few people to discover that I could easily have been writing this foreword from the other side's point of view. Not much was made of it at the time – even I didn't find out until much later – but in 1962 Matt Busby had a chat with his pal, Bill Shankly, about the possibility of taking myself and Chris Lawler to Old Trafford. A fee of £50,000 was mentioned, a lot of cash for two teenagers who had never played League football, and it must have made our manager scratch his head a bit. Of course, I'm a Liverpudlian through and through and wouldn't have wanted to go, but if the boss had accepted I might not have had much choice. Thank goodness, he declined, and in the end I think he got pretty reasonable service out of the two of us.

Still, it was a nice pat on the head to be wanted by Manchester United, which brings me to the passionate rivalry between the two sets of Reds. Some people compare it to the emotion engendered by the Merseyside derby, but the two situations are not the same at all.

The Liverpool-Everton contest is a local one, and carries with it more than a century of tradition. It seems to me entirely natural that there's a lot of pleasure in beating opposition from your own home town. Okay, it leaves the losers with a feeling of disgrace, of being second-class citizens on Merseyside, but somehow it seems part of the way of life and essentially a family affair.

In contrast, the United-Liverpool matches give rise to real hatred among extremists on each side of the divide. I suppose there has always been a certain rivalry between Manchester and Liverpool as cities and it is understandable that that should be extended to football. But the raw malice which is frequently on display is completely unacceptable. The chants about United's Munich disaster and our tragedy at Hillsborough are utterly sick and beyond the realms of sport.

I suppose it stems from recent history. In the 1960s both had great teams, but after that United spent a long time in Liverpool's shadow. We won so much and they didn't. Feelings ran high and battles of words between the fans became ever more bitter. More recently United have held the upper hand and their supporters, understandably enough, are twisting the knife.

So there has been jealousy and gloating on both sides, and that can never be a recipe for harmony. Some supporters get so wound up that they assume the clubs are at war, yet this has never extended to the players and staff. In my day there was never a problem having a drink after the game with the likes of Nobby Stiles, Bobby Charlton and Denis Law, and there was never any nastiness carried over from the action on the pitch.

In fact, I used to have a lot of pride in all teams from the north-west doing well. My attitude was that if Liverpool couldn't win something, then let it be Everton; if not Everton, then Manchester United. At least that meant success for our region. At one time the fans thought that way, too, but there has been a dangerous change.

On the positive side, Liverpool versus Manchester United provides a massive sporting occasion, a really dramatic spectacle with two of the country's finest sides locked in combat.

To some people it's the most important aspect of their lives, and good luck to them. They exemplify the spirit behind Shanks' famous saying about football being more important than life or death. As for me, I am as disappointed as anyone if Liverpool lose but I try not to let it get me down. It might take a day to get over it but you have to let it go. After all, there's always the next time.

CHAPTER ONE:

A TALE OF TWO TITANS

JUST say the words: Manchester United against Liverpool. The very phrase conjures up grandeur and drama, feverish intensity and fierce pride, not forgetting the downright excellence of English football at its compelling best. But before examining the sporting context of this irresistible fixture, it is apposite to picture two vividly contrasting yet inextricably linked scenes.

In the first, during the spring of 1963, a small boy from Manchester is standing on the Kop, that most awesome expression of Liverpool's passion for soccer. His accent is broadest Openshaw, and in case there is the slightest doubt about his allegiance, he is proudly decked out in United scarf, bobble hat and badges. He has travelled the thirty miles down the East Lancs Road to watch his favourites – Denis Law, Bobby Charlton and the rest – take on Bill Shankly's Reds at Anfield and, though kick-off is more than an hour away, his face is alight with wholesome expectation. Suddenly he is the centre of attention. A gaggle of figures in full Liverpool regalia close around him and one hulking fellow, perhaps a stevedore from the docks which had been the city's commercial lifeline for so long, leans over the lad and says, 'Hey, son, can you see all right?' There is no hint of malice or intimidation, only genuine concern that the young United fan should enjoy a decent view of the action. That lad, whose name is Cliff Butler and who is now the vastly knowledgeable and widely respected editor of the Old Trafford club's matchday programme, never forgot the gesture. For him, and for the vast silent majority, it sums up, simply but eloquently, what watching football should be all about.

For the second vignette, we must leap forward nearly a quarter of a century, to February 1986 when once again Manchester United are at Anfield. As the coach bearing the visiting players arrives at the stadium it is surrounded by milling supporters, but this time there is something seriously wrong. Many of the faces turned towards Bryan Robson and company are contorted by what looks frighteningly like hatred. The footballers are doing their best to remain outwardly impassive to this startling display of emotion when a brick clatters into the side of the vehicle, close to where Mark Hughes is sitting. There is genuine alarm among the United party, who are almost engulfed by the mob as they embark on the short walk from coach to dressing room. Now the situation escalates dramatically as the players are sprayed with tear gas. Choking and shocked, they are shepherded by quick-thinking manager Ron Atkinson down a corridor to reach fresh air and sanctuary on the pitch, where they gasp to catch their breath and paw desperately at their eyes. Though severely shaken by the experience, the players recover quickly, but several children caught in the cloud of gas are not so lucky. They are rushed to hospital for emergency treatment, their day out at the big match ended in one horrifically traumatic moment. The incongruity with the experience of the young Cliff Butler back in 1963 is as stark as it is poignant.

In truth, these are extremes and that mindless act of 1986 was, mercifully, an

The benign face of Matt Busby, the former Liverpool wing-half who turned Manchester United into an institution revered around the world.

isolated incident. But the two accounts offer persuasive evidence of the changing atmosphere of what has come to stand alone as the most riveting, if sometimes overwrought, regular encounter in the English game.

The title of this book, *Red and Raw,* was chosen advisedly. As immeasurably improved communications have made the world a smaller place, Manchester United v Liverpool has replaced the traditional local derbies as the premier example of unalloyed tribalism. Neither faction has been more blameworthy than the other, the unwelcome churlishness being as marked at Old Trafford as at Anfield, and to their credit the clubs themselves have made efforts to defuse the tension. But still it persists.

Of course, local rivalry has always existed outside of the sporting arena. Nowhere else in the country do two such huge cities sit so closely together as Liverpool and Manchester. Indeed, taking into account the conurbations of St Helens, which is part of Merseyside, and Wigan, which falls under the aegis of Greater Manchester, the big two are practically at garden-fence proximity. And naturally enough, when neighbours are involved in close competition, then feelings run high.

Yet until the middle and late 1960s there was no specific contention between the two Red clans, no more animosity than might be exchanged with Bolton, Preston or Wolves. But the abolition of the footballers' maximum wage rendered the big-city outfits ever more powerful, and under the inspired guidance of Matt Busby and Bill Shankly respectively, United and Liverpool dominated the decade. United won the FA Cup in 1963, topped the League in 1965 and 1967 and claimed the European Cup in 1968; Liverpool, after lifting the Second Division title in 1962, went on to take the Championship in 1964 and 1966, and the FA Cup in 1965.

All this success coincided with a change in the nature of the media, which was dwelling increasingly on the utterances of prominent individuals (the wonderful Shankly was the most quotable man in football history) which in turn had the effect of shifting arguments on to a new and more personal level. With ever more information available and endless hot air expended, supporters' passions and prejudices were more readily fanned; a more cynical, win-at-all-costs mentality became prevalent.

Players from both sides recall the 1960s as overwhelmingly stimulating, especially in Liverpool where the Beatles were making an indelible mark on popular culture. These veteran Reds admit that the competition between the two clubs was intense, but stress that, certainly in the early part of the decade, there was no vestige of unpleasantness either on or off the pitch. Indeed, there were close friendships forged between the Anfield and Old Trafford contingents and Paddy Crerand once said that if United couldn't win a trophy then he hoped it went to Liverpool, an admirable sentiment with which Tommy Smith concurs in his foreword to this book.

Happily, in the main, amiable relations have persisted between the participants to this day, but it has been a different story where many of the spectators have been concerned. Nationwide hooliganism became rife in the early 1970s and violent skirmishes between United and Liverpool followers were not rare. But the astonishing depth of disregard between the two north-western camps was due to more than merely a manifestation of a national trend.

From this distance, it seems obvious that the pair's divergent fortunes in the 1970s and 1980s contributed massively to the degenerating situation. United's decline in the wake of the Busby era, culminating in their relegation in 1974, coincided with the start of the Merseysiders' climb towards a hitherto unscaled peak of dominance.

Liverpool icon Bill Shankly, soccer obsessive and splinteringly acerbic sage, whose admiration for the more stately Busby was immense.

Thus when the Mancunians were at their lowest ebb, the Scousers rubbed their noses in the dirt. To put it bluntly, there was envy on one side and arrogance on the other, ugly emotions massaged perpetually by the natural cut-and-thrust of a game which thrives on furious action and, increasingly, media-led controversy. Even when United bounced straight back into the top flight and bested Liverpool on many an individual occasion, still it was the Merseysiders who laid regular claim to the prize that mattered most, the one which decided who was cock of the north, the League Championship.

But it wasn't as simple as that. Though beyond any sane argument Liverpool were, by continuous weight of achievement, the most successful club by far, they were never the biggest. That was always Manchester United. No matter how humdrum the Old Trafford team might have been at any given juncture – and they sent out a few distinctly poor combinations – the Red Devils were always top of the tree in terms of glamour and worldwide support. Partly through the legacy of goodwill bestowed on them by the Munich air disaster, partly because of the enlightened and entertaining approach of Matt Busby over a quarter of a century, United were special, somehow beyond the logic of everyday sporting reality.

And how that rankled among the Anfield legions, who became increasingly outraged that their heroes did not, as they saw it, ever receive the full and unreserved credit for their mastery of the English scene. In the same way that Manchester City had railed against the

When Shanks retired in 1974, Kopites left him in no doubt about their feelings.

reverence still accorded to United in the early 1970s, even though the Blues were demonstrably a superior side, so Liverpool recoiled with similar perceived injustice, and thus the gulf between Scousers and Mancs continued to widen. As the years went on, moronic chants about the Munich and Hillsborough tragedies abounded, and earlier bile mushroomed with terrifying ease into full-fledged hatred.

By the mid-1990s, of course, the balance of power had altered radically. Then United, revived so inspirationally and comprehensively by Alex Ferguson, were the best as well as the biggest, leaving the Merseysiders feeling more jaundiced than ever. And, human nature being what it is, the Old Trafford brigade did not exercise undue grace in greeting their serial triumphs. Instead there was a gleeful element of paying the Liverpudlians back for all the years of suffering under the Anfield cudgel. Undoubtedly, the sweetest triumphs of all were those inflicted upon the old enemy, and how Fergie's Red Army crowed.

To exacerbate matters, the current relative fortunes of the two cities seem to be at dramatic variance. Whereas once Liverpool was one of the world's leading ports, with all the consequent bustle, prosperity and optimism that entailed, now the docks and their way of life have been swept away, creating widespread unemployment and a feeling – hotly denied in some quarters but difficult to gainsay – that it is a problem-racked community struggling to find a new identity.

Against that Manchester has emerged as the undisputed capital of the north-west, commercially vibrant, overflowing with investment, its own considerable social problems notwithstanding. It is blessed with thrusting new developments such as the

Nynex, the biggest indoor arena in Europe; the gigantic Arndale and Trafford shopping complexes; and the Metro transport system. Airports are the modern equivalents of the old shipping ports, and Manchester's Ringway is immense, serving the whole of the region. In sombre contrast, Liverpool's Speke is like a bus stop, without even a daily service to London in mid-1998. In addition, where once Merseyside was the centre for youth culture, now that mantle has passed to Manchester, which boasts the most extensive university campus in Europe. Many people go from Liverpool to Manchester to do their shopping; indeed, some even go from Liverpool to Warrington! As one born-and-bred Scouser put it, 'I love my city and it saddens me that it is in danger of becoming a commercial backwater. But it's a fact that few of the investors who pour up the M6 are interested in turning left …'

However, the game is a great, if fundamentally superficial leveller, and at the time of writing Liverpool were being inspired afresh by new national hero Michael Owen. Maybe the soccer scales were shifting, maybe not. By the time this reaches the bookshelves, the reader might be rather wiser on that count.

Airy predictions are worth little, but what seems certain is that the two sets of Reds will remain among the leading powers in the land for the foreseeable future, even after the inevitable advent of a European Super League has diluted the appeal of the domestic scene. Whatever happens to football in the early years of the twenty-first century, surely the pull of Manchester United v Liverpool will be as insistent as ever. Undoubtedly every man, woman and child who ever witnessed this clash of the Titans from the Kop or the Stretford End will wish it to survive and prosper as an enduring symbol of the British game at its most potent.

But how splendid it would be if it ceased to be tainted by unsavoury negatives, if it could embody the spirit of Matt Busby and Bill Shankly, close friends who could temper pride with humility and draw the line between healthy rivalry and festering resentment. For all his sparkling rhetoric, there is no doubt that, deep down, Shanks knew perfectly well where football really stood in relation to matters of life and death.

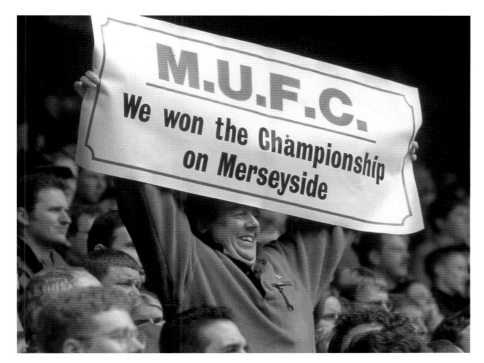

Get the message, Liverpool? Payback time for United fans in the spring of 1997.

CHAPTER TWO:

A RED RITUAL RESUMES 1946/7 – 1949/50

W HEN the six years of untold horror and miserable self–denial of war were at an end, entertainment was high on the agenda of the fun–starved masses. Top–class football offered a simple, cheap and joyful diversion and, though still reeling from the depredations of the conflict themselves, Manchester United and Liverpool were eager to meet the demand.

Of the two, the Mancunians had the hardest struggle to ready themselves for a return to League action in the early autumn of 1946. The club was debt–ridden and Old Trafford had been so comprehensively ravaged by Hitler's bombs – the main stand, the offices and the dressing rooms were all rendered unusable – that they had made arrangements to play their home matches at Maine Road, the headquarters of Manchester City. But they had a spring in their step, thanks mainly to a new and enterprising young manager, a certain Matt Busby.

Albert Stubbins, worshipped on Tyneside, equally adored on Merseyside.

Ironically, the visionary Scot had been an ever–present in Liverpool's side during the last campaign before the war, but when the Anfield club offered him a coaching post in 1945 he turned it down in favour of the senior job with United. He relished the prospect of being in total control – an alien concept to most boards of directors at that time, but one on which he insisted – and soon he moulded the gifted squad of players he had inherited into one of the most attractive the British game had seen.

Some thirty miles west, the Merseysiders were in buoyant mood, too. They had organised a pre–season tour of Canada and the United States, boss George Kay enthusing about the benefits of Californian sunshine, fresh orange juice and man–size American steaks on his footballers, whose physiques had been affected by rationing. They returned to England heavier by an average of seven pounds per man, and won two of their first three matches before facing Manchester United at Maine Road.

The series of encounters which was to thunder across the pages of modern football history began with what remains, at the time of writing, the most one–sided meeting between the two clubs since the war. Busby's new team trounced his old one 5–0. *[See Classic Clash Number One on page 18.]*

Leslie Edwards of the *Liverpool Daily Post* was correct in describing his own admirably unbiased report of proceedings as melancholy reading for Merseysiders, but in one respect he was wrong. He referred to a defeat for which there could be no salve, adding rather enigmatically that scarcely had the game finished before George Kay left in search of a stranger who would be mightily welcome. That stranger turned out to be Albert Stubbins, Newcastle's dynamic red–haired centre–forward who had been expected to join Everton but who was now whisked from the Toffees' clutches following a late cloak–and–dagger dash to Tyneside by Liverpool's canny chairman Billy McConnell.

The £12,000 signing of the personable Stubbins, English football's leading scorer in wartime competitions, proved to be a stroke of inspiration. Immensely skilful and deceptively powerful for a such a slim fellow, he combined exhilaratingly with the prolific inside–forward Jack Balmer and the multi–talented Billy Liddell, whom many shrewd judges describe as the finest of all Liverpool footballers. By the time United travelled for the return fixture in early May, the Anfield outfit had an outside chance of the title, which, back in September, Busby's men had been tipped to claim with ease and for which they were still among the favourites.

Charlie Mitten, a dashing destroyer on the left flank of Busby's first enchanting team.

On a sunny but blustery spring afternoon, the visitors took the eye with their delightful on–the–floor football, but Liverpool's industry, speed and penetration proved more than a match for it. In the event a thrilling game was decided by Stubbins' twelfth–minute goal, after which the hosts' defence, in which right–half Bob Paisley was outstanding, held firm in the face of sustained pressure. Subsequent newspaper headlines referred to 'the luckless Mancunians' but that was of little consequence to the jubilant Kopites.

Just how crucial that victory turned out to be was apparent when the final League table revealed the Anfield Reds to be Champions by a single point ... from Manchester United. Kay's team had finished the season with thirteen points out of a possible fourteen, with joint top–scorers Stubbins and Balmer notching twenty–four goals each. Albert Stubbins, not surprisingly, had become an instant folk–hero, the crowds enthralled by his derring–do on the park and warming to his modest and gentlemanly demeanour off it. It was a shame for both player and club that he never really settled away from his native Tyneside and after one more bountiful term he became markedly less effective. Even so, he remains one of the most popular figures in Merseyside sporting history.

It is fascinating to ponder on the contrast in crowd atmosphere between the late 1940s and more recent times. Jack Crompton, who from his position between United's posts was well placed to pick up on fans' rumblings, remembers one incident which illustrates the essentially good–natured flavour of the earlier era.

'Back then it was a more physical game for goalkeepers and when you caught the ball you had to protect yourself forcibly from charging forwards,' he recalls. 'One day at Anfield I had to stand up to Billy Liddell, a lovely character off the pitch but a right handful during a game, and I ended up flattening him. Now Billy was a huge favourite with the Liverpool supporters and they weren't best pleased with my treatment of their hero. As he got to his feet, I heard a voice not far behind me shout something like "Hey Crompton, we'll f***ing get you after the match." I just grinned to myself and put it out of my mind, because if you worried every time someone swore at you then you'd never walk on to a football field again.

'But after the game I was walking outside the ground with Johnny Carey when we were approached by four big fellows. Suddenly I remembered the voice in the crowd

Stan Pearson (right) is thwarted by the combined efforts of Liverpool keeper Ray Minshull and wing-half Bob Paisley in an FA Cup clash at Goodison Park in January 1948. United won 3-0, but they had not seen the last of Mr Paisley . . .

and wondered what we were in for. Then one of them said to me, "It's okay, Jack, there's no one here. We heard what those silly buggers shouted at you and we thought we'd come along to make sure the sides were equal." And the best part of it was that these four men were Scousers!

'I thought it was wonderful that they had gone out of their way to look after an opposing player, but that sort of generous feeling was typical of the way the Liverpool and United camps behaved towards one another at that time. Somewhat healthier than modern developments, wouldn't you say?'

Although, some half a century later, such a climate seems agreeably wholesome, not all old-time footballing occasions oozed sweetness and light. For instance, when the Red brigades met at Maine Road in August 1947 it was a tetchy, scrappy affair, with United triumphing 2-0 following a controversial first-half opening goal by Johnny Morris, which the visitors swore was offside. A Stan Pearson strike in the second period clinched the points, but the last hour of the game was marred by the misfortune of Liverpool right-back Jim Harley, who suffered a serious ankle injury while tackling United's left-wing flier, Charlie Mitten.

Happily the fare was considerably more entertaining in the Anfield rematch only a week later. This time, perhaps with a gently delivered flea in their collective ear, Busby's men hit prime form. With the all-star forward line interchanging positions with bewildering rapidity and precision, they surged into a two-goal interval lead through Mitten and Pearson, and when Jack Rowley spurned a chance to make the game safe from the penalty spot, there could not have been a soul among the full house who gave Liverpool a chance of making the centre-forward pay for his carelessness. One reporter described the Merseysiders as lackadaisical, adding, 'With one or two exceptions they played like fellows who had just got up from a lobster supper banquet.' After the break, though, it was United who were pink with embarrassment as an opportunistic strike from the persistent Stubbins, a penalty from Balmer and a subsequent dogged rearguard action earned the home side an unexpected point.

Jack Crompton remembers that day with a good–natured grimace. 'As I ran to the Kop end for the second half, a little group of United fans shouted to me "Come on Jack, we can take this lot, no trouble." But twenty minutes later, with the score at 2–2, I was hailed by a big, raucous Liverpudlian voice saying "Hey Crompton, you're on your own now. Those silly sods have buggered off!"'

However, that slip by United could not disguise the fact that while Liverpool were a workmanlike outfit blessed with several outstanding players, the Red Devils of that era were truly a vintage crew. Indeed, no less canny an observer than Bob Paisley, towards the end of his long life in football, described them as one of the finest teams he had ever seen.

It was a combination without a weakness: Jack Crompton was reliable between the sticks; full–backs Johnny Carey and John Aston were calm, masterful and possessed skills which would have shamed many First Division forwards; stopper Allenby Chilton was rocklike and ruthless, while wing–halves Henry Cockburn and either John Anderson or Jack Warner buzzed productively. But what made this United so special was an attack which made the purists drool. Jimmy 'Old Brittle Bones' Delaney and Charlie Mitten were wingers who could captivate and destroy; inside–forwards Johnny Morris and Stan Pearson were makers and takers of chances, both of them mixing subtle, stealthy skills with deceptive strength; chief marksman Jack 'Gunner' Rowley was a dreadnought, but an intelligent one with a light touch when necessary. If Busby's dazzlers had a fault as a unit it was that they lacked that last ounce of ruthlessness which converts near things into trophies, hence their frustrating record of finishing as First Division runners–up in four out of the first five post–war seasons.

In the 1947/8 season, though, they made ample amends in the FA Cup, numbering Liverpool among their victims in a fourth–round tie played at Goodison Park, even though the Mancunians had been drawn at home. (This anomaly was due to Manchester City, who were still United's regular hosts as Old Trafford was not yet refurbished, having a home tie with Chelsea on the same day.)

Having travelled across Stanley Park to the home of the Blues, George Kay's Reds were beaten 3–0, with Rowley, Morris and Mitten netting in the space of five first–half minutes. In fact, such was United's dominance that they could have doubled the tally but for the brilliance of Ray Minshull in the Liverpool goal.

The attendance exceeded 74,000, with an estimated 15,000 locked out, and the East Lancs Road was clogged by westward–bound traffic all morning. Certainly, those who invested £1 for the return plane trip from Ringway to Speke, laid on by an enterprising charter company employing eight–seater Rapides, enjoyed a less frustrating journey.

The following season saw the devotion of the fans tested in a manner which was commonplace at that time but has since receded into history – the playing of back–to–back fixtures against the same opponents over Christmas. Although Maine Road could have accommodated many thousands more for the barren draw on 25 December, the gate was only just short of 48,000, while more than 53,000

'Gentleman' John Carey, the United skipper and a cultured defender who contested a succession of stirring personal duels with Liverpool hero Billy Liddell.

Division One
11 September 1946
at Maine Road

MANCHESTER UNITED 5

Pearson 12, 17, 85; Rowley 37;
Mitten 49

Jack Crompton, Johnny Carey, Billy
McGlen, Jack Warner, Allenby Chilton,
Henry Cockburn, Jimmy Delaney, Stan
Pearson, Johnny Hanlon, Jack Rowley,
Charlie Mitten.

LIVERPOOL 0

Charlie Ashcroft, Jim Harley, Barney
Ramsden, Phil Taylor, Laurie Hughes, Bob
Paisley, Berry Nieuwenhuys, Jack Balmer,
Bill Jones, Willie Fagan, Bob Priday.

Half-time: 3-0 Attendance: 41,657

WHEN Manchester United annihilated Liverpool in their opening post-war encounter, there seemed little standing between rookie manager Matt Busby's men and the first League Championship of the new era. That afternoon at Maine Road the Merseysiders beavered frenziedly, effervescing with energy apparently garnered from the diet of Texas T-Bones enjoyed on their recent trip to North America, but they were outclassed comprehensively by a United side which flowed like molasses over glass.

The Red Devils performed with a rhythmical smoothness which was beautiful to behold. Indeed, some of the moves involving the right-wing pair of Delaney and Pearson were utterly breathtaking, while Rowley and Mitten were hardly less effective on the left. True, injury had deprived the visitors of Welsh international goalkeeper Cyril Sidlow and Billy Liddell, that most powerful of flankmen, but even after making allowances for the absence of two such influential figures, Liverpool's showing was a major disappointment.

United began the game as they meant to continue, sweeping the ball from player to player with deft precision. So dominant were they in the early stages that it was nearly fifteen minutes before the home custodian, the ever-steady Crompton, received a touch of the ball. By then Pearson had already hammered his side into a lead which he doubled after seventeen minutes and which Rowley consolidated to make it 3-0 shortly before the interval. After the break, for all the Merseysiders' exertions, Busby's lovely team played exhibition stuff, Mitten adding a fourth goal before the endlessly inventive Pearson completed his hat-trick. In the opposite direction there was only one worthwhile shot – from Bob Paisley – and where Manchester meshed like a well-oiled machine, their opponents resembled a disparate collection of unacquainted cogs and wheels. Phil Taylor, another man destined to manage the club, laboured nobly in the Anfield cause, but he was simply overrun.

This was the first of three United teams assembled by the future Sir Matt which genuinely merited the overused adjective 'great'. Though the mists of time are closing around this oldest combination, rendering meaningful comparison ever more difficult, there is no shortage of respected judges who maintain stoutly that it was even more entertaining than the Busby Babes of the 1950s or the Best-Law-Charlton creation of a decade later.

This overwhelming victory left United with maximum points after their first four League games, and it seemed unlikely that any team in the land would live with them. But for the remainder of the campaign, though they continued to serve up exhilarating fare, they could not maintain their early-season consistency, so that when they arrived at Anfield nearly eight months later the Championship was still up for grabs.

United's Stan Pearson, a beguiling mixture of subtle visionary and unflashy technician.

crammed into Anfield forty–eight hours later to see second–half goals from Stan Pearson and the bustling Ronnie Burke ease United to victory.

For the players, two games so close together were less than welcome, for social reasons as well as the likelihood of having to face the second encounter suffering from a knock which had not had time to clear up. However, the situation was accepted as part of a way of life which, overall, was eminently rewarding. Indeed, if there were any gripes about unreasonable conditions, Matt Busby made a point of reminding his men that if anybody wanted to opt out he would have no difficulty in finding others who would work on Christmas Day in order to enjoy two months paid holiday in the summer.

Jack Crompton recalls, 'It was a bit awkward for family men, especially if we were playing down south, and weather conditions were not always ideal for long–distance travelling. At least when we played Liverpool we didn't have far to go and could spend some time with the children on Christmas morning. There had to be a bit of self–restraint when it came to the seasonal festivities, but I think the players were sensible about that. Well, most of them were!'

In 1949/50 a gap of six months separated the Reds' two meetings, the first of which, at Anfield in September, saw a fabulous team goal cap a typically gutsy Liverpool performance and capture a well–deserved point from their more expansively talented opponents. In the early stages United had purred ominously, and when Mitten nodded them ahead a minute before the break, a Manchester victory seemed something of a foregone conclusion.

But the Merseysiders held on gamely until fourteen minutes from time when they produced an equalizer as exquisite as it was unexpected. After a sharp interchange of passes between Phil Taylor and Jimmy Payne, the ball arrived at the feet of Bob Paisley in the left–half position. With characteristic lack of fuss, the man destined one day to become the most successful manager in the history of English soccer played a one–two with Liddell before dispatching a through-ball for which the Scottish wingman raced with his marker, Johnny Carey. Though near to exhaustion from earlier efforts, the brilliant Billy outstripped the Irishman and squeezed a centre from the byline to Stubbins. With the Geordie off balance and with his back to goal, there seemed little danger, but with sudden balletic agility he spun like a scarlet top to turn the ball past the dumbfounded Crompton.

The Red Devils' goalkeeper Jack Crompton, who received backing from an unexpected source at Anfield.

By the time the two clubs' paths crossed again in March, United were reinstalled at Old Trafford and four points clear at the top of the First Division. Not for the first time in recent years, the title seemed theirs for the taking, but thanks mainly to an inspired display by visiting goalkeeper Cyril Sidlow the scoresheet remained blank. It seemed a disappointing yet hardly disastrous result for the Mancunians, yet it proved to be a turning point in their season. Thereafter they won only one of their last nine matches and slumped to fourth in the table. As for Liverpool, they made it to Wembley where they lost the FA Cup Final, after spirited resistance, to an Arsenal side inspired by Merseysider Joe Mercer. Now the 1950s beckoned, a decade in which the two sets of Reds would experience wildly contrasting fortunes. On the one hand would be creeping mediocrity culminating in relegation; on the other an upward spiral of scintillating success finally marred by the starkest of tragedies.

CHAPTER THREE:
OUT WITH THE OLD
1950/51 – 1953/4

Opposite: The magnificent Billy Liddell, a lovely man who could always find time to be kind to a young opponent before a game . . . only to run the rookie ragged when the action commenced!

AS the second half of the century got under way, the fortunes of Manchester United and Liverpool were poised to surge dramatically in opposite directions. Soon the Red Devils would claim that elusive first Championship under Matt Busby before undergoing a youthful revolution that would fire the imagination of the sporting world. In sombre contrast, the Merseysiders would change managers, decline from a frustratingly ordinary First Division outfit into one which was frankly feeble, then slip limply out of the top flight.

In the summer of 1950, as Liverpool boss George Kay struggled with both ill-health and an increasingly evident need to reinvigorate a side which looked some way off being potential title challengers, the news spotlight concentrated mainly on England's shock elimination from the World Cup and their shattering defeat by the USA. But no sooner had that almost surreal reverse been assimilated into the nation's footballing consciousness than an off-the-field controversy at Old Trafford shifted the focus of public attention.

Charlie Mitten, seduced by the promise of riches untold, had opted to defy the authorities by walking out on United to sample life in Colombia. Some denounced him as disloyal but, in the era of soccer slaves, when players earned perhaps £12 a week while their skills made vast fortunes for their clubs, his decision was entirely understandable. Sadly, Charlie's El Dorado was to prove illusive. He was destined to return to England after just one South American campaign and was compelled to pursue his career away from Old Trafford.

Meanwhile, how United could have used Mitten's extrovert talents as their title quest resumed in 1950/51. With Jimmy Delaney nearing the end of his extravagantly bountiful Indian summer – he re-crossed the border, joining Aberdeen at the grand old age of thirty-six in November 1950 – Busby faced the future without the star flankmen who had been such crucially important constituents of his first wonderful team.

However, Jimmy did enjoy one last outing against Liverpool, on a stormy Anfield evening in August, although shortly before half-past six it seemed certain that the game must be called off. Thunderclouds bunched so densely over Merseyside that the stadium, not equipped with floodlights at the time, was plunged into near-darkness. Kopites, drenched on their walk to the ground and now steaming in the crush on the famous terrace, added to the eeriness of the scene by lighting thousands of matches and waving them in the gloom.

Then suddenly, as if some celestial switch had been flicked, the blackness lifted and what turned out to be an enthralling, high-quality contest got under way. Billy Liddell and Johnny Carey fought out many a personal duel during this era, both enjoying their individual triumphs, and this time it was the turn of Liverpool's dashing Scot to claim the ascendancy. Though the poise of the United skipper served him well during close-range exchanges, Billy defied the muddy conditions to run at his

Roger Byrne, accurately earmarked by Matt Busby for an illustrious future. The self-assured Mancunian was destined to captain United and win thirty-three successive caps for England before dying in the Munich disaster.

adversary and succeeded in outstripping him often enough to cause chaos in the visiting defence.

Duly Liddell eluded his marker to open the scoring and though Jack Rowley equalized slightly against the run of play, a rare mistake by new Manchester goalkeeper Reg Allen, who turned a cross from Cyril Done into his own net, gave George Kay's team a 2-1 interval lead. The second period produced no further score, but it was not without incident. Liddell for Liverpool and Stan Pearson for United both rattled the frame of the goal, and Jack Balmer netted with a spectacularly adroit twisting header, only for the strike to be ruled out for an earlier handling offence. Unusually for that time, Liverpool players protested so vociferously to the referee that one of them, Phil Taylor, was booked. Nevertheless they took the points and deservedly so in a game on which one reporter commented, 'This was a royal treat. No one could complain about football these days if this stuff were commonplace.'

Sod's law applying to soccer as to all other walks of life, when the two teams met only seven days later at Old Trafford, they produced a drab defensive encounter in which, with Liddell absent due to injury, only United's John Downie managed to break the deadlock.

Before the two northern giants would meet again, the Anfield men would be under new leadership. The faithful, quiet, endlessly industrious Mancunian George Kay, who had held the managerial reins for fifteen years and had guided Liverpool to the first post-war Championship, succumbed finally to the advancing ravages of illness and retired in February 1951. Tragically, he had only three years to live.

Kay's replacement, ironically another Manchester man, was Don Welsh, a former Charlton Athletic marksman who had become a popular Anfield figure while guesting for the Reds during the war. He took over a side which boasted a doughty defence – in which full-backs Ray Lambert and Eddie Spicer, stopper Laurie Hughes and wing-halves Bill Jones and Bob Paisley were all exceedingly capable – but which, despite the perennial magnificence of Liddell, lacked consistency in attack.

Accordingly they were ensconced in mid-table when next they met the Red Devils, who were, as ever, title-aspirants, in November 1951. The teams played out a goalless draw which was entertaining enough, but for United the significance of the occasion stretched well beyond the gaining of an away point. Making their debuts that day were two young men whose contribution to the Old Trafford cause would pass into club legend: Roger Byrne and Jackie Blanchflower.

For the versatile eighteen-year-old Blanchflower, who played at right-half, it proved a painful experience as he suffered a split eye in the first half and needed stitches at the interval. As he recalled later, with the modesty and wit which were both typical of the man, 'I think my eye problem was due to all the blinking from watching Billy Liddell run past me! That fellow was quick enough to catch pigeons and he was powerful, too. Without a doubt, he was one of the finest forwards I ever faced.'

Jackie couldn't have performed badly, though, because he was selected for the next match only to tear a knee cartilage in training and spend the rest of the season on the sidelines. Eventually, of course, he excelled at inside-forward, wing-half and centre-half, before injuries sustained at Munich signalled a brutal end to his playing days.

The impact of twenty-two-year-old left-back Byrne was even more marked. His self-assured and pacy policing of Liverpool outside-right Brian Jackson earned him widespread plaudits, none more appreciated than one from his own manager. Matt Busby, always cautious when publicly assessing the prospects of his youthful charges, declared, 'Let Roger Byrne get the feel of things for about three First Division matches. If he gets on as well as I expect, then I am prepared to say that he is a certainty to play for England.'

As events transpired, Roger was ever present for the remainder of the campaign, despite switching to the left wing in the spring. Thereafter he rose to become club skipper and a fixture in the number three shirts of both United and England before his life was snuffed out in its prime on a slushy German runway.

Other new United faces since the previous term were those of wingers Johnny Berry and Ernie Bond, replacing the eminent old firm of Delaney and Mitten. Unlike most of the additions to Busby's forces at this time, Berry was already an experienced professional, a shrewd capture from Birmingham City that summer. A buzzing, feisty performer who presaged the modern midfielder in his willingness to battle back when his defence was under pressure, he matured into a flankman of international class and would have won far more than his mere four England caps but for the presence of Stanley Matthews and Tom Finney. Berry's career ended in the air disaster of 1958, when he was maimed and after which he never played again. And Bond? After some enterprising early displays, such as in this meeting with Liverpool, he slipped out of the reckoning and his footballing days ended anti-climactically with Cowdenbeath.

Come April 1952 and Liverpool were looking ever more ordinary, while United were showing signs of blowing yet another Championship. After overcoming Wolves in mid-March to stretch their run of unbeaten League games to sixteen, they had appeared to be sitting pretty. But unexpected defeats at Huddersfield and Portsmouth, and a draw at Burnley, had raised real doubts about their ability to take the title pressure.

It was in this ominous climate of uncertainty that they played host to the Merseysiders, but United supporters worn down by a succession of Championship near-misses need not have worried. Though the first quarter pulsated with hectic action which could have produced goals at either end, home nerves were calmed by a Byrne penalty after thirty minutes. Then three strikes by Downie, Byrne and Rowley in an eight-minute spell early in the second period sealed the points and set up a triumphant finale to the Red Devils' season.

The main contributor to the 4-0 blood-letting was Roger Byrne, who was relishing his spell on the left flank, even if the subsequent newspaper headline 'United find winger Byrne has Mitten touch' seemed a trifle excessive. His success in an advanced role underlined the tactical boldness which characterized Busby's thinking that term, during which he had also moved captain Carey from right-back to right-half to telling effect. Carey's switch resulted in an extended first-team opportunity in the number two shirt for Salford-born Tommy McNulty, who would eventually join Liverpool in February 1954 as Anfield fortunes continued to nosedive. For now, though, Tommy could bask in the glory of an accomplished performance against the great Liddell, one which Don Welsh doubtless remembered as he went in search of new recruits to boost his faltering combination.

Having disposed of their fellow Reds United romped to the title, taking seven points from their last four games of the season and scoring seventeen goals in the process. After finishing as runners-up four times in the previous five campaigns, the Old Trafford camp was both ecstatic and relieved. It had begun to look as if, for all their attractive endeavour, there was a fatal flaw in the club's make-up when it came to lifting the premier domestic prize. Now that ghost had been laid, although there was an element of regret that only five of the memorable 1948 vintage – Carey, Cockburn, Chilton, Rowley and Pearson – remained as regulars to share in the accolades.

Some pundits predicted that the title breakthrough would lead to a period of United dominance in the League, but such theories were scotched by a severely lacklustre start to 1952/3, a sorry state of affairs which their manager was not prepared to tolerate for long. Confident that he had assembled a phenomenal pool of rookie talent, Busby began to pitch the youngsters into First Division action.

Bill Foulkes, a miner who played part-time football from the day he arrived at Old

Division One

22 August 1953

at Anfield

LIVERPOOL 4

Bimpson 20, 54, 58; Jones 44

Charlie Ashcroft, Ray Lambert, Eddie Spicer, Phil Taylor, Laurie Hughes, Bob Paisley, Jimmy Payne, Kevin Baron, Louis Bimpson, Bill Jones, Billy Liddell.

MANCHESTER UNITED 4

Rowley 9; Byrne 48 (pen); Lewis 60 Taylor 83

Jack Crompton, John Aston, Roger Byrne, Don Gibson, Allenby Chilton, Henry Cockburn, Johnny Berry, Jack Rowley, Tommy Taylor, Eddie Lewis, David Pegg.

Half-time: 2-1 Attendance: 48,442

This was the highest-scoring of all post-war meetings between Liverpool and Manchester United, and although the Red Devils trailed three times, they deserved their point in the end. Indeed, during the final minutes of this hectic encounter it seemed that the visitors might even steal victory, a possibility which prompted the police to form a thin but determined blue line in front of some 20,000 frustrated Kopites.

United started brightly and took the lead after nine minutes when Rowley freed Pegg on the left, then charged into the box to ram the winger's precise centre high into Ashcroft's net. The hosts responded with gusto and equalized in somewhat bizarre manner on twenty minutes when Crompton jammed a Liddell cross against the bar, where it remained for perhaps two seconds before it dropped and was forced home by Bimpson.

Chances proliferated at either end for the remainder of a breathless first half but there was no further breakthrough until a minute before the interval. Then Crompton, who was having an uncharacteristically erratic afternoon, lost the ball, thus allowing Liddell to set up a comfortable finish for Jones.

United levelled three minutes after the resumption when Lambert was adjudged to have fouled the rampaging Taylor in the box and Byrne converted coolly from the spot. The Kop roared its disapproval, but Liverpudlian discontent was short-lived. After fifty-four and fifty-eight minutes Bimpson scored from Liddell corners, thus completing a combative hat-trick and giving his side what looked certain to be a winning lead.

Not so. On the hour, Lewis lobbed a reply from a Berry corner to complete a frenetic spell of four goals in twelve minutes and set up a rousing finale. Now United poured forward in search of an equalizer but were denied repeatedly by the acrobatic Ashcroft. Then Liverpool hit back with another wave of attacks during which an overhead kick from Bimpson hit the crossbar.

Another goal seemed inevitable but at which end would it arrive? The answer was provided in the eighty-third minute when Rowley nodded on a Chilton free-kick and Taylor bundled the ball past Ashcroft, flattening the goalkeeper in the process. The Kop howled for a free-kick but the referee, after lengthy consultation with his linesman, gave the goal and it was 4-4.

At this point, with United hell-bent on a winner and the home fans furious, the police made their precautionary move. However, justice was done when the final whistle went without further score. Liverpool, having beaten Portsmouth in their opening game, had now held their own against the powerful Mancunians and given little indication that they would be facing demotion in the spring. As for United, they had shown character and resilience in recovering from a 4-2 deficit, but anxieties about defensive frailties would have to be addressed.

Louis Bimpson, a lion-hearted bustler whose hat-trick jolted United but was not enough to defeat them.

25

Bill Foulkes, whose little white lie in Matt Busby's office launched the indomitable Lancastrian on an illustrious career.

Trafford as a seventeen year old in 1949 until he won a full England cap and turned professional in 1954, was one of the 'Busby Babes'. Yet the man who became the central colossus of the Red Devils' rearguard during the 1960s, and who compiled nearly 700 senior appearances for the club during an illustrious career, made his debut at Liverpool in December 1952 in rather uncertain circumstances.

He explains: 'I had been nowhere near the first team as a defender and they had been trying me out as a striker with the reserves, for whom I had scored a few goals. Then just as I was about to get my senior chance up front I injured my ankle in training and I was still struggling for fitness when our coach, Bert Whalley, told me Matt Busby wanted to see me in his office.

'To be honest I feared the worst. I had not been playing and I thought I might be in for the old heave-ho. But when I went in the Boss was cheerful and asked about my ankle. Though it was still very painful, I told him it was great. He said "Let me see you jump," so right in front of his desk I leapt as high as possible and didn't show the pain I felt when I landed. He said "That's good, I'm thinking of playing you on Saturday." Now I knew the reserves were at Old Trafford and I thought that was what he meant. Then the boss said "You live in the area, at St Helens, so you had better make your way straight to the ground." I replied that I thought the reserves were at home, but then he stunned me by saying "No, I want you in the first team at Liverpool." I could have fallen through the floor!'

Though Bill believed he had kidded the great man, Matt probably had a fair idea of what was going on. Even so, he was prepared to risk him in the unfamiliar role of right-back in direct opposition to the formidable Billy Liddell.

Foulkes recalls the game. 'Billy was a real gentleman. He knew it was my debut and he was very kind to me before the game. He introduced himself and wished me well, but then he ran me into the ground, as it was his job to do. He was a powerful man but also very skilful and I found it a very hard examination. He scored the first goal of the game and they were leading at half-time, but we came back to win 2-1 through John Aston and Stan Pearson. It was a very good result as we had been having an indifferent time in the League. After the game my ankle was blown up like a balloon. I'm sure I got through on adrenaline but I must have played reasonably well because I was picked for the next game at Chelsea. At least Matt Busby knew I had the necessary desire to put myself through the pain barrier.'

Playing on the opposite side to Foulkes was another young defender destined to give prodigious service to his employers. Ronnie Moran was making only his third senior appearance for Liverpool that day but he was to remain at Anfield for the next forty-five years, a tower of strength as player, coach, caretaker manager and general factotum, a massive lasting influence throughout the golden era of the most successful club in the history of the English game.

However, such were Liverpool's ills in 1952/3 that far more than one promising young defender was going to be needed to put matters right. Don Welsh and his players strove manfully but there was a less-than-dynamic atmosphere about the club's administration that spelled danger. The Reds had not been out of the top flight since 1905 but now the spectre of relegation, for so long unthinkable, was beginning to attain the proportions of a realistic threat.

Indeed, when they arrived at Old Trafford in April 1953, the need for points was urgent, but after only ten minutes it was pretty clear that none would be forthcoming. United started like world beaters, cutting through the visitors' resistance like a scythe through grass, and early goals from Pearson and Rowley effectively ended the game as a genuine contest. A few valiant sallies from Liddell, as ever Liverpool's most potent menace, were foiled by Crompton and it was left to Berry to tie up proceedings for United when he ran half the length of the field to score ten minutes from the end.

Ronnie Moran, near the outset of nearly half a century of priceless, if sometimes unobtrusive service to the Anfield cause.

A late strike by Sammy Smyth was little consolation to the Merseysiders, who now needed to beat Chelsea in their final fixture to be assured of First Division football the following season. After much huffing and puffing they managed it, but the feeling of relief was tinged significantly with unavoidable foreboding. An appalling succession of injuries had hindered their efforts in 1952/3, but there was no disguising the fact that, Liddell excepted, they were chronically short of attacking quality.

Liverpool's moment of truth arrived in 1953/4, though not before a bright start which included sharing eight goals with United at Anfield in August *(see Classic Clash Number Two on page 25)*. That false dawn was followed by an early-autumn slump from which they never recovered, their sorry plight underlined savagely by their Old Trafford annihilation in December. United won 5-1 with Tommy Taylor and Jackie Blanchflower plundering a brace apiece and Dennis Viollet completing the rout, while seventeen-year-old wing-half Duncan Edwards bestrode the pitch like a leviathan. Louis Bimpson contributed the solitary forlorn reply.

Liverpool's misfortunes deepened when Eddie Spicer broke a leg in attempting to prevent Taylor's first goal, causing Liddell to move to left-back and removing any vestige of offensive enterprise. It was the Reds' eighteenth consecutive away defeat in the League and there was little doubt that they were the First Division's poorest team. They managed only nine wins all season and finished bottom of the table, leaving the Manchester United-Liverpool fixture in abeyance for the foreseeable future.

CHAPTER FOUR:

HEAVEN, HELL AND A NEW MESSIAH 1954/5 – 1962/3

T HE paths of Manchester United and Liverpool did not cross during the second half of the 1950s, the unavoidable upshot of the Merseysiders' sorry fall from First Division grace in 1954. However, the next half-decade cannot be passed over lightly as the tumultuous events of that period are relevant to the events of the 1960s.

For Matt Busby and his club, there was the glorious rise of the Babes, encompassing two successive League titles and pioneering forays into Europe, a triumphant progress brought to a savage halt by the calamity of the Munich air disaster. Meanwhile the Merseysiders endured a maddening sojourn in the lower flight, repeatedly missing out narrowly on promotion but rarely, until the arrival of Bill Shankly, shaking off an aura of ordinariness which was little short of criminal for an institution blessed with such passionate followers.

United's story takes precedence here, as it is unquestionably the more momentous. Having already pinned his faith on home-nurtured youth, and augmented it through the judicious purchases of centre-forward Tommy Taylor from Barnsley and right-winger Johnny Berry from Birmingham City, Busby was not faint-hearted in putting his policy to the test. Thus by mid-decade the final vestiges of his marvellous class of 1948 – Messrs Chilton, Cockburn, Pearson and Rowley – had been phased out and the new generation reigned supreme.

It is not easy, some forty years on, to appreciate the precise position of the Busby Babes in the national psyche. Though the genial but deceptively steely Matt cut an avuncular figure far removed from the rock'n'roll culture which was burgeoning in the late 1950s, his sparkling team was the footballing embodiment of that wider movement. Of course, they were not rebels as such, but they were youthful, they were refreshing and they were exhilaratingly precocious. On the field they were wonderfully entertaining, threatening to sweep all before them for the

Tommy Taylor, the buccaneering Manchester United and England spearhead whose prime was beckoning when he lost his life at Munich.

foreseeable future. Off it they melded magnificently, a group of boys growing up, living and working as one unit, exuding a swashbuckling 'one-for-all-and-all-for-one' mentality which bred matchless team spirit, the like of which no coach could forge by his own will.

The names of Duncan Edwards and company would have passed into football folklore merely on the strength of their Championship endeavours of 1955/6 and 1956/7, but they were to become chiselled indelibly on the memories of a wider audience as a result of the horrific accident on the way home from a European Cup tie in Belgrade in February 1958. Among the twenty-three people who lost their lives at Munich were eight players and three key club officials. Two further players,

Johnny Berry and Jackie Blanchflower, sustained injuries that meant they never returned to the game; two more, the immensely promising wingers Albert Scanlon and Kenny Morgans, were never the same again; and Matt Busby himself came agonizingly close to death. The subsequent rebuilding job, in which Matt was aided inspirationally by his assistant Jimmy Murphy, took a good five years to come anywhere near completion, by which time Liverpool had returned to the top flight.

But what of the Anfielders in the intervening period? Well, after one season of coming to terms with life at the lower level, they became regular challengers for promotion but, mortifyingly, were perpetual nearly-men. Their record of Second Division finishes in the five years from 1955/6 reads third, third, fourth, fourth, third and third. Don Welsh, who managed the club from 1951 to 1956 and former captain Phil Taylor, who was in charge from 1956 to 1959, were hard-working,

Bill Shankly, aged 46 in 1959, just before he grabbed Liverpool FC by the scruff of the neck.

honest fellows who produced teams which were passably entertaining but which lacked the vital spark needed to make them special. Throughout that infuriating interlude they possessed only one truly outstanding performer in Billy Liddell, hence the tag 'Liddellpool', which was highly complimentary to the revered Scot but damning where the club's overall ambition and self-esteem was concerned. There were some very good players, such as Ronnie Moran and Alan A'Court, but also a plethora of sound but unremarkable journeymen, and some who were just not up to it.

But the main reason Anfield slipped into the doldrums and remained there for so long was the board's readiness to accept second best. It was an attitude which had allowed not only the team to stagnate, but also the stadium and the training ground at Melwood to run down. This began to change on 14 December 1959, the day Bill Shankly walked through the door to become manager.

It is tempting to suppose that Shanks' effect was instant. In fact, while he hit the place like a blast of cleansing air, making it clear to people at all levels of the club that they must change their outlook or go, it was impossible to achieve the necessary wide-ranging transformation overnight.

First he insisted on physical improvements to the premises which, while making due allowances for the depredations of the war years, he branded a disgrace. Then he set to work on a playing staff which he felt was unworthy of the Liverpool fans, that gritty, humorous, soccer-mad multitude on which he based his belief that the club's potential was literally limitless. Within weeks of his arrival he had drafted a list of twenty-four professionals who were surplus to his requirements and within a year he was rid of them all.

Throughout this frequently painful process, he was fortunate to have a backroom brigade of Reuben Bennett, Bob Paisley and Joe Fagan, each of whom he had assessed quickly as being of the highest quality. In addition, he had the moral backing of an old friend and role model, a certain Matt Busby. During Bill's early years as Liverpool boss, there was many a lengthy and heartfelt discussion between the two men, particularly during a low period when Shanks was contemplating resignation on a point of principle. Matt went a long way towards convincing his countryman that he should stay – though there might be a few United fans who would see this as Busby's biggest mistake! They remained close for the rest of their careers, their comradeship never tainted by the sometimes bitter enmity between obsessive sections of their clubs' supporters.

Shankly himself was a truly remarkable man, a footballing evangelist who demanded that his fervour be shared by all who worked with him. He regarded the task of sparking the Reds' renaissance as his life's labour and by the time he retired in 1974, prematurely as he admitted later, he had achieved that and more. Bill was a lifelong socialist and he extended the tenets of his politics into every aspect of his job. He employed a collective system in which there was no room for temperamental fancy dans and in which each man strove for his comrades while receiving similar support in return. It sounds devastatingly, almost ridiculously simple and Bill maintained that was its beauty. As he explained, 'No one was asked to do more than anyone else. We were a team. We shared the ball, we shared the game, we shared the worries. No one had to do it on his own.'

Even so, Shankly would not have left Huddersfield, who were a big club at the time, for Anfield but for his instinctive affinity with the people of Liverpool. He was moved overwhelmingly by the indomitable good cheer with which so many Scousers accepted the devastating hardships of enforced unemployment. As he put it, 'If I wanted a workforce I would pick it from Merseyside and we would wipe the floor with everybody. All they need is to be treated like human beings. The people here have a hard life but they have a big spirit. When they're on your side and all working together, then they take some beating.'

And so, ultimately, did his team, but in early 1960 those days were way in the future as he buckled down to transform the mindset of Liverpool FC, whose directors seemed satisfied with Second Division safety and regular gates of 30,000. Roger Hunt, whose Anfield arrival had preceded Shankly's by only three months, remembers the situation vividly. 'So many people seemed to be content just jogging along, doing reasonably well and never spending much in the transfer market. But Bill Shankly was different. He sensed what could be achieved and, as a passionate man himself, he felt keenly the longing of the fans.'

At first, money was a problem. He wanted top players, the likes of Jack Charlton at Leeds United and Heart of Midlothian's Dave Mackay, but attempts to sign them foundered on parsimony. That was to alter with the arrival on the board of Eric Sawyer of the Littlewoods Pools company, a shrewd financier who recognized the necessity of speculating to accumulate.

But before that overdue enlightenment was to dawn, Shanks had to get on with the job in hand, using the comparatively meagre assets available to him. One of his earliest tests, some six weeks after becoming Liverpool boss, was a fourth-round FA Cup encounter with Manchester United at Anfield.

At this juncture, United's playing strength was still below par as a result of Munich, though the Red Devils had astounded pundits by finishing as Championship runners-up in 1958/9, the first full campaign after the crash. That was a fantastic achievement, based on a free-scoring forward line of Warren Bradley, Albert Quixall, Dennis Viollet, Bobby Charlton and Albert Scanlon, but it was a one-off effort rather than the result of steady development and the early months of 1959/60 revealed that more reconstruction work was necessary.

For instance, crucially important performers such as Charlton and defender Bill Foulkes had been suffering patchy form, almost certainly due to delayed trauma from the accident, and the team had a distinctly mid-table look about it. Against that Liverpool were riding pretty high in the Second Division, having taken seven points from their previous four League games and, given home advantage, were regarded as slight favourites when the two sets of Reds met for the first time in more than half a decade.

However, a selection of the after-match headlines reveals that Merseyside expectations of taking a prestigious scalp were rudely dashed. 'Charlton back in world class', 'Bobby justifies Busby's faith' and 'Bang-Bang Charlton back on target' reflect the most popular journalistic angle, while 'Manchester United's class tells before the end' was less jaunty but more comprehensively informative.

In front of England manager Walter Winterbottom and more than 56,000 fans, Charlton chose this day to reaffirm his credentials as one of the most talented footballers of his generation. For weeks he had appeared listless and lacking in self-belief, a pale shadow of the 'Bobby Dazzler' beloved of the Old Trafford faithful, but now he was back to his enchanting best.

Unfazed by the quagmire into which Anfield had deteriorated as rain fell steadily throughout the afternoon, the unassuming son of a Geordie miner stamped his quality on proceedings after thirteen minutes. Picking up a skidding pass from Dennis Viollet in midfield, he swayed with graceful ease past would-be tackles from Johnny Wheeler and John Molyneux before planting a twenty-yard shot beyond keeper Bert Slater and into the far corner of the net. It was almost the prototype Charlton effort: the instinctive ball control and the swerving run which wrong-footed defenders while they were still several yards away from an ideal position to challenge. However, on this occasion the trademark howitzer, that demoralising weapon which was to make him his country's most prolific scorer, was substituted by a deliberate placement, which proved equally effective.

Until that moment Liverpool had been on top, and had Roger Hunt's first-minute shot not been cleared off the line by the splendid Maurice Setters then the action may have unfolded along different lines. Indeed, even after falling behind, the Second Division outfit were far from finished and they equalized after thirty-six minutes when Johnny Wheeler smacked home from twenty yards after Harry Gregg had lost a Ronnie Moran free-kick. But a minute before the interval, another Charlton contribution – this time a thudding left-footer from a Bradley cross – restored United's lead and left their hosts sorely deflated. Thereafter Bobby, now brimming with confidence, might have scored three or four as he terrorized the Reds' rearguard, though it was left to Bradley to complete the scoring with a scorching shot off the underside of the crossbar.

It had been a stirring show by Manchester and pundits predicted it might prove a turning point in their post-Munich rehabilitation and a staging post on the way to Wembley that term. In both cases they were wrong. A single-goal defeat at the hands of Sheffield Wednesday ended their FA Cup interest in the next round, and it was to take another four years of painstaking consolidation before they re-emerged as realistic title contenders.

Bobby Charlton, the quiet boy with thunder in his boots whose timely return to form shattered Liverpool's FA Cup ambitions in January 1960.

Meanwhile Liverpool were being reinvented by Bill Shankly. As cash became steadily more available he made canny excursions into the transfer market, unearthing such gems as centre-forward Ian St John from Motherwell, stopper Ron Yeats from Dundee United and wing-halves Gordon Milne and Willie Stevenson from

Preston North End and Glasgow Rangers respectively. They combined so effectively with local lads such as Ronnie Moran, Gerry Byrne and Chris Lawler (all defenders), the versatile Tommy Smith and forwards Ian Callaghan, Roger Hunt, Jimmy Melia and Alan A'Court that before long Shanks had assembled a side which could live with the best.

While undergoing constant tinkering and improvement, Liverpool finished a distant third in Bill's first two Anfield springtimes, but during 1961/2 they dominated the Second Division, claiming the Championship with five matches to spare and by an eventual eight-point margin, thus issuing a chilling warning to the top flight that a new power was abroad in the land.

That season Roger Hunt struck forty-one League goals and earned his first full England call-up. It was a period he relished. 'It was a pleasure to play for Liverpool in 1961/2. A goalscorer can't ask for more than to be part of a good side which believes in going forward and does so at every opportunity. I gelled immediately with Ian St John, who had joined us at the start of the season. He was a terrific, unselfish player and we seemed to be able to read each other's minds. The fact that he tended to drift back into midfield to pick up the ball early meant I was more an out-and-out striker than a conventional inside-forward, but with two wingers offering super service – Alan A'Court on one side and either Kevin Lewis or Ian Callaghan on the other – that was no hardship.'

Naturally enough, with Liverpool having finally achieved promotion after such a long and monumentally frustrating wait, expectations of the Anfielders were massive as the 1962/3 campaign got under way. Imagine, then, the apprehension which swept through the legions of Reds supporters when their team kicked off with two reverses and a draw, and won a mere four of their first sixteen games. In this atmosphere of foreboding Liverpool faced United at Old Trafford in November 1962, the resultant 3-3 draw offering a measure of relief to the beleaguered Merseysiders, who actually came within a few seconds of victory *(see Classic Clash Number Three on page 34)*.

It proved a hugely significant turning point. In the months that followed, Shankly's men, in whom he had retained faith throughout their tribulations, became truly formidable opponents, losing only one of their next seventeen matches. Indeed, but for that dreadful start, they might have offered a realistic challenge for the Championship pennant which ended up across Stanley Park with Everton.

Certainly, when United visited in April, Liverpool were not the type of side any relegation candidate would relish facing – and the unexpected, unpalatable but unavoidable truth was that, despite investing heavily in Torino striker Denis Law and wing-half Pat Crerand of Celtic, the Red Devils were far from certain of avoiding the ignominy of the drop.

As if added spice were needed in such a tense situation, both clubs were through to the semi-finals of the FA Cup and their League meeting was seen as a possible rehearsal for Wembley. In the event it turned out to be a sour, bad-tempered affair containing very little in the way of entertainment, very much a case of flat beer after the champagne of the six-goal thriller back in early winter. At one point the niggles looked likely to get out of hand, with St John and Law squaring up to each other and Moran and Nobby Stiles, whose less-than-cordial gestures to the Kop were missed by the referee, having a spirited difference of opinion. Happily both confrontations ended up with handshakes.

Football-wise, Stiles was guilty of two horrendous first-half misses within a minute of each other, leaving St John to steal the limelight with a seventy-second-minute winner. The result saw Liverpool move up to sixth place in the table while United wallowed in nineteenth, only a point clear of the relegation slot. Two weeks later, Lancashire's dream of a Red Rose FA Cup Final was shattered when Liverpool were bested by a numbingly negative but doggedly effective Leicester City, though United did their bit, going through against Southampton.

Come season's end, which the fearful winter delayed by several weeks, the Merseysiders were in eighth position, highly creditable for their first term back among the elite and offering immense hope for the future. United managed to scuffle clear of danger and, by way of ample consolation, lifted the FA Cup with a gala performance against the Filberts. With Liverpool comprehensively revived and the Red Devils on the verge of following suit, the scene was set for a series of epic duels.

The pugnacious but subtly skilful Ian St John, a Scottish centre-forward whose all-consuming desire for success matched Shankly's own. He was a key figure in the Anfield revolution.

Division One

10 November 1962

at Old Trafford

MANCHESTER UNITED 3

Herd 39; Quixall 69 (pen); Giles 90

Harry Gregg, Seamus Brennan, Noel Cantwell, Nobby Stiles, Bill Foulkes, Maurice Setters, Johnny Giles, Albert Quixall, David Herd, Denis Law, Bobby Charlton.

LIVERPOOL 3

St John 51; Melia 85; Moran 89

Tommy Lawrence, Gerry Byrne, Ronnie Moran, Gordon Milne, Ron Yeats, Willie Stevenson, Ian Callaghan, Roger Hunt, Ian St John, Jimmy Melia, Alan A'Court.

Half-time: 1-0 Attendance: 43,810

This match was a newspaperman's nightmare. Not that the serried ranks of frantic scribblers in Old Trafford's bulging press box did not appreciate the enthralling story which unfolded before them, merely that the timing of key events proved a little inconvenient. When United led 2-1 with five minutes left, most of the reporters, with stringent deadlines uppermost in their minds, had their yarns already written. When Melia equalized they would have embarked philosophically on rapid rewrites, then when Moran gave Liverpool the lead in sensational manner the feverish clattering of typewriter keys would have been punctuated by language of a distinctly industrial nature. But when Giles levelled with twenty seconds remaining, necessitating a third rejig in five minutes, hair would have been torn and the ears of innocent copy takers assaulted in a most ungentlemanly manner.

Still, it was all in a good cause. This gale-blown meeting between a star-studded United still in the throes of post-Munich reconstruction and newly-promoted Liverpool, struggling temporarily near the foot of the First Division table, was one for the memory bank.

United's new star, Law, was unexpectedly quiet in the wake of his four-goal demolition of Ipswich Town the previous week, being comprehensively shackled by the efficient Milne, yet the Red Devils had the better of the first half. Thus it was no more than they merited when Herd was sent clear by the back-on-form Quixall to furnish a thirty-ninth-minute lead.

However, the visitors hit back six minutes after the break when Gregg failed to hold a low shot from Callaghan and St John popped in the rebound. Thereafter Liverpool displayed admirable courage and enterprise and could feel slightly hard-done-by when Quixall restored United's advantage with a sixty-ninth-minute penalty, awarded after Melia shunted into Giles from behind.

Now Shankly's men, maybe fired by what they perceived as an unjust spot-kick, lifted their game and put their hosts under sustained pressure. It seemed destined not to pay off until five minutes from time when Melia atoned for his earlier misdemeanour by forcing in a close-range shot from Yeats' downward header.

It seemed that the tables had been well and truly turned after Setters fouled Hunt in the eighty-ninth minute and Moran beat Gregg with a fulminating twenty-yard free-kick, but the drama had yet to reach its climax. That arrived with practically the last kick of the match when Giles gulled both

Yeats and Moran before beating Lawrence with a clever cross-shot on the run.

When the final whistle blew, Liverpool were the more disappointed but their spirits would soon rise as they set off on a sequence of nine straight wins which lifted them out of the danger zone. In contrast, United would sink perilously close to the relegation trapdoor before making good their eleventh-hour escape.

Left: Liverpool goalkeeper Tommy Lawrence is seated as David Herd opens the scoring.

Below: The white-shirted Ian St John squeezes the Merseysiders' first equalizer past diving custodian Harry Gregg. A hectic climax was to follow.

CHAPTER FIVE:

A TIME OF LEGEND
1963/4 – 1968/9

FROM chronic under-achievers in the Second Division at the tail-end of the 1950s to genuine challengers for the League title in less than half a decade, Liverpool had travelled a long way under the zealous stewardship of Bill Shankly. With painstaking attention to detail, never signing a man about whose character he entertained the slightest doubt, he had constructed a dashing team indelibly imbued with the work ethic and possessing far more flair than was widely reckoned.

For a time, both before and after Anfield became a regular repository for silverware, Liverpool were the target of certain southern-based critics who disparaged them for a so-called lack of panache, referring to them as a machine. In fact, Shanks, that high priest of socialist collectivism in both football and life in general, accepted that particular tag as a compliment, though he took barbed exception – and understandably so – to sneering implications that his side was boring, in some way less worthy than those with more spectacularly gifted individuals, such as Tottenham Hotspur or Manchester United.

As he told that excellent writer John Roberts, who helped him with his autobiography in 1976, 'They said we were predictable. Well, I think anybody who is unpredictable is a waste of time. Being predictable is not too bad. Joe Louis (the great heavyweight boxer) was predictable. He would knock men down on the floor. Goodbye! We were predictable but the opposition couldn't stop us!'

In any case, the suggestion that Bill's team lacked artistry was a calumny, as any unbiased assessor of winger Peter Thompson, deep-lying centre-forward Ian St John or sweet-passing wing-half Willie Stevenson would have to acknowledge. What Liverpool were not was flashy – and they didn't need to be. The side was built on a strong Caledonian spine of goalkeeper Tommy Lawrence, man-mountain Ron Yeats at centre-half and St John leading the forward line. Arrayed around them was a collection of individuals who were all tough, could all control the ball without fuss and pass it accurately, and were all able to apply those assets with intelligence.

Matt Busby's United, meanwhile, appeared considerably less methodical, although they could never have known such sustained success by being quite the 'off-the-cuff' outfit of popular legend. What made them special, of course, was the presence of three world-class performers in Bobby Charlton, Denis Law and George Best, vividly contrasting talents but each of them, in footballing terms, a genius. The English game has known many marvellous players, and the influx of foreigners in the 1990s has increased the numbers of perceived 'greats' dramatically. But no other club has been able to boast a trinity of contemporaries quite so ravishingly endowed as United's in the 1960s. Add to them such accomplished performers as Pat Crerand, Nobby Stiles, Bill Foulkes and Tony Dunne, and the full picture of Matt Busby's fabulous post-Munich reconstruction begins to emerge.

One man arguably better placed than any other to compare the relative merits of Liverpool and United in the early and middle 1960s is Phil Chisnall, who remains unique in that he played under Busby, Shankly and Alf Ramsey, three of the most revered soccer bosses of all. As a precociously gifted young inside-forward, Mancunian Phil had signed for his hometown club and looked set to play an integral part in United's post-Munich reconstruction. He displayed such rich promise that he won Under-23 international honours and was described by England manager Alf Ramsey as 'probably the best passer of a ball in the country.' However, the white-hot competition for places at Old Trafford eased him out of contention, and after making nearly half a century of senior appearances as a Red Devil he accepted a £25,000 move to Liverpool in April 1964.

He recalls: 'I was only twenty-two and nowhere near as worldly-wise as young men are today, so I suppose I felt rather overawed to be sitting in a room beside Matt Busby and Bill Shankly while they discussed my future. I was told I didn't have to go, but it was flattering to be wanted by Liverpool, who were another great club and had just won the League. I was just going to get married and it seemed all part of a fresh start. Looking back it might have been a mistake to leave Old Trafford but I have never agonized over it.'

In the event, despite Shanks' prediction that he might be something special, Phil never made the Anfield grade, eventually continuing his career at a less exalted level with Southend United and Stockport County. But his three-and-a-half years at Anfield left him in a position to make fascinating comparisons between life with the two giants.

'Some of the differences were amazing. It might seem a bit of a cliche, but things were far more laid back at United. Matt Busby would tell us that we wouldn't be at Old Trafford if we weren't good footballers, so just go out and

George Best, Denis Law and an empty net . . . what Liverpool nightmares are made of. The Irishman applies the final touch at Old Trafford in October 1965, with Tommy Lawrence and his defenders helpless to intervene. United took the points in this battle, but the season's Championship war was won by the Merseysiders.

express ourselves. At Anfield there was far greater emphasis on teamwork and, in particular, fitness. I had heard about Liverpool's strenuous training methods before I moved, so I was quite surprised on the first day when we did some loosening-up exercises and then went for a fairly long run. It seemed pretty rigorous but nothing I couldn't handle and I turned to another young lad and said, "Well, that wasn't too bad." He just stared at me and replied, "We haven't even started yet!" Then came the most intensive individual routines I have ever experienced. Each of us was put under pressure and stretched to the limit. The training was so hard that the matches became easy in comparison, which was exactly what was intended. The result was that Liverpool were the fittest team around and they would steamroller opponents in the second half. That's why they scored so many late goals. When I was at Old Trafford I used to have breakfast before going to work. I never did that in all my time with Liverpool. I'd never have kept it down!

'Yet, for all that, United used to beat Liverpool as often as not because of their fabulous ability. Don't misunderstand me: obviously United needed a certain standard of fitness and a certain amount of method, but they didn't concentrate on it anything like as intensely as Liverpool did.'

As for the rivalry between the two camps, Phil found it hard to reconcile with the relationship between the two managers. 'They were very close, almost seeming like father and son. Bill Shankly looked up to Matt Busby as a hero. He would come through to Manchester to see the boss nearly every week. Despite all the palaver with the fans, they were great buddies. That was the reality.'

Despite the fact that Shanks was the younger man, Busby's junior in terms of both experience and achievement, circumstances dictated that come late November 1963 his team seemed approximately a year ahead of his mentor's in achieving the blend and consistency which are the hallmarks of League Champions. Some five weeks earlier United had risen briefly to the First Division summit only to fall away alarmingly, while the Merseysiders were looking increasingly ominous. Thus it came as no surprise that when the north-west's two rising powers collided at Old Trafford a month before Christmas it was Liverpool who came out on top, shading a gripping game by its only goal.

Above: Phil Chisnall, who had to make alternative breakfast arrangements after leaving Old Trafford for Anfield.

Opposite: Alf Arrowsmith, a Mancunian who was not popular in his home town after his two goals scuppered United's title challenge.

Before the kick-off there was a sickening indication of mindless trends in crowd behaviour when a minute's silence for President Kennedy, who had been assassinated the day before in Dallas, was interrupted by several morons on the Stretford End terrace.

Happily, their loutish contribution was quickly forgotten as a splendid contest got under way. But while Liverpool were never less than positive and Albert Quixall, who had been out of sorts in recent matches, showed his most incisive attacking form of the season for United, for most of the first half the dominant figures were defenders.

The game turned on an incident a minute before the interval. Peter Thompson swung over a wickedly curving corner, home goalkeeper Harry Gregg attempted to pluck it from the head of Ron Yeats and the two collided with horrifying force. The ball ran loose and a third player, Maurice Setters, was hurt as he hacked it off the line, but while he and Yeats were able to continue after treatment, poor Gregg suffered a broken collarbone.

The days of substitutes had not yet dawned, so centre-forward David Herd took over between the posts, as he recalls with a rueful grin: 'I don't know why I volunteered for the job. I must have been mad. Did I enjoy it? No, I did not!' All the genial Scottish international can remember of the occasion was conceding the goal, in the seventy-fifth minute, to the fearsome Yeats. 'The ball came over from a corner – I think Ian Callaghan took it – and I stayed on my line when I should have gone out to take it. Ron met it with his head and I didn't have a chance.'

In fact, Herd does himself an injustice. Yeats' effort would have taxed any regular keeper to the limit, and what has slipped the valiant deputy's mind is his sterling work throughout a second half in which Liverpool attempted to cash in on Gregg's absence. David made several saves of which Harry would have been proud, including one spectacular full-length dive to deflect a scorcher from Jimmy Melia. As Matt Busby joked afterwards, 'He'll be in goal for our next training session and if he makes any more stops like the one from Melia he can stay there until Harry gets back!'

Looking back at the game, United made no concessions to adversity and created as many chances as Liverpool but without making one count. The setback in the Championship race was compounded by the loss of the courageous Gregg, who had returned to the action, albeit as a passenger on the wing, with his arm in a sling. A survivor of the Munich disaster, he was a magnificent keeper, arguably United's finest ever until the advent of Peter Schmeichel, but he was plagued by injuries throughout his career, missing out on two League titles and an FA Cup triumph as a result.

Yeats' goal, his first since his arrival at Anfield from Dundee United two-and-a-half years earlier, left Shankly gleeful and not disposed to understatement. 'Ron Yeats is the

Division One
4 April 1964
at Anfield

LIVERPOOL 3

Callaghan 6; Arrowsmith 39, 52

Tommy Lawrence, Gerry Byrne,
Ronnie Moran, Gordon Milne, Ron Yeats,
Willie Stevenson, Ian Callaghan,
Roger Hunt, Ian St John,
Alf Arrowsmith, Peter Thompson.

MANCHESTER UNITED 0

Harry Gregg, Seamus Brennan,
Tony Dunne, Pat Crerand, Bill Foulkes,
Maurice Setters, George Best,
Nobby Stiles, David Herd, Denis Law,
Bobby Charlton.

Half-time: 2-0   Attendance: 52,559

IT was the day the English footballing public finally woke up to the inescapable truth that Bill Shankly's Liverpool were going to win the League – and that they would make worthy champions. Had United triumphed – and, frankly, there was never any question of that – they would have moved within a point of Bill Shankly's men, but now they stood five points adrift and effectively out of the title reckoning.

In thrashing the Red Devils, their main rivals for the crown, Liverpool's teamwork was matchless, their conviction unshakeable. At no time on this tumultuous Anfield afternoon did there appear the merest shred of doubt about the outcome.

The hosts began at a gallop, Gregg being forced into early saves from Arrowsmith and Hunt, and there was time for only one defiant gesture from the visitors – a scorching drive from Herd which narrowly cleared Lawrence's bar – before Liverpool took the lead. Thompson's steepling corner was fumbled by Gregg as he was challenged by Yeats and the ball ran loose to Hunt. The England marksman, so often vilified for lack of intricacy in his footwork, confounded his critics with a slick backheel to Callaghan who netted his first goal for four months with an emphatic narrow-angled drive.

Now United saw their Championship dream begin to crumble and they contrived a brief flurry of attacks in response, but they were without cohesion and Liverpool soaked them up comfortably before firmly quelling the rebellion with a second goal after thirty-nine minutes. A Callaghan shot was blocked on the line by Law – whose presence between his own posts says much about the way the game was going – only for the winger to regain possession before crossing for Arrowsmith to head home. By this time Gregg was hampered by an injury sustained in a collision with St John, but the fittest of custodians would not have repelled the young striker's perfectly placed effort.

Seven minutes after the break any lingering doubt about the outcome was erased when Arrowsmith, a Mancunian by birth, rounded off a sweet five-man move by directing an awkwardly bouncing ball into goal from ten yards.

Thereafter, with the Merseysiders coasting, United became increasingly frustrated. Not surprisingly the combative Law was booked following a tussle with his Scottish international colleague St John and Setters was fortunate to escape similar censure. Long before the end, Red Devil was upbraiding Red Devil, which the Kop was quick to spot and to jeer, and when the final whistle came it was a blessed relief to Matt Busby's side.

Every Liverpool man had been at or near the top of his game, particularly Milne, who had blotted out Law while still endeavouring to make a creative contribution, and the veteran Moran, who reacted to recent claims that he was past his best by giving arguably his most accomplished performance of the season.

Overall, though, the lasting impression was of the collective excellence of the champions-elect. Rarely had they practised what their manager preached to more telling effect.

Not for the first time, United owe a huge debt to Nobby Stiles (right), who clears their lines at Anfield in October 1964. Watching with contrasting emotions are (left to right) the Mancunians' prostrate keeper Pat Dunne, United defender Bill Foulkes and Liverpool raiders Roger Hunt and Chris Lawler. The visitors won 2-0.

greatest centre-half in the world today,' he said. 'George Young used to do a terrific job for Rangers and Scotland, but Ron is even better.' Whether or not the Liverpool boss was indulging in deliberate hyperbole, the comment underlined his immense and genuine regard for his skipper, the defensive cornerstone of his Red revolution.

Victory in Manchester was a telling step on the road to title glory but it was a barnstorming run of springtime form, including a 3-0 tanning of United in the return game *(see Classic Clash Number Four, on page 39)*, which made certain the coveted Championship pennant was fluttering over Anfield at season's end. As Busby led his well-beaten side out of the dressing-room, he called to Shankly, 'Congratulations Bill. See that you make a good job of it now.' It was an illuminating moment, typical both of the times and of the warmth between the two men. Who could imagine such a greeting being passed between the two managers today?

The Liverpool boss wasn't a boaster but he bristled with justifiable pride in his achievement, taking care to stress the part played in it by Messrs Paisley, Fagan and Bennett, to whom he was as close as family in their working lives without ever extending their relationships away from football.

What made him happiest was the certainty that, after years of comparative neglect, solid long-term foundations had been laid and that he should be able to entertain the people of Liverpool royally for the foreseeable future. Busby, too, could be pleased with his campaign. Finishing as runners-up to the resurgent Anfielders was no disgrace, and he believed that his team was on the verge of something big.

Just how big began to become apparent during the following autumn and early winter when a scintillating sequence of thirteen wins and a draw from fourteen matches underlined United's pedigree as title contenders. Their victims included Liverpool, who were finding the mantle of Champions so onerous that they managed only five wins in the opening three months of the new term.

The Red brigades' Hallowe'en meeting at Anfield provoked a truly ghoulish response from a stridently vocal faction of the home fans. Having become accustomed to their side sweeping all before them, a 2-0 defeat at Mancunian hands was deemed unacceptable and was greeted with an excess of bile directed at their own players, including England marksman Roger Hunt. Such treatment was as unjustified as it was idiotic, for no one tried harder than the loyal, likeable Hunt, a man who had scored freely throughout the club's renaissance and would continue to do so for another half-decade. Indeed, that season he contributed thirty-seven goals in all senior competitions and for 'slanderous comments to descend on the poor fellow's head', as one reporter put it, was unforgivable.

The Kopites' ire extended to their opponents, too, and Nobby Stiles, who was booked for kicking the ball into the crowd, was pelted with pennies as he lay injured in the United goalmouth after clearing a shot from Chris Lawler off the line.

The game itself was brimming with good football, with United holding sway throughout the first period and deserving the thirty-fifth-minute lead provided by David Herd. They dominated the next quarter, too, with Charlton and Crerand at their irresistibly creative best, but after the Scot had lobbed a delightful second goal on sixty-five minutes, Liverpool responded with a frenetic grandstand finish which might have yielded a reply. As the action hotted up, so did a few tempers and Yeats was mighty fortunate to escape being sent off after he appeared to butt Herd in the face, both ball and referee having departed the immediate scene.

Happily, there was no malice in the incident and more than thirty years later the two men still engage in occasional sporting encounters. David explains: 'I bump into Ron on the golf course from time to time, and we'll enjoy a natter about how we used to battle in the old days. He was a fine centre-half, absolutely dominant in the air, so we used to keep the ball on the ground or play it in to the near post. They didn't come much tougher than Ron; he didn't take many prisoners!'

To return to 1964/5, the points accrued from that tempestuous encounter lifted United above Tommy Docherty's Chelsea to the top of the League, which is where they were when they completed the double over the Merseysiders with a 3-0 victory in April. [See Classic Clash Number Five on page 42]. Shanks was not amused, as Tommy Smith recounts: 'It was only the week before we faced Leeds in the FA Cup Final and he seemed to think the prospect of Wembley might have affected some of us. He might have been right. Whatever, as we walked into the dressing room he was ranting and raving, and feeling everybody's shirt to make sure they had been sweating. He was fearsome that day.'

He was a happy man a week later, though, when his Reds overcame Don Revie's side to lift the Cup for the first time in Liverpool's history. When he spoke of it years later, his passion was undiluted. 'Grown men were crying and it was the greatest feeling any human being could have to see what we had done. There have been many proud moments. Wonderful, fantastic moments. But that was the greatest day.' Having compensated thus for slipping out of the title race, Liverpool rounded off their season by perishing gloriously and controversially in the semi-final of the European Cup against Inter Milan.

As for United, two days after disposing of the Merseysiders they beat Arsenal to take the title back to Old Trafford for the first time in eight years. Busby had

Division One
24 April 1965
at Old Trafford

MANCHESTER UNITED 3

Law 40, 57; Connelly 81

Pat Dunne, Seamus Brennan, Tony Dunne, Pat Crerand, Bill Foulkes, Nobby Stiles, John Connelly, Bobby Charlton, Noel Cantwell, Denis Law, George Best.

LIVERPOOL 0

Tommy Lawrence, Chris Lawler, Gerry Byrne, Geoff Strong, Ron Yeats, Willie Stevenson, Bobby Graham, Roger Hunt, Phil Chisnall, Tommy Smith, Peter Thompson.

Half-time: 1-0 Attendance: 55,772

This comprehensive trouncing of Liverpool by Manchester United offered a neat symmetry with the corresponding fixture of the previous campaign. Then the Merseysiders had outplayed their ancient foes to the tune of 3-0 and gone on to take the Championship; now the roles were precisely reversed.

This time United might have made the scoreline lastingly embarrassing, rather than merely unpalatable for their fellow Lancastrians. They squandered countless opportunities, they had two 'goals' disallowed and man-of-the-match Bobby Charlton twice threatened to bring the woodwork down around Tommy Lawrence's ears by striking the post with fearsome force. In addition, the besieged custodian made a series of blinding saves.

In fairness it should be pointed out that Liverpool's FA Cup Final date with Leeds, just one week hence, must have been playing on their minds, and injury had deprived them of three key players in Ian St John, Ian Callaghan and Gordon Milne.

The traffic was virtually all one way from the first whistle with Pat Dunne in the Manchester goal touching the ball only twice in half-an-hour, and then only thanks to back-passes from his own defenders. However, over-anxiety in front of goal was letting down a United side clearly feeling the strain of being poised on the threshold of the club's first title since the Munich disaster and the visitors' fortifications held firm until the forty-minute mark.

Then, at last, the almost non-stop pressure paid off when Yeats misheaded a Connelly cross to Law, who transferred the ball from chest to foot in one blinding blur of movement before netting from a distance of ten yards. Old Trafford erupted with a gigantic roar of relief and United finally settled into the smooth, sophisticated passing rhythm which had become their trademark.

The second half was akin to an exhibition as Charlton and Crerand dominated midfield, Best and Connelly ran amok on the flanks and Cantwell laboured nobly as leader of the line in the absence of David Herd.

And then there was Law, who afforded a glimpse of the inspiration which made him so special when he accelerated suddenly beyond his markers to throw himself headlong at a cross from Crerand in the fifty-seventh minute. He finished in a crumpled heap in the back of the net, but the ball was nestling beside him and United were two goals to the good.

For the next fifteen minutes the Mancunians were reduced to ten men while Law had stitches inserted in a knee wound and briefly the storm abated around the Liverpool goal. The excellent Thompson, who vied with Lawrence as Liverpool's most influential figure, took advantage of the lull to pose some attacking threat of his own. But then the Scot returned, normal service was resumed and Connelly added a third goal from close range after eighty-one minutes.

So the final tally was three when it might have been six, seven or eight, and the Liverpudlians went home with their respectability intact. But only just.

completed a remarkable rebuilding job and been rewarded with the premier domestic prize.

For both of England's most fanatically supported clubs, the future was beckoning alluringly and it was appropriate that they should meet next in the Charity Shield, that traditional friendly reserved for high achievers. In the 1960s the fixture was staged at the home of the Championship-holders which, on this humid, late-summer's afternoon, enabled cricket fans from the other Old Trafford to take a couple of hours off from watching Lancashire take a whacking from Championship-chasing Northamptonshire.

Though the cut and thrust of recent League encounters was inevitably missing, United and Liverpool served up an entertaining contest, sharing four goals and the custody of the Shield for the next year. Twice the home side led, through Best and Herd only to be pegged back by strikes from Stevenson, and Yeats, though it was the visitors who finished the stronger and who provided the game's only truly memorable moment in the form of their first equalizer. Willie Stevenson, a tough but cultured wing-half who spent his early career as a Glasgow Ranger languishing in the shadow of Jim Baxter, dribbled impudently past four opponents before netting from the edge of the box. Shankly praised the manoeuvre lavishly, only regretting that it had not come in a game when points were at stake.

Certainly the Merseysiders could have done with such a decisive intervention at Old Trafford in October, when United fielded Best, Law and Charlton as a central trio and gave a first-half display that verged on the lyrical. The Irishman, at his most irrepressibly inventive, put them in front after eighteen minutes, following a defensive mix-up involving Yeats and Smith. If that was messy, then ample compensation for the purists was not long in coming. Eight minutes before the break, Charlton picked up the ball in midfield and sent a devastating diagonal through-pass which rendered the entire Liverpool back four helpless. Seeing Law bearing down from the left flank, Lawrence sprinted from between his posts to intercept but Denis won the race and stroked the ball past the diving custodian with a touch of gossamer-light perfection.

That was the end of the scoring but not the incident. At half-time fighting broke out in the crowd, a policeman's helmet was seen hurtling through the air and four fans from the Liverpool section, including a small boy, were thrown out of the ground. When the action resumed on the pitch, it might have been a different match. Unusually for that era, United had decided to defend their lead which resulted in the hitherto out-of-sorts visitors launching a succession of attacks. Play became unduly physical, Stiles was hit by a missile from the terraces and more supporters were ejected. What had been beautiful had turned ugly, but at least the Champions, who had made a lacklustre start to the defence of their crown, could console themselves with the points. Liverpool, who had been in much better fettle and would go on to regain the title, would have to wait until New Year's Day to gain recompense.

They did so with a late winner from the excellent Gordon Milne – whose buzzing midfield contribution rarely seemed to be appreciated by the fans until he was absent – cementing the Reds' position at the top of the table *(see Classic Clash Number Six on page 45)*. For United it marked the end of a ten-match unbeaten sequence and proved a watershed in a season in which they promised much but finished empty-handed, losing FA Cup and European Cup semi-finals along the way. Liverpool won the League at a canter and came close to a marvellous double, going down to a bizarre goal from Libuda of Borussia Dortmund in the final of the European Cup-Winners' Cup at Hampden Park.

In 1966/7 the Shankly-Busby title monopoly continued, this time United claiming the prize. Both clashes between the two clubs ended all-square, though they were radically different in character. The first, at Old Trafford in December, was an exciting contest from which the Red Devils were content to emerge with the one point which kept them

Opposite: Not this time, Georgie! Tommy Smith raises his arm to claim an infringement as the inspirational Best dispatches the ball goalwards.

on top of the table after being deprived of Law and Stiles through injury and illness. Meanwhile Liverpool, desperate to recover from a 5-1 midweek mauling by Ajax in Amsterdam, were equally satisfied to share four goals, all of which came in the first half.

The stars were George Best and Ian St John, who each scored twice, with the little Irishman shading the headlines for knocking Ron Yeats to the ground in retaliation for a perceived foul. Remarkably he got away with a booking.

It was classic end-to-end fare with St John capitalizing on a typically incisive Milne through-ball after thirteen minutes. Best responded with a slashing cross-shot three minutes later and a twenty-seventh-minute penalty after Yeats had upended young Jim Ryan, then 'The Saint' swivelled sweetly on a Thompson corner seconds before the interval. Yet for all that hectic action, the enduring image of the game was one of pure comedy. When the hard-working Herd crossed invitingly into the Liverpool goalmouth, Charlton pulled back his lethal left foot and a sensational strike seemed imminent. But Bobby failed to connect and the ball struck his standing right foot before bouncing to safety, leaving the great man with egg, and an apologetic grin, on his face. Park footballers everywhere could take comfort from the proof that, on occasion, even this most graceful of performers could look like a donkey!

There were no such laughs, and no goals, when the clubs met again, at Anfield in March. For Liverpool victory was imperative to wipe out the Red Devils' two-point lead at the top of the First Division, while a draw would be enough for the visitors to retain the title initiative. In a ragged, rugged encounter marred by a buffeting wind and a plague of over-physical challenges, United got their wish. Not for the first time Ron Yeats and Denis Law were less than cordial in their attentions to one another, and Liverpool's new signing from Blackpool, Emlyn Hughes, made two tackles which would have been more appropriate on a rugby pitch. Some of the spectators got into the spirit of things by fighting behind a goal, a space appearing in the crowd as if by magic to accommodate the combatants.

The most impressive forward on view was Ian Callaghan, the Merseysiders' workaholic right-winger, but he was shadowed faithfully by young Bobby Noble, whose hugely promising career was ended by a car crash only a month later. Ian reflects: 'There was nothing worth remembering about that game, but I recall Bobby as being potentially outstanding. He had not been in the side for very long but people were already talking about him as an England possible. What happened to him was so tragic.'

Callaghan debunked the popular myth that Matt Busby's wonderfully attractive sides relied on breathtaking attack to the detriment of their defence. 'They had some of the hardest opponents I ever faced. Three that stick in my memory are Tony Dunne, Nobby Stiles and Bill Foulkes. Tony was so quick to recover if you did get past him and read the game well; Nobby was fantastically underrated, a very good all-round footballer as well as a ball-winner; as for Bill, he didn't say much but you knew you had been in a game after facing him. Everyone at Liverpool had great regard for the United defence.'

In turn, Cally himself was one of the most respected figures in the game, excelling first as an out-and-out flankman under Bill Shankly, then serving Bob Paisley as a dynamically chugging midfielder, all the while maintaining an unbesmirched reputation for sportsmanship. His readiness to work and subjugate his own interests to those of the team was used frequently by Shankly against United, especially at Old Trafford when the Merseysiders' rearguard was likely to be under most pressure.

He recalls: 'It started when Bobby Charlton was their outside-left. I used to play on the right so I was in direct opposition, and Bill got me to drop back to block the service to Bobby. It limited me a bit as an attacker but we were playing to a formula and that was my job. I never had any problems with that. After all, Bobby, George Best and Denis Law were special players who demanded special attention. Bill didn't pretend otherwise. On a Friday morning he would tell us what great players they were, then make the point that

Opposite: Gordon Milne (right) pops up to ensure justice is done with a late winner. Goalkeeper Harry Gregg is grounded in the melee, while retaining their feet if not their equilibrium are (left to right) United's Bobby Charlton, Bill Foulkes and Noel Cantwell, and Liverpool's Roger Hunt.

Division One
1 January 1966
at Anfield

LIVERPOOL 2

Smith 39; Milne 88

Tommy Lawrence, Chris Lawler,
Gerry Byrne, Gordon Milne, Ron Yeats,
Willie Stevenson, Ian Callaghan,
Roger Hunt, Ian St John, Tommy Smith,
Peter Thompson.

MANCHESTER UNITED 1

Law 2

Harry Gregg, Tony Dunne, Noel Cantwell,
Pat Crerand, Bill Foulkes, Nobby Stiles,
George Best, Denis Law, Bobby Charlton,
David Herd, John Connelly.

Half-time: 1-1 Attendance: 53,970

H ERE was a match which throbbed with passion from first to final whistle, a tempestuous encounter which opened with United snatching the lead after two minutes and closed with League leaders Liverpool grabbing a richly deserved winner with only 120 seconds to spare. In between there was non-stop incident, with the biggest losers being the thousands of fans turned away when the gates were locked forty-five minutes before kick-off.

That opening goal owed nothing to the visitors' famous flowing football and everything to the fiery opportunism of Denis Law. Gregg launched a long clearance downfield, Law outfought Yeats to gain possession, then dodged round the courageously advancing Lawrence before planting the ball into the unguarded net.

The effect was like a wasp stinging a raging bull. Now wave after wave of Liverpool attacks threatened to engulf white-shirted United in a red tide and although Matt Busby's boys engineered an occasional threat on the break, an

equalizer seemed inevitable long before it materialized in the thirty-ninth minute.

In fact, the manner of its arrival was something of a surprise as the scorer, Tommy Smith, recalls: 'We were 1-0 down and Shanks was going off his head, when I got the ball and I nutmegged George Best. Really! For a split second I didn't know what to do, whether to shout "Yes!" or to pass it to one of the other lads. In the end I mis-hit a shot from about twenty yards. It was low and slow and Harry Gregg had time to throw his hat on it. But he was late going down and it crept in between his hand and the post. I could hardly believe it.'

During the second half United's goal was under constant siege, and as the match wore on towards its pulsating conclusion the catalogue of personal duels which seemed in danger of going out of control began to lengthen. For starters there was Law and Smith, Yeats and Law, Smith and Stiles, St John and Law, Smith and Best – the names of the usual suspects were predictably prominent. At one point Smith executed a rugby tackle on David Herd, an offence for which he

would be dismissed in the 1990s, but he escaped without even a caution. However, Tommy's physical zealotry could not conceal his accomplishment as a footballer and one over-excited Merseyside-based reporter even compared him to Duncan Edwards, a ludicrous parallel but illustrative of the Anfield iron man's majestic form on the day.

Another conspicuous contributor to the Liverpool cause was Ian St John, who had six clear scoring opportunities, only to hit the bar twice, miss one sitter and see three goal-bound efforts frustrated by magnificent Gregg saves.

In the end, with the Kop seething with frustration, the glory went to Gordon Milne, who had scored the winner against title rivals Leeds only three days earlier. With only two minutes to go, Gerry Byrne drove a twenty-five yarder into the crowded United goalmouth and Milne deflected it deftly into the net. The eruption of joy and relief was frightening in its intensity, and the Mancunians' faint hopes of retaining their Championship had taken a near-fatal blow.

if we could contain those three by starving them of possession, then we should have no trouble with the rest of them. He was great at kidology!'

There are many illustrations of the off-the-field closeness of the two camps in the 1960s, few more endearing than the friendship between Shankly and Charlton. Cally recalls: 'When we were due to play at Old Trafford, we would stay the Friday evening at a hotel in Lymm, Cheshire, just round the corner from where Bobby lived. On the morning of a match Shanks was not a fellow to lie in bed; he wanted to be up and doing. So he got into the habit of going for a walk and one morning he ended up at Bobby's house. The story goes that Bobby happened to peer out of the bedroom window and saw someone prowling in his garden. On closer examination it turned out to be Bill so he went downstairs in his dressing gown and let him in. They ended up talking football over a cup of tea, and that became a regular thing whenever we were in the area, even if we were playing City. There was a great mutual respect there. Bobby thought the world of Shanks and everybody at Liverpool felt the same about Matt Busby. There was a real bond between the clubs and friendships were made then that continue today, mainly on the golf course. That's the way it should be. The hostility which has crept into the modern game, mostly among fans it should be said, is completely unwarranted.'

Not that there was any lack of psychological warfare in the 1960s, as Cally points out. 'Bill was renowned for the way he would wind people up, and there was the famous "This Is Anfield" sign at the entrance to the players' tunnel. Obviously that wasn't Matt Busby's style, but I always remember there was a particular smell at United. They had a liniment that whiffed like nothing else. It seeped through the corridors and you were aware of it as soon as you arrived. It was distinctive and let you know where you were. Maybe it was a subtle form of intimidation, a way of saying "This is Old Trafford and it's going to be hard."'

The 1967/8 season was to bring ultimate glory for United, when they became the first English club to lift the European Cup, and anti-climax for Liverpool, but as the meetings between them demonstrated, in reality there was very little to choose between the two teams.

Both matches resulted in 2-1 away wins, the first going the way of the Red Devils in November. They arrived at Anfield a point behind their table-topping hosts and when Liverpool mounted an early barrage it seemed unlikely that the positions would be reversed by teatime. However, United survived the onslaught and the genius Best put them two up by half-time, thanks to a glancing header in the eighteenth minute and the adroit conversion of a raking Crerand pass in the fortieth. In both instances, Lawrence might have been unhappy with his judgement.

After the break the Reds set about rescuing their 100 per cent home record with gusto, but United had laid canny plans for a lengthy rearguard action and carried them out to the letter. The main ploy consisted of stemming the supply of passes to wingers Callaghan and Thompson, thus forcing a frontal assault with which the majestic Foulkes was eminently capable of dealing. With the abrasive John Fitzpatrick operating as an extra defender, the visitors' goal remained intact until the eighty-third minute, when Hunt scored after neat work by Tony Hateley. But it was a classic case of too little, too late.

Mancunian fans taunted the Liverpudlians with earthy corruptions of the Kop's own chants and, astonishingly given the increasingly hostile atmosphere between the two clans, were greeted with nothing more than silent disdain.

Both clubs remained in the title race when their paths crossed again at Old Trafford in April, with both United and Manchester City beginning the day with a two-point advantage over the Merseysiders. However, Busby's side had been faltering of late, their attention possibly diverted by their European adventure, and Shanks sniffed an upset, announcing to his team before the kick-off: 'Boys, I don't think we'll

have much trouble today. They look tired, dog tired.'

After only three minutes his assessment looked cock-eyed. Yeats miscued a free-kick straight to the feet of Charlton, who hit a long pass to the right flank, where Hughes' fumble allowed Best to stride on and beat Lawrence at his leisure. However, the Liverpool skipper lost little time in making amends, heading against Alex Stepney's post only six minutes later and netting the rebound. Then, just after the quarter-hour mark, Hateley set up Hunt for what proved to be the winner. Hunt remembers the occasion as if it were yesterday: 'The sun was shining, we were both in the running for the title and the atmosphere was fabulous. This was what Manchester United v Liverpool was all about. I recall the one-two with Tony and sidefooting past Stepney, though at that early stage I didn't think it would be the decisive goal. We played well and deserved our victory in the end, but we owed a big debt to Tommy Lawrence. He was superb that day as he often was, although he didn't get his fair share of recognition. A lot of people dismissed him as a bit cumbersome, but in fact he could move really quickly and, having been an outfield player until he was fourteen, he could read the game really well. That was ideal for us because our defence used to push up and Tommy acted as a kind of sweeper. It

United's David Sadler is outnumbered by a Liverpool posse of (left to right) Tommy Lawrence, Emlyn Hughes and Tommy Smith, and the ball squirms to safety at Anfield in March 1967.

wasn't very often that he was caught out.' Sadly, for his pains on this occasion, Tommy was showered with missiles by idiots in the Stretford End.

Another memory of the day comes from United centre-half David Sadler. 'I was in direct opposition to Tony Hateley, who was extremely effective in the air. Before the game Matt Busby pulled me to one side and told me not to allow him free headers, so I made sure I gave myself an extra yard in which to jump. The problem is that Liverpool, obviously scenting Matt's ploy, starting dropping the ball in to his feet. With me allowing him space, it was probably the best game Hateley ever had on the floor!'

At twenty to five that evening, all three contenders had forty-five points, with Liverpool and United slated as joint favourites, but to widespread surprise Joe Mercer's City compiled an excellent late run to frustrate both of them and claim the Championship. For Busby and his team there was more than ample compensation in the form of the European Cup, very much their Holy Grail. Meanwhile Shankly, who was beginning to ring the changes to his vintage combination of mid-decade, finished the season empty-handed but with high hopes of improvement in 1968/9.

He achieved it, too – his club's sixty-one points being enough to win many a title, but not this time when an outstanding Leeds side compiled a then record sixty-seven. Certainly Bill's Reds outclassed United at Anfield in October but, sadly, the game was a travesty with the visitors fielding seven reserves in advance of their World Club Championship second-leg confrontation with Estudiantes of Argentina. Matt Busby declared that all the absentees were genuinely injured, but that was of little consolation to the massive crowd who witnessed a non-event.

Liverpool, fresh from scoring eleven goals in their previous three League outings, were excessively profligate in front of the posts, contenting themselves with St John's header after fourteen minutes and new marksman Alun Evans' late strike. For United, debutant centre-half Steve James and young midfielder Carlo Sartori showed promise, but it was a miserably unequal contest played out to an accompaniment of obscene chants from both sets of supporters. The watching Argentinians, whose knowledge of colloquial English was mercifully minute, can hardly have been impressed. They might, though, have appreciated the Kop's joke at the expense of Nobby Stiles, who had been dubbed 'El Bandido' following his dubious dismissal for alleged dissent in Buenos Aires. After Nobby had gesticulated with characteristic eloquence when a decision displeased him, the great terrace roared as one man: 'That is why you get sent off!'

Inestimably more entertaining fare was on offer when Liverpool travelled to Old Trafford in December, at which time the fortunes of the two protagonists were at considerable variance. The Merseysiders led the First Division by four points and were looking for their seventh successive victory; United, having lost their violent showdown with Estudiantes, were enduring their poorest campaign since their brush with relegation in 1963.

However, Bobby Charlton and company, producing their most attractive football of the season despite a treacherous frozen surface, overcame their all-conquering visitors thanks to a single strike by Denis Law. So dominant were United that they might have added several more goals but for a heroic display by keeper Tommy Lawrence, of whom Hugh McIlvanney wrote, 'He could not go down to feet more often if he had a shoeshine concession.' Even Lawrence was helpless to prevent the fifty-third-minute score, which arrived at the end of a deadly passing sequence which had become a familiar nightmare to defenders of that era. The way it went was: Charlton-Best-Law-goal!

At the end of that season, with Liverpool a gallant second in the First Division and United a mediocre eleventh, the two clubs were at a crossroads. The Merseysiders would regroup under Shankly, eventually going on to scale new heights; but for their old rivals, the storm clouds were gathering.

CHAPTER SIX:

FOOTBALL APOCALYPSE 1969/70 – 1973/4

I N January 1970, Sir Matt Busby announced his intention of passing over the reins of his beloved football team to another man at the end of the season. He was sixty years old, had been through untold trauma, had assembled three magnificent teams and had attained his lifetime's ambition. Now a new era was beginning at Old Trafford and, with results already declining and no shortage of signs that the going would become increasingly choppy, it was time for a change.

After a frenzy of speculation about his likely successor, there came news in springtime that Wilf McGuinness, United's reserve team trainer and former Busby Babe, would be promoted from within. In some quarters the loquacious thirty-one-year-old Mancunian was described as the luckiest man in football; other, sager observers opined the opposite.

Superficially it was every prospective manager's dream to be placed in charge of Manchester United, one of the world's biggest clubs. But what was he faced with? Some of the stars were close to their sell-by dates, many of the youngsters were not up to the standard of past vintages and the transfer market was fraught with peril for such an inexperienced operator. In addition, Wilf had a legend looking over his shoulder – Sir Matt had moved 'upstairs' to become general manager – and the new man found it difficult to command the respect of certain senior players.

Despite this unpromising climate, United were showing signs of recovering from a dreadful start to the campaign when they entertained an ominously rampant Liverpool in mid-September. Thus far Shankly's side had taken sixteen points from a possible eighteen and, as they looked down on the rest of the division, there was an air of looming omnipotence about them.

George Best didn't give a fig. Though disillusioned by behind-the-scenes developments at Old Trafford, and reportedly not on the best of terms with co-star Bobby Charlton, he turned on a world-class display which inspired an unexpected home victory. The Irishman was everywhere, a bewildering, untameable presence who constantly wrought havoc, switching positions to create chances for himself and others, never allowing the Merseysiders' normally ultra-efficient rearguard to impose its customary command. Meanwhile, in almost surreal counterpoint to the twinkle-toed fashion icon, there was Charlton, looking old and stern and austere, still enchantingly creative in his distribution but frequently busying himself with the more menial of midfield duties. For their part, Liverpool ran ferociously, stabbed their simple passes with their usual economy, but for all the dynamism offered by the splendid trio of Smith, Hughes and Callaghan, they failed conspicuously to thrill.

Morgan and Best rapped the woodwork for United and Hunt did the same for Liverpool, before the decisive moment came after sixty-seven minutes. Naturally it involved Best, who beat Yeats in the air – no mean feat in itself – to feed Alan Gowling, whose pass sent Morgan through to shoot past Lawrence. One reporter concluded his report with the imprecation, 'See Best while you can for you will not

Tommy Smith, 'The Anfield Iron', in 1970.
His formidable hardness was legendary, but his admirable all-round ability was not always appreciated.

see another one like him'. Some thirty years on, his judgement seems pretty sound.

As the season wore on United stabilized without ever looking likely to break into the leading group, while Liverpool were far more consistent. Mortifyingly for their fans, though, they fell behind Harry Catterick's exhilaratingly resurgent Everton. However, having taken over as First Division leaders by trouncing the Toffees 3-0 at Goodison only a week before their return rendezvous with McGuinness' men in December, the Kopites could be excused for drooling at the prospect of another major scalp. Hence their dismay, and the football world's astonishment, when the Mancunians racked up the most emphatic Anfield triumph in their history.

They deserved it, too. Prompted cannily by recalled veteran playmaker Pat Crerand, ponderously slow but still remarkably sharp of brain and touch, United delivered their soundest all-round performance of a patchy season. The damage began with a Yeats own goal after twenty minutes, but when the dynamic Emlyn Hughes popped in an equalizer five minutes later the general consensus was that the visitors had shot their bolt. Not so. Second-half strikes from Ian Ure and Morgan served as appetizers to Charlton's crowning glory. Playing a slick one-two with Morgan with six minutes left, Bobby bludgeoned a twelve-yard howitzer of such savagery that Lawrence's prevailing emotion must have been relief to have escaped with his life.

For thirty-one-year-old Roger Hunt, the game carried a lasting significance, even though he appeared only for the last fifteen minutes as a substitute for Ian Ross as the Reds desperately sought a way back into contention. He didn't know it at the time but it was to be the last of his 489 senior outings in ten illustrious years at Anfield and soon he would be a Bolton Wanderer. During his golden decade 'Sir Roger' notched a barely credible 285 senior goals, a club record until it was overhauled by Ian Rush, and he remains the top League scorer with 245. He recalls: 'To be honest, I didn't make much of an impact that day, I didn't really have a chance. We were well beaten and it wasn't the way I would have chosen to go out after all that time. Overall, though, I can't possibly complain. I had a marvellous time with Liverpool. The games against United were some of the most exciting and they were always special for me because I was born and lived all my life halfway between the two cities. Just as many friends and neighbours supported United as followed Liverpool, so the interest was intense.'

Had they realized they had just witnessed Roger's competitive swansong in a red shirt, the Anfield faithful would have bid an emotional farewell. As it was, the Kop, who frequently had the edge on the Stretford End where magnanimity in defeat was concerned, applauded Charlton's fabulous effort nobly and even Shankly admitted, 'It was a great goal, a great performance.'

What this rare praise could not do, however, was disguise the inescapable truth that while Liverpool remained a formidable force, albeit one undergoing a period of transition, United were sliding inexorably towards mediocrity and worse.

Nevertheless, in the summer of 1970 Wilf McGuinness, who had led the Red Devils to the semi-finals of both domestic cup competitions and eighth place in the League in his first term at the helm, was promoted from chief coach to manager.

Yet again United began the new season at less of a lick than Liverpool, so that when the two met at Anfield in September the visitors already had ground to make up. They started brightly and took a twentieth-minute lead through Brian Kidd, but they were flattering to deceive. Two minutes later Alun Evans seized on a rebound from Ian Ure to equalize and thereafter the Reds, driven on by the dreadnought Hughes and the brilliant Thompson, dominated the match. Only young keeper Jimmy Rimmer, whose long-term Old Trafford future was to be blighted by the continuing excellence of Stepney, kept his side in contention by making a succession of superb saves as the shots rained in. With David Sadler also outstanding, the visitors survived a second-half siege to leave with a point. One name which deserved a mention in dispatches was a composed full-back called Roy Evans, who was enjoying a rare senior outing before retiring to become one of the League's youngest coaches.

Tommy Smith faulted himself for Kidd's goal – he backed off instead of attacking a long centre from Stiles – but the man who was to run Arsenal's Frank McLintock mightily close in the Footballer of the Year poll gave a typically assertive overall display. What remains most vividly in his mind, though, was the pleasing contribution of rookie midfielder John McLaughlin, the mention of whom makes him smile affectionately.

'John had a lot of skill and did well that day with his passing. His only problem was that he was very slight. Bob Paisley used to make sure that he ate well, always feeding him up and sending steaks to his house. Then one day John went to see the manager and asked for a Saturday off because he had to get married. Shanks raised his eyebrows, called Paisley in and said, "Bob, what have we done? We've bred a monster here!"'

The laughs were not coming as easily at Old Trafford. Come December, with the team in disarray, McGuinness was relieved of his duties and Busby resumed control until a new manager could be found. The venerated Scot presided over a marked upturn in fortunes culminating in a top-half finish, but the long-term auguries were not good, as Liverpool's embarrassingly easy win at Old Trafford in April emphasized only too clearly.

Division One:
25 September 1971
at Anfield

LIVERPOOL 2
Graham 8; Hall 25

Ray Clemence, Chris Lawler,
Alec Lindsay, Ian Ross, Larry Lloyd,
Emlyn Hughes, Kevin Keegan,
Brian Hall, Steve Heighway,
Bobby Graham, Ian Callaghan.

MANCHESTER UNITED 2
Law 53; Charlton 72

Alex Stepney, Tommy O'Neil, Francis
Burns, Alan Gowling, Steve James,
David Sadler, Willie Morgan, Brian Kidd,
Bobby Charlton, Denis Law,
George Best.

Half-time: 2-0 Attendance: 55,642

'We played enough football to have won half-a-dozen games' observed Bill Shankly after Manchester United came back from a first-half battering to claim a point, and it would have been a brave man who argued the odds with the seething Liverpool boss. But not even Shanks at his most irascible could legitimately have denied the skill and composure with which the visitors levered themselves off the ropes, nor the awesome quality of Bobby Charlton's sensational equalizer.

Liverpool, who started the game four points adrift of Frank O'Farrell's side, began at breakneck pace and soon United were reeling in the face of non-stop, frenetic but precisely executed attacks. Messrs Keegan, Graham and Heighway, who was demonstrating vividly that he was no one-season wonder, presented constantly moving targets which the Mancunian defenders could not pin down and it seemed only a matter of time before home domination yielded a breakthrough.

So it proved with Liverpool taking a two-goal lead, yet ironically both successful strikes were out-and-out flukes. After eight minutes Bobby Graham accidentally deflected home a twenty-yard shot from Ian Callaghan which keeper Alex Stepney had seemed to have covered; then Ian Ross' twenty-fifth-minute cross hit Brian Hall's back and crept over the line with Stepney hopelessly wrong-footed.

Still, Liverpool were well worth their advantage and at half-time it seemed possible that United might be facing humiliation. However, steadied at the back by the impressive David Sadler – who was almost serene while the storm raged around him – they began mounting meaningful attacks of their own, and George Best set up Denis Law to reduce the arrears from close range after fifty-three minutes.

The Reds complained, claiming Kidd had impeded Hughes in the build-up, but their troubles were only just beginning. On seventy-two minutes Best, who was becoming increasingly irrepressible as his 300th League outing progressed, back-heeled to Charlton just outside the angle of the penalty box and the England veteran beat Ray Clemence with a rising right-footer from twenty yards.

It was one of the goals of the season and fit to save any match, but three minutes later it appeared that Liverpool were in front again when Graham netted after Steve James had handled in the box. Even when the referee whistled and gestured to the spot where the supposed offence had occurred, it seemed the Kopites' joy would be delayed only for the length of time it would take to convert a penalty. However, the official had ruled offside against Keegan and Anfield recoiled with perceived injustice. Thereafter, what had always been a game with a brisk physical edge became even more abrasive as United protected their point vigorously, and at times ruthlessly.

Later Manchester skipper Charlton was generous in his praise of Liverpool's whirlwind start. 'They were so fast it was unbelievable. It was not just Kevin Keegan, who does look a very fine player, it was all of them.' As for Shanks, he was breathing fire, most of it in the direction of the referee, but found consolation in his team's performance: 'If we continue to play like that we shall come to no harm,' he opined. How right he was.

52

The visitors were due to meet soon-to-be-crowned Champions Arsenal in the FA Cup Final and were without Larry Lloyd and Emlyn Hughes, who were on international duty, but it was United who played more like a team distracted by thoughts of Wembley. Inspired by the tearaway attacker Steve Heighway, plucked from non-League obscurity to become the English game's discovery of the season, the Merseysiders won 2-0 at a canter. Heighway himself scored the first goal after twenty minutes and then pressurized centre-half Paul Edwards into deflecting a long ball from Smith past the stranded Stepney on the hour. Grins Tommy, 'The ball just grazed Edwards' head, and although I claimed the goal they wouldn't let me have it. Stevie was brilliant that day, he went through them like a dose of salts. That was one of the few times I can remember United fans booing their own side.'

Wembley brought extra-time heartache for Liverpool, who failed narrowly to prevent Arsenal securing the League and Cup double, but 1971/2 saw Shankly continue the process of transforming a good team into one which would lift trophies on a regular basis. The new ace in his pack was Kevin Keegan, a £35,000 acquisition from Scunthorpe who, according to Shankly, turned the club upside down with his burning desire to succeed. The young winger-turned-striker went straight into the first team, giving the side a new dimension with his non-stop movement, nimble footballing brain and utter fearlessness.

While Liverpool were close to lift-off, United were experiencing a false dawn, albeit a richly entertaining one. Under new boss Frank O'Farrell they began 1971/2 in swashbuckling style, their 2-2 draw at Anfield *(see Classic Clash Number Seven on page 52)* representing one of only nine points dropped in the first half of the League campaign. But while the Best-inspired Red Devils were piling up an enviable lead at the top of the table, there was no shortage of shrewd judges who maintained that they were in a false position, that they were fundamentally a poor team relying too heavily on one wonderful player. Sadly for all who espoused the Old Trafford cause, the prophets of doom were spot on.

After Christmas they plummeted, managing only five more wins and finishing in eighth position, their abysmal form during the second period of a 3-0 home defeat by Championship-chasing Liverpool in April being indicative of their plight. To be fair, United held their own in the first half with both of O'Farrell's flagship signings doing well. Martin Buchan, the immaculate Scottish defender who was privately appalled by the standard of some of his new team-mates, coped coolly with the threat of Keegan, while strong-running flankman Ian Storey-Moore augmented the ever-present threat of Best at the other end.

But after the break the home side caved in as the Merseysiders, who had claimed nineteen out of the previous twenty possible points, ran amok. The rout began just before the hour with a header by Chris Lawler, taking the full-back's career total to an amazing fifty-three; two minutes later John Toshack nodded number two, and the rampant Emlyn Hughes netted a thirty-yarder via a post with five minutes left.

Tommy Smith remembers the visit. 'Long before the end their fans were upset, which wasn't surprising. They seemed on a downward spiral and it was pretty obvious that if they didn't do something about it quickly they were going to be relegated.' The sourest note of the afternoon was struck by the Stretford End, who barracked Keegan constantly for no apparent reason. Presumably they were jealous, but whatever their motivation it offered a telling comparison with the Kop's generosity to Bobby Charlton two seasons earlier.

Understandably, the travelling Scousers taunted the home fans mercilessly, but their most frequently repeated refrain, 'We're gonna win the League', did not prove an accurate prediction. They lost out by a point to Brian Clough's Derby County but their time would come – and soon.

The 1972/3 season began excruciatingly for Manchester United with a home

Opposite: Kevin Keegan's attempted overhead kick is blocked by Tommy O'Neil as the white-shirted visitors defend in depth. Onlookers (from left) are Liverpool's Brian Hall and United's Steve James and David Sadler.

defeat by Ipswich Town. There then followed a midweek visit to a Liverpool side already buoyant from an opening-day victory over Manchester City. United lost, and though the score was only 2-0, they lost badly. The Reds, looking decidedly Champion-like, roared into instant attack and Stepney had already been forced into several desperate saves when he was beaten after twelve minutes. The architect was the evergreen Callaghan, whose delicate lob was converted by Toshack from the angle of the penalty area. Eight minutes later the Welshman robbed Buchan and set up Heighway for the second, and it was game over. Thereafter, inexplicably to Kopites scenting the humiliation of their bitterest rivals, the Merseysiders took their collective boot off the pedal and cruised. Many of the home fans, perhaps feeling cheated, resorted to a prolonged 'concert' of obscenities which nullified the Liverpudlian claim, which hitherto had been justified, that their repertoire was wholesome compared to that of their Mancunian counterparts.

The return fixture fell less than two months later and it seemed likely that a massacre was in prospect. While Liverpool were purring along smoothly at the top of the League, United were on the bottom, and the behaviour of the Old Trafford fans before kick-off suggested fear and panic in the ranks. As soon as the visiting contingent at the scoreboard end began their inevitable chants, groups of home 'supporters' attempted to infiltrate them. The police struggled vainly to keep them apart, skirmishes broke out and soon reinforcements were pouring over the Stretford End wall and running the length of the pitch to join in the battle. At one time it seemed possible that the game might be called off – which may have been the troublemakers' twisted motive – and there were still interlopers on the grass when the players ran out.

Once the action got under way the expected pattern began to emerge, with Liverpool moving more purposefully, but gradually the annihilation scenario began to recede. O'Farrell's men were playing with more pride and confidence than at any previous time that term and as the interval approached territorial honours were about even. Then came two decisions by referee Bill Castle which shaped the destiny of the match.

After forty-one minutes it seemed that the deadlock would be broken when Heighway sprinted into the United box and was upended by Stepney, only for vociferous penalty claims to be waved away. Some 180 seconds later, with the visitors still smarting, the official massaged a fistful of salt into their perceived wound. Bobby Charlton crossed into the area, Ted MacDougall brought the ball under control and the defenders screamed for handball. Mr Castle was unmoved, United's £200,000 marksman slipped past big Larry Lloyd and let loose a shot which Ray Clemence could only parry to the feet of Wyn Davies. The Welshman netted and the underdogs trooped off for their half-time mug of tea a goal to the good.

Returning with their new-found resolve undiminished, they increased their lead on fifty-four minutes when MacDougall supplied a smart finish following a penetrating through-pass from right-back Tommy O'Neil. Thereafter they played better than for many a month, with Buchan in serene control at the back and Charlton demonstrating that reports of his imminent demise had been exaggerated. Indeed, after Tony Dunne had been invalided out of the action, Bobby proved a capable deputy at left-back, the very epitome of the calm elder statesman stepping in to defuse a potential crisis.

Final proof that nothing was going to fall for Liverpool arrived when Peter Cormack, their most enterprising player, nodded a late chance against the bar and Keegan smashed the rebound over.

Tommy Smith, whose characteristic blend of uncompromising aggression and underrated skill had been as effective as ever, was philosophical about a reverse in which his former colleague Ted MacDougall, who had started his career at Anfield but failed

Opposite: Kevin Keegan, an irrepressible jack-in-the-box who gave Liverpool a new dimension in the early 1970s.

Division One

22 December 1973

at Anfield

LIVERPOOL 2

Keegan 30 (pen); Heighway 66

Ray Clemence, Tommy Smith, Roy Evans, Phil Thompson, Larry Lloyd, Emlyn Hughes, Kevin Keegan, Peter Cormack, Alan Waddle, Steve Heighway, Ian Callaghan.

MANCHESTER UNITED 0

Alex Stepney, Martin Buchan, Tony Young, Brian Greenhoff, Arnold Sidebottom, Clive Griffiths, Willie Morgan, Lou Macari, Brian Kidd, George Graham, George Best. Sub: Sammy McIlroy for Kidd (45).

Half-time: 1-0 Attendance: 40,420

WHAT was surely the most abject combination ever to run out at Anfield in the name of Manchester United looked exactly what they were – a team about to part company with the top flight. As a unit they lacked both pattern and passion, as individuals most of them under-performed horribly. They were ripe to be massacred and Liverpool, as if remembering it was the season of goodwill, let them off ludicrously lightly.

United boss Tommy Docherty was facing his second successive relegation-haunted Christmas, but whereas during the previous term he had only recently inherited a lamentable mess, this time he had to take responsibility for his men's embarrassingly feeble display.

There were honourable exceptions, notably goalkeeper Alex Stepney, who pulled off near-miracles to limit the victory margin to two, and Martin Buchan, that most self-assured of defenders, who performed admirably and sometimes appeared to be asking himself

what on earth he was doing among such a motley crew. Meanwhile Willie Morgan posed the only vestige of attacking threat, subjecting a young full-back named Roy Evans to some torrid moments.

In their situation going into the match – perilously close to the foot of the table with just fourteen points from nineteen games and only one win in their last dozen attempts – United needed all the defensive fortitude they could muster, but were handicapped by the absence through injury of centre-backs Jim Holton and Steve James. In contrast, Liverpool, with almost twice as many points and unbeaten in eight games, were riding high and entertaining realistic hopes of a title tilt.

Occasionally such confrontations confound all predictions, but not this time. Somehow the visitors kept the scoresheet blank through a first half-hour of total Liverpool domination, but then they fell behind in confusing fashion. Kevin Keegan headed a cross into the air and Alan Waddle poked out a leg from the resultant melee and prodded the ball goalwards. He claimed it had crossed the line before a hand scooped it away; the referee disagreed but declared that the hand did not belong to Stepney and awarded a penalty from which Keegan sent the keeper the wrong way.

Still United showed not the slightest hint of attacking enterprise and Liverpool walked all over them. Tommy Smith, freed of all defensive duties, and Ian Callaghan were outstanding as the Reds swarmed forward unceasingly. Chance after chance went begging with Waddle the

main culprit, missing at least four before he made amends by nodding on a Callaghan cross for Steve Heighway to lash the ball in from six yards after sixty-six minutes. Thereafter all the home side managed was to demonstrate their need for shooting practice, allowing Docherty's team to slink home with a respectable scoreline which failed utterly to reflect their pathetic performance.

Hope in their hearts and plenty to sing about; the Kop in the 1970s.

to make the grade, had been so instrumental. 'Quite simply, it was Ted's day. It must have been the best game he ever played, certainly for Manchester United. He was a pace merchant and he gave Larry Lloyd the runaround. Ted was a nice fella, too, but he couldn't trap a bag of cement. The boss lambasted us for letting him take us apart. The big joke afterwards was "Why did we sell MacDougall?"'

United fans hoping, praying, that this spirited display would herald a recovery had their hopes brutally dashed. The general trend continued to be downwards and, after a 5-0 thrashing by Crystal Palace at Selhurst Park in mid-December, Frank O'Farrell was sacked. He had never been close to the players – Denis Law said later that he had arrived a stranger and left a stranger – but he was a decent man and it was difficult not to feel sorry for him. His rebuilding task, onerous enough anyway, had been rendered immeasurably more difficult by the distracting, self-destructive antics of George Best. Arguably, too, he was not helped by the awe-inspiring presence of Matt Busby on the board, even if, as he insisted, the former boss never interfered.

For the remainder of the campaign, followers of Liverpool and Manchester United might have been inhabiting different planets. While the Merseysiders went on to claim their first Championship for seven years, adding the UEFA Cup for good measure, the Mancunians were engaged in a gruesome struggle against demotion. Led by new boss Tommy Docherty, they escaped the drop which, given the state of the club when he took over, was a major achievement in itself.

Docherty's desire to do what he termed the top job in football, and for which he forsook the reins of the Scottish national team, was never in question; what worried many observers was his volatility and his ruthlessness. Under Tommy there was a bewildering turnover of players, and soon Old Trafford resembled a Caledonian enclave as 'The Doc's Tartan Army' was assembled. Along the way there were well-publicized spats with a host of household names; at least, went the theory, life with Docherty could never be dull.

Actually, it could, as the fans discovered to their dismay when the 1973/4 season got under way. For the bulk of that season, the Doc's side was not only extremely poor, it was also excruciatingly drab, as it demonstrated with numbing clarity in the goalless draw with Shanks' champs in late September. Unquestionably Docherty had tightened the defence, but seemingly at huge cost to attacking options, which seemed non-existent against Tommy Smith and company.

With Liverpool – already six points off the blistering pace being set by Leeds – Champions surprisingly anonymous for a team containing the likes of Keegan and Heighway, the contest simply atrophied. Perhaps it would have been different had Chris Lawler's third-minute headed 'goal' not been disallowed because Peter Cormack was offside, but it seemed that United, with the honourable exception of Willie Morgan, were always happy to settle for a point. Big Jim Holton and Steve James were magnificent at the heart of the home rearguard and they received lusty support from vigorous colleagues but the title-holders might have been expected to show the wit to break them down. As Erland Clouston put it in the *Liverpool Echo:* 'If word gets round the League that you can hold Liverpool with a couple of big lads and some hefty tackling, then we are in for some gruelling afternoons at Anfield.'

Afterwards, when pressed for an opinion on United's negativity, Bill Shankly was uncharacteristically diplomatic, refusing to be drawn into criticism of his friend and countryman, Docherty. His expression, though, left little doubt as to his private opinion.

A fascinating sidelight on the United v Liverpool experience is provided by George Buchan, brother of Martin, who made one of his only three appearances for United (all as a substitute) in that glum stalemate. After coming on to replace George Graham, the gutsy little forward got into an immediate tussle with Emlyn Hughes. 'He kicked me and I swore at him. He said something along the lines of "Who are you to be treating me like that? What have you won?" What impressed me about that was that he had done his homework, even on someone like me who was not exactly a prominent member of the United side. It showed total professionalism.'

Buchan Junior, who would soon move on to Bury despite impressing the Old Trafford coaching staff with his pace, remarked, too, on the heated relationship between the two sets of fans. 'I had always been used to passion in football. Believe me, having played in Protestant versus Catholic five-a-sides back home in Aberdeen I knew how worked up people could get. But that was rivalry, not hatred. Watching some of the supporters when United played Liverpool I could sense raw hatred. I couldn't begin to understand it.'

Any notion that Yuletide niceties might counteract the prevailing hostility were dispelled when the teams met on Merseyside three days before Christmas. The atmosphere was poisonous as Liverpool won with almost contemptuous ease. *(See Classic Clash Number Eight on page 55.)* As the end of the season approached, apocalyptic events were brewing at both Old Trafford and Anfield. One, hitherto unthinkable but utterly deserved, was the relegation of Manchester United to the Second Division for the first time since the war; the other, which stunned the football world and numbed the Red half of Merseyside, was the sudden retirement of Bill Shankly.

The first is easily explained. The Red Devils were not good enough to stay up, so they went down. It was deeply painful to all who loved the club, but it had been coming for some time. In the end it proved to have a cleansing effect. Put bluntly, it did United good to discover they had no divine right to a place among the elite.

But Shankly's decision, made in the wake of a comfortable FA Cup Final triumph over Newcastle, came into a different category. It was both shocking and mysterious. Having put together a second splendid side, why would a man as obsessed with football as Bill stand back and watch another man take over his creation? True, he was sixty, so perhaps his own profoundly moving explanation that he was 'tired with all the years', should be accepted at face value. Yet there was little doubt in subsequent seasons, as he watched his former lieutenant Bob Paisley compile a matchless catalogue of triumphs, that he regretted his hasty departure. However, what it proved was the timeless adage that no individual is more important than the club; not even the man who made it.

CHAPTER SEVEN:

THE NEW AGE
1975/6 – 1980/81

ENGLISH football was deprived of its most compelling spectacle for only one season. Having jettisoned the negative approach adopted throughout most of their relegation season, Manchester United were reborn. Indeed, they emerged as the brightest, boldest, most downright entertaining new force to hit the domestic game for many a long day, romping away with the Second Division title and captivating crowds up and down the land with their swashbuckling commitment to fast-and-furious attack. Their style was hailed as romantic and for bringing about an overdue return to traditional football values. Tommy Docherty deserved massive credit for his enterprise.

United's head-turning renaissance acted as a gauntlet to the top-flight's ruling class, but although it turned out that these precocious Red Devils had a thing or two to learn, they did themselves and their manager proud throughout a vintage 1975/6 campaign.

In United's absence, Liverpool had not exactly been idle. Bob Paisley, whom many observers saw as an eternal lieutenant, had acceded to Shankly's Anfield throne. He had been reluctant to make the step, even attempting to change his predecessor's mind about retiring, and a common view was that he was on a hiding to nothing. The theory went that if he succeeded then he would merely have taken advantage of Bill's foundations and that if he failed then he would have squandered a golden legacy. Never has the calibre of a football man been so chronically underestimated. After underlining that he was no extrovert and would not be attempting to capture the fans' affection by aping Shanks, he simply got on with the job.

When no silverware accrued that season – although Liverpool finished only two points behind the Champions, Derby County – doubts were expressed. But Bob of the Boot Room was unmoved. He had been making subtle adjustments to his squad, acquiring Terry McDermott and Phil Neal and converting Ray Kennedy from under-achieving marksman to a midfield role in which he would earn fulfilment. Come the 1975/6 season Paisley was ready for United and everyone else.

The renewal of hostilities at Anfield in November proved to be an uplifting affair, both off and on the pitch. In an era when hooliganism was widespread, trouble had been seen as a distinct possibility, but the Merseysiders' new wall, built to separate factions at the Anfield Road end, suffered no assault as supporters' exchanges remained, for the most part, good humoured. As for the game, Liverpool put down Docherty's upstarts 3-1, but not before the Mancunians had played some of the most adventurous football played by any visitors to the Reds' citadel since pre-Shankly days.

United paid dearly for two individual errors. After twelve minutes their rookie goalkeeper, the genial Irishman Paddy Roche, caught a cross from Ian Callaghan, then dropped it as he cannoned into central defender Brian Greenhoff. The ball ran loose to Steve Heighway who had only to place it in the unguarded net. Then, a minute after half-time, Stewart Houston lost the plot as his colleagues employed the offside trap and Kevin Keegan sent John Toshack in to score.

United reacted not with cowed acceptance of Liverpool's superiority but with wave upon wave of hell-for-leather attacks which yielded a goal for winger Steve Coppell. A draw seemed possible but other chances were spurned and the home side clinched the victory when Toshack and Keegan indulged in a touch of head-tennis telepathy which resulted in Keegan bundling the ball past the hapless Roche. In the end, for all the fire and hunger of Docherty's young braves, Liverpool nous had prevailed, and deservedly so, in a smashing game. Defeat saw United knocked off the First Division's top spot and slide to fifth, while their conquerors climbed above them to fourth.

Come February and the return at Old Trafford, Liverpool had reached the summit – on goal difference from United. This time the outcome was goalless, but only after another absorbing contest in which the hosts did most of the attacking but the visitors, efficient, patient and panic-proof, stood their corner in time-honoured manner. Maybe Sammy McIlroy, Stuart Pearson and Gerry Daly should have snatched something from a succession of openings, but the Mersey men Ray Clemence, Tommy Smith, Emlyn Hughes and Phil Thompson all performed so majestically in defence that none of them deserved to finish on the losing side. Typically, too, Liverpool broke out in the final quarter and might have poached both points.

Right-back Smith remembers the night for his confrontation with United's new goal-scoring flankman Gordon Hill. 'There were always one or two wingers I thought I could get to with a little psychology, and Gordon was one of them. On his day he was brilliant, but he rarely was against us. This time I shouted to Jimmy Case, who was playing in front of me "Send him down the line and I'll kick him over the stand." Of course, I was only messing around. But in the first minute

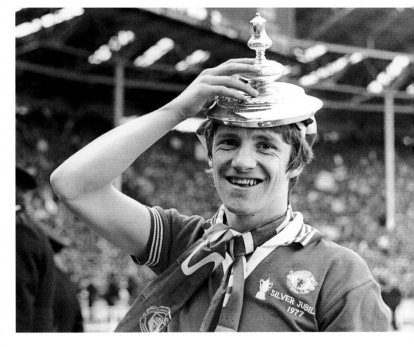

United's Gordon Hill at Wembley in 1977, on a day when his grin was wider than that of his old rival, Tommy Smith.

he cut inside and I whacked him. Afterwards he seemed to be playing left-back. Funny, that!'

Gordon chuckles at the recollection. 'Tommy liked a bit of banter. It certainly didn't upset me. The fact was that one day he would have me in his pocket, but the next time I'd turn him inside out so that he'd need dizzy pills. Either he'd do his job well or I'd do mine, but there was never any hard feelings. He was a super player and I'd have had him in my team any time.'

Either of these fine teams would have made worthy Champions, which was of little consolation to United when the title ended up at Anfield. The Red Devils' innocence and verve had been an overwhelmingly refreshing addition to the First Division, but in the end Liverpool's experience and organization made them the better all-round team. In fact, Bob Paisley, who emulated Shanks' double of three years earlier by placing the UEFA Cup alongside the League crown, was on the verge of assembling a genuinely great side. United? They seemed sure to assuage their League disappointment by sweeping aside Second Division Southampton in the FA Cup Final, but they failed to do themselves justice at Wembley, and lost 1-0. Docherty mouthed the conventional platitude about being back the next year. As it turned out, to Liverpool's cost, he was right.

Before then, though, there were League battles to fight, and the Merseysiders dominated both League encounters during 1976/7, even though the two games produced only one goal between them. At Old Trafford in February the scoresheet was blank, the corner tally of 16-4 in Liverpool's favour producing a more accurate reflection of what happened. Ian Callaghan, who hit the overworked Alex Stepney's post near the end, and Steve Heighway were outstanding as United were paralysed in front of their own fans. Indeed, so one-sided was the game that the normally reticent Paisley remarked that the hosts had looked like a Third Division outfit while Docherty could only agree with that bleak assessment.

The result left Liverpool behind League pacesetters Ipswich only on goal difference but having played three games more; by the time the Red Devils arrived at Anfield in early May the position was transformed, with the Merseysiders needing only four points from as many games to retain their title. The first two of those were garnered with almost embarrassing ease against a visiting side deprived by injury of their regular centre-backs, Martin Buchan and Brian Greenhoff. Keegan scored the only goal of a strangely low-key contest with a fifteenth-minute header, but Liverpool's territorial advantage was overwhelming with the gallant Stepney again standing between his team and a rout. All United managed to win that night was the toss for the choice of colours in the FA Cup Final, deputy skipper Lou Macari's call ensuring that Doc's Devils would play in their customary red.

All known form pointed to a comprehensive Liverpool victory at Wembley but United claimed the Cup and prevented a unique treble. *(See Classic Clash Number Nine on pages 62-3.)* Two of the strikers who played that day, David Johnson of Liverpool and United's Jimmy Greenhoff, recall the game with contrasting emotions.

For the affable but immensely dedicated 'Johnno', a Scouser through and through, it was a day of unmitigated anguish. 'We'd won the League with some lovely football

Something of a curiosity: Bobby Charlton at Anfield in 1977, resplendent in the white shirt of . . . Liverpool. No, United's maestro was not making a sensational comeback for the enemy, he was taking part in a testimonial match for Tommy Smith. Here Bobby tussles with his chum Ian Callaghan, for so long a footballing adversary, now a rival on the golf course.

but this game was so frenetic that precious little good stuff was actually played. I was up front with Kevin Keegan, but there wasn't much service from the bylines so I ran about all afternoon like a blue-assed fly without having a serious effort at goal. No sooner had I been substituted for Cally than he put in a beautiful cross! What can you do?'

Afterwards Ray Clemence was criticized for walking off without completing a lap of honour with his team-mates, but he was not alone. 'I went with him,' admits David. 'It wasn't lack of respect for the fans or United, just the huge disappointment of losing such a massive game and, in my case, being taken off. You know you've done your best but there's still an unavoidable sense of letting people down. I have never known a Liverpool dressing room so low. It was crushing. But we had the European Cup Final coming up so we had to get hold of our feelings and swallow them quickly. On the train back north, Bob Paisley, Joe Fagan and Ronnie Moran began to build us up again. What was gone was gone, look to the next game. That's always been the Liverpool way, win or lose, and it worked pretty well, didn't it? Four days later we won the really big one.'

Meanwhile Jimmy Greenhoff, who had joined the club he had followed as a boy from Stoke the previous November, might have been on a different planet. 'My winner was a bit of luck and I knew it, but that didn't matter. I had been through seven losing semi-finals, including replays, with Leeds and Stoke so this was an overdue experience. When United had lost to Southampton the year before I had gone to watch because my brother, Brian, was playing. I went to the reception that evening, too, and saw how flat everyone was. To play a part in putting things right a year later was absolutely fantastic.'

United in joy. Jimmy Greenhoff (left) and younger brother Brian nurse the FA Cup, secured at Liverpool's expense, courtesy of Jimmy's breastbone at Wembley in 1977.

MANCHESTER UNITED 2

Pearson 50; J Greenhoff 55

Alex Stepney, Jimmy Nicholl, Arthur Albiston, Brian Greenhoff, Martin Buchan, Sammy McIlroy, Lou Macari, Steve Coppell, Stuart Pearson, Jimmy Greenhoff, Gordon Hill. Sub: David McCreery for Hill (82).

LIVERPOOL 1

Case 52

Ray Clemence, Phil Neal, Joey Jones, Tommy Smith, Emlyn Hughes, Ray Kennedy, Jimmy Case, Terry McDermott, Steve Heighway, David Johnson, Kevin Keegan. Sub: Ian Callaghan for Johnson (63).

Half-time: 0-0 Attendance: 100,000

IT was the day Manchester United won the FA Cup with a fluke goal and Liverpool were deprived of a unique place in football history. Had the Merseysiders prevailed, and until half-time it seemed pretty inevitable that they would, Bob Paisley would have presided over the club's first League and FA Cup double, which was momentous enough in itself. But four days later in Rome they had a date with Borussia Moenchengladbach for the European Cup Final, which they went on to win. Thus, from an Anfield perspective, fate had cheated the Reds of an incomparable treble by means of a bizarre rebound from the chest of Jimmy Greenhoff. Of course, the Old Trafford camp can contend that they were beginning belatedly to find their form and they might have won anyway. But try telling that to Tommy Smith, who swears to this day that the United marksman yanked his shirt in the lead-up to that almost surreally dramatic winner.

Naturally enough, the pre-match hype had concentrated mainly on Liverpool's treble aspirations, but United were not exactly pressure-free, either. Following yet another Championship failure – they had finished a distant sixth – and remembering they had lost the previous year's final to Second Division Southampton, the Red Devils were undisputed underdogs and in desperate need of solid achievement. If they failed here, while their arch rivals experienced their finest hour, it would be utterly devastating to Mancunian morale. Though their customary outward bravado proclaimed otherwise, many a foot soldier in Tommy Docherty's Red Army approached the day with a dark sense of foreboding.

The mood was lightened considerably when the team line-ups revealed that United's captain, Martin Buchan, had passed a late fitness test. The thought of facing Kevin Keegan, out to shine in his final match on home soil for Liverpool before his controversial move to Hamburg, without their most accomplished defender was not an appealing one; especially as the rearguard had been notionally weakened already by the introduction of rookie left-back Arthur Albiston in place of the injured Stewart Houston. As for Liverpool, they were without long-term injury casualty Phil Thompson at the heart of their defence and had excluded thirty-five-year-old Ian Callaghan from their midfield, perhaps with one eye on Rome. In addition, they had selected England international David Johnson as Keegan's front-running partner in preference to David Fairclough, who had played in both semi-final clashes with Everton.

On a stiflingly hot afternoon, Liverpool began the more convincingly, scampering eagerly around Wembley's green acres as if they wanted the job effectively completed by half-time. United's formidably mobile twin spearhead of Stuart Pearson and Greenhoff the elder were comfortably held in check, as were wingers Steve Coppell and Gordon Hill, while the white-shirted Merseysiders' midfield trio of Jimmy Case, Terry McDermott and Ray Kennedy were in dominant mode. Only one clear opening was fashioned, when Kennedy headed against the foot of Alex Stepney's post three minutes before the break, but all the interval talk was of the likelihood of Liverpool victory.

The tide, however, was about to turn. United, beginning the second half positively, at last began to pose an attacking threat and nineteen-year-old Albiston showed the way with an enterprising fifty-yard dash, leaving Smith and Phil Neal in his wake before marring the effect with an inaccurate cross. Suddenly the game had a different feel and United took a shock fiftieth-minute lead. Sammy McIlroy headed towards Greenhoff near halfway and the hitherto excellent Emlyn Hughes hesitated disastrously; Jimmy nodded on in turn to Pearson, who sprinted unstoppably into the box before beating Ray Clemence at his near post with a low drive.

Greenhoff recalls: 'Stuart's great pace gave them no chance and his finish was out of this world. It never got the recognition it should have done. They say no keeper should be beaten at his near post but you have to leave a bit of room. It was just a perfect shot.'

Liverpool responded like the champions they were, equalizing only two minutes later. Joey Jones delivered a high cross from the left to Case, who controlled the dropping ball exquisitely on his

thigh, then swivelled to crash a fulminating half-volley into the top corner of the net via Stepney's fingertips. It was a regal strike, fit to turn any game, and it seemed to underline the inevitablity of a Merseyside triumph. United had had their moment, they had let their advantage slip and now were about to be devoured.

Not exactly. Just 180 seconds later Lou Macari headed on to Jimmy Greenhoff in the Liverpool box, where he tangled with Smith. The ball ran loose to Macari who shot, rather wildly, from ten yards. It was going well wide when it hit the chest of the stumbling Greenhoff, who was trying to get out of the way, and looped serenely but unstoppably beyond Clemence and Neal into the net.

It's a freakish moment imprinted forever on Jimmy's memory. 'I put Tommy under pressure and tried to shuffle my feet to unnerve him.

As the ball spun away I tried to protect it with my body, then tried my damndest to get out of the way because I was in Lou's line of vision. Then his shot hit me and skewed into goal. I thought "Thank you very much, I'll have that." I didn't think I impeded Tommy and neither did the referee.'

Tommy took the opposite view. 'I think he fouled me, that he pulled me round, but it's a long time ago and there are no grudges. The shame is that after controlling most of the game we didn't do ourselves justice. The fact that United's goal came so quickly after ours took the stuffing out of us. From that point the game seemed to get harder.'

Even so, there was more than half an hour left for Liverpool to repair the damage but, despite changing the focus of their attack by replacing Johnson with Callaghan, the nearest they came

to an equalizer was when Kennedy scraped the crossbar with a brisk left-footer two minutes from the end.

For Bob Paisley, then, a dream had died, but soon there would be rich consolation in Rome. For the Doc, there was the joy of finally winning at Wembley at his eighth attempt as player and manager, but who could have believed that he would be out of Old Trafford before another season began?

Okay, so the goal resulted from an outlandish deflection but Lou Macari is not bothered as he salutes United's winner. Emlyn Hughes (right) appeals in vain for a foul on Tommy Smith.

Alex Stepney is a model of sympathetic restraint as he embraces a clearly distraught Emlyn Hughes after the final whistle in the 1977 FA Cup Final.

There was joy unconfined, too, for the youngest man afield, United's nineteen-year-old left-back Arthur Albiston, who had deputized nobly for the injured Stewart Houston. 'I felt a bit of an impostor because Stewart had played in all the rounds. Somehow I felt I hadn't earned the right to play, which is why I offered my medal to Stewart at the end. He didn't take it though.'

In the after-match euphoria the talk was of how the Doc could lead United on a realistic pursuit of Liverpool's crown in 1977/8 but before the new term began he had been sacked for conducting a love affair with Mary Brown, the wife of the club physiotherapist, Laurie. On a personal level, Tommy went on to know contentment, marrying his sweetheart and starting a new family. Professionally, though, he had to deal with the undying frustration of never knowing how his flamboyant young United side might have developed under his continued tutelage.

Bob Paisley had no such agonizing to do. After Liverpool's golden night in Rome when they put Borussia Moenchengladbach so emphatically to the sword, all he had to consider was how to follow becoming European Champions. The answer he came up with was to become European Champions again, this time by beating FC Bruges at Wembley, an astounding achievement marred only slightly by disappointment at failing to retain the League title.

Before then, though, Liverpool would face United three times, starting with the Charity Shield at Wembley in August. The occasion, which was entertaining enough though not graced by a goal, was dominated by interest in the Merseysiders' replacement for departed hero Kevin Keegan. Kenny Dalglish, for whom they had paid Celtic a British record fee of £440,000, made an accomplished, unflashy debut, slotting expertly into the Reds' smooth pattern. United had a new face, too, in manager Dave Sexton, recruited from Queen's Park Rangers in the wake of Docherty's dismissal. How this admirable but unassuming fellow would cope with life in the Manchester United goldfish bowl was the subject of widespread speculation.

Jimmy Greenhoff recalls the day with a grimace. 'I was feeling fitter than at any time in my career. We had just got back from Norway, where we'd had a fantastic time and I'd scored five goals in my last match. I made a pretty fair start against

Liverpool, too. But then, after beating Phil Thompson in a sprint, I went to lob Ray Clemence and the turf seemed to give way under my feet. I'd strained knee ligaments which meant, after completing all my pre-season training, I was further back than square one and I didn't play again until October.'

When he did return, the opposition was again Liverpool, then third in the table, and seventh-placed United were impeccable value for a 2-0 home victory. Bob Paisley had been worried that his men were becoming jaded due to too many social commitments as European Champions, and after smartly taken second-half strikes from Lou Macari and Sammy McIlroy had settled matters, the Anfield boss was mercilessly scathing of his charges. 'Our running and movement off the ball was rubbish. Too many experienced players were hiding out there.' One relatively green recruit didn't do so well, either. Playing in only his second game for the Reds since his transfer from Partick Thistle, Alan Hansen looked classy in possession but he dallied on the ball deplorably, one bloomer resulting in a United 'goal' that was disallowed for offside. It's not a game he would remember with relish but, as he recalled much later, it taught him a valuable lesson.

But as impressive as United had looked at Old Trafford, Liverpool were more polished still in the return at a rain-lashed Anfield in late February when the four most expensive players in Britain were on show. For United £500,000 centre-half Gordon McQueen, who was making his debut after signing from Leeds, and £350,000 Joe Jordan did nothing to further their reputations. For the hosts £440,000 Kenny

Back at Wembley less than three months on for the Charity Shield, Jimmy Greenhoff (left) races for possession with Phil Thompson. Seconds later the United striker was writhing in agony on the turf, the victim of a knee strain.

Dalglish was unobtrusively excellent, but the man who ran the show was midfield general-cum-enforcer Graeme Souness, recruited from Middlesbrough for £352,000 in January.

Apart from opening the scoring after thirty-eight minutes with a coruscating volley from Terry McDermott's cross, he passed and tackled majestically throughout, and found time for copious verbal inspiration as well. In general, Liverpool were in charge, their second-half strikes from Ray Kennedy and Jimmy Case eliciting only one response, from Sammy McIlroy on the hour. Though the visitors stuck to their guns manfully, they were outplayed and Benfica scouts looking for weaknesses ahead of their European Cup encounter with Liverpool must have quailed. The lightest moment of the afternoon came when a wild kick from Jordan shredded Emlyn Hughes' shorts. On rushed coach Ronnie Moran with a spare pair, but he did not depart before administering a public 'spanking' to the beaming England veteran.

The extent to which Manchester United lagged behind the double European Champions, though never admitted by their fans at the time, was illustrated with emphatic eloquence at Old Trafford on Boxing Day 1978. That season's Liverpool combination remains, for many contemporary observers, the club's best ever – and that's quite a compliment. Despite two shock away defeats by Arsenal and Bristol City, they held a handsome First Division lead and some of their football, notably in their 7-0 drubbing of Tottenham, had been utterly breathtaking. There wasn't a weakness in the side, but the stuff of greatness sprang from the midfield axis of Jimmy Case on the right, Graeme Souness in the middle, Ray Kennedy on the left and Terry McDermott absolutely everywhere. Each member of this now-hallowed quartet was an accomplished technical performer, each one was a feisty character and each one would work his socks off for the common cause. Their off-the-ball movement was simple but ceaseless, their understanding of team needs total, their effect devastating. United perished to a Kennedy header (five minutes), a Case tap-in after a fizzing Dalglish shot (twenty-four minutes) and a mazy run past several defenders capped by an acute-angled shot from David Fairclough.

For 'Supersub', a tag which he detested but with which he was saddled throughout his career, it was his first start of the season and Paisley believed it would massage his confidence. Oddly, though, David was rarely as effective from the first whistle as he was after rising from the bench, and he never scaled the heights expected of him.

Dave Sexton, whose team struggled gamely but who never came close to upsetting the visitors' magisterial stride, summed up with honesty: 'They are as good as most teams in Europe and should be a cert for the title.'

Given this position of acknowledged pre-eminence, it was understandable that the Champions-elect were taken aback by the fire-and-brimstone opening made by United when the two clubs were thrown together at Maine Road on FA Cup semi-final day. Like religious zealots determined to prevail or perish for their cause, they threw themselves at Liverpool and it was with considerable relief that the favourites greeted Kenny Dalglish's sumptuous eighteenth-minute intervention, a twisting run past Buchan, McIlroy and Bailey to open the scoring against the run of play.

United refused to yield, however, and two minutes later Jimmy Greenhoff crossed, Clemence and Hansen exchanged 'After you' messages and Jordan flicked an equalizer at the near post. The white-shirted Red Devils kept up their frenzied momentum but had a lucky break when McDermott struck the post with a thirty-eighth-minute penalty awarded for a push by Buchan on Dalglish. Bailey dived the wrong way but, according to Terry later, 'the post moved six inches!'

Thereafter the spirited underdogs continued to growl, the ever-deepening mire imposing restrictions on Liverpool's normal passing game, and it was no more than United deserved when Brian Greenhoff put them in front following another lapse by Hansen in the fifty-sixth minute. Now, gradually, the Merseysiders began to wrest the

initiative from the increasingly leg-weary Mancunians, who found themselves pinned inside their own half for lengthy periods. The siege intensified to epic proportions during the last quarter-of-an-hour and when Hansen was on hand to thump home after Bailey could not hold Thompson's eighty-second-minute cross, there seemed no way that United, now deflated as well as beleaguered, could possibly survive. But somehow they did. Chances proliferated – Dalglish and Heighway were especially profligate – but at the end of an afternoon of raw passion, a draw was a fair result.

Dave Sexton, an extremely modest man by nature, was justifiably proud on this occasion, singling out his recent acquisition from Wrexham, Mickey Thomas, for special praise, the little midfielder having run himself into the Maine Road mud as well as testing Clemence and company with a series of wicked crosses. In the aftermath it was tempting to believe that Sexton's heroes had shot their bolt, as David Johnson recalls: 'Towards the end we had pulverized them. They'd had their chance and blown it. We felt that we'd been to Manchester and should have won; now we'd murder them at Goodison. But another day, another dollar, as they say ...' Indeed! The United bolt remained unshot and their chance decidedly unblown. *(See Classic Clash Number Ten on page 68).*

Yet if Merseyside fans had been guilty of over-confidence prior to the Goodison Park replay, won so memorably by Jimmy Greenhoff's late header, then so were many Mancunians in advance of their Wembley date with Arsenal. When Liverpool were defeated it felt as if the Cup was already as good as lifted; in fact, the Gunners triumphed 3-2 in the most dramatic of finishes, leaving the crestfallen Old Trafford hordes to face a summer pondering what might have been.

Even encircled as he is here at Anfield in February 1978, Kenny Dalglish could strike fear into defenders' hearts. His Mancunian minders are (left to right) Jimmy Nicholl, Gordon McQueen, keeper Paddy Roche, Arthur Albiston and Sammy McIlroy. Liverpool won 3-1.

FA Cup semi-final replay
4 April 1979
at Goodison Park

MANCHESTER UNITED 1

J Greenhoff 79

Gary Bailey, Jimmy Nicholl, Arthur Albiston, Gordon McQueen, Martin Buchan, Sammy McIlroy, Lou Macari, Mickey Thomas, Steve Coppell, Jimmy Greenhoff, Joe Jordan.
Sub: Andy Ritchie for Macari (78).

LIVERPOOL 0

Ray Clemence, Phil Neal, Emlyn Hughes, Phil Thompson, Alan Hansen, Terry McDermott, Graeme Souness, Ray Kennedy, Steve Heighway, Kenny Dalglish, David Johnson.
Sub: Jimmy Case for Johnson (82).

Half-time: 0-0 Attendance: 53,069

ONCE again Jimmy Greenhoff was Liverpool's FA Cup executioner but this time, unlike at Wembley two years earlier, there could be no cries of 'Foul!' or 'Fluke!' from the Anfield camp. True, fortune favoured United as they held on in the latter stages of the first instalment of the semi-final at Maine Road the previous Saturday, and they were pinned back by the rampant Reds for much of the second period at Goodison. But overall they deserved to win for their unquenchable spirit, for keeping their heads when they might have been overrun, and for taking their chance when it came with deadly aplomb.

Going into this game, few pundits favoured the Mancunians' chances of standing between the Champions-elect and their latest tilt at the League and FA Cup double. After all, United had led until near the end in Manchester and let the advantage slip; now, back on Merseyside, the superior class of Bob Paisley's marvels would surely tell.

This very point had been made publicly by Graeme Souness – not, perhaps, the wisest of tactics as the Red Devils began at searing pace, as if they had a point to prove. Indeed, only Ray Clemence kept the favourites in contention as he made brilliant early saves from Lou Macari, Joe Jordan and Steve Coppell; then Gordon McQueen shot over a gaping goal and Jordan thumped a header against the underside of the bar, all by the midway point of the first half. Gradually, though, Liverpool reasserted themselves and after Ray Kennedy had rapped Gary Bailey's woodwork, Kenny Dalglish went agonizingly close with a diving header.

After the interval, Souness and company began to assume their expected control of proceedings and when that most combative of playmakers went close after seventy-five minutes, it seemed likely that, for United, the end was nigh.

Quite the reverse. Three minutes after that miss, Jordan found Mickey Thomas free on the left and the mercurial Welshman crossed into the Liverpool goalmouth where Greenhoff had given Emlyn Hughes the slip. Jimmy allowed the ball to bounce and as Clemence charged out, more to distract his opponent than with any realistic hope of making a save, the United marksman directed a precision header between Ray and his right-hand post.

It remains one of Jimmy's favourite memories. 'It seemed an age before the ball bounced. At first I didn't know whether to take it on my chest or head it, but then Clemence committed himself and my mind was made up. I made a bit of a fool of myself with the goal celebration; teeth gritted, tongue out, arm waving, the lot, but it was a wonderful moment. Afterwards I could hardly take my eyes off the big clock they had at Goodison and the hands didn't seem to move. That twelve minutes felt the longest in my life!'

While Greenhoff and company cavorted in the Goodison mud, the Liverpool lads trudged off disconsolately. For the second time in two years they had been within touching distance of the coveted double, only for the old enemy to intervene.

To make matters worse, a month before Wembley, United had been firmly shown their place in the First Division pecking order, being swept aside imperiously at Anfield by a Liverpool side in unstoppable mid-gallop towards the club's eleventh title. Sexton's team had striven as manfully as ever, but they were barely in contention, certainly not after Dalglish had nodded his twenty-second goal of the season after thirty-six minutes and Phil Neal had doubled the lead two minutes after the break. After that, there were passages of play when the hosts appeared to toy with their adversaries, stroking the ball around with practised ease.

The game held particular significance for Alan Kennedy, who had arrived at Anfield from Newcastle for £330,000 at the beginning of the season. The rugged left-back, who rejoiced in the nickname of 'Barney Rubble', recalls: 'It was my first game for Liverpool against United and, for a little spell, Steve Coppell had been giving me a hard time. But I can recall winning the ball off him and just having time to look up and see Kenny at the far post. When he scored from my cross it was a great tonic for me, as a new boy, to dispossess England's right-winger and then lay on a goal in such an important game.' Thus Liverpool finished top of the First Division pile yet again, though the full extent of their domination had hardly begun.

In 1979/80, too, they set the pace, with United clinging gamely, if not always elegantly, to their coat-tails and the Merseysiders' superior quality was such that it was something of a surprise for the pair to be level on points going into their Boxing Day meeting at Anfield. The match was billed as a telling examination of United's Championship credentials. It was a test they failed dismally.

Boosted by the summer signing of England schemer Ray Wilkins from Chelsea, the Red Devils had improved their consistency – hence their exalted position in the table – but Liverpool, who had gone fifty-two games since their last home defeat, simply outclassed them. Somehow contriving to play their usual flowing game despite driving wind and rain, they went ahead on fifteen minutes following a six-man move rounded off by the increasingly magisterial centre-back Alan Hansen. His one-two interchange with Ray Kennedy prior to his clinical low finish past Gary Bailey was a study in precision.

Thereafter United huffed and puffed valiantly but, in truth, it was only the athletic Bailey who kept them in contention. Indeed, he almost compounded his defensive excellence by furnishing his side with a bizarre equalizer after seventy-three minutes, when his long clearance was caught by the gale, bounced once on the edge of Ray Clemence's penalty box and again on his crossbar. On the run of play it would have been a travesty, but Bailey had done enough to earn some personal good fortune.

What cruel irony, then, when he was at fault with Liverpool's second goal five minutes from time, allowing a fierce volley from David Johnson to squirm between his legs. The Kop was merciless, chorusing sarcastically 'We all agree, Bailey is better than Shilton'. As his team's best player on the day by far, he deserved better than that.

In the circumstances it was remarkable that the title issue was still alive when Liverpool checked in at Old Trafford in early April – and by the end of an afternoon of pulsating drama it was clear that the contest had more mileage still. Yet after Kenny Dalglish gave Gordon McQueen the slip to net from a narrow angle after fourteen minutes, the Championship race seemed virtually done and dusted.

But that all changed with a twang of a hamstring. Alan Kennedy takes up the tale. 'I was beating Steve Coppell in a chase for the ball when, suddenly, I felt like I'd been shot in the back of my leg. My hamstring had gone and I pulled up. He crossed, Mickey Thomas scored and the whole atmosphere changed.'

That was after twenty minutes and United, scenting a whiff of hope, began to turn up the pressure. The experienced visitors, not prone to panic, soaked it up serenely until a decisive sixty-fifth-minute intervention by a thirty-three-year-old veteran whose career had been written off by two specialists.

Opposite: Jimmy Greenhoff (number eight) steers an exquisite header past Ray Clemence to earn United, very much the underdogs, a place in the 1979 FA Cup Final.

Alan Hansen sends Anfield into yuletide raptures, netting early in this encounter on Boxing Day 1979 despite the attentions of Stewart Houston (left) and Martin Buchan. Liverpool won 2-0.

Jimmy Greenhoff remembers: 'I had been out for nearly a year with a succession of pelvic injuries. Two men had told me I shouldn't play again, but a third held out some hope so here I was. Still, I'd not had a full game for the first team, only one for the reserves and not much training when Dave Sexton asked me to face Liverpool. I told him I was nowhere near fit, but he needed me so I gave it a go. I felt shattered during the game, too, but then this corner came over from the right, Joe Jordan nodded it towards goal and I got a little deflection with my head to send it past Ray Clemence. It was enough to win, and it just about kept our faint Championship hopes alive. In the end we hung on until the final Saturday of the season, though I must be honest and say that Liverpool always had a bit in hand.

They were a truly great side.'

Even so, United's effort had been immensely creditable and raised optimism for 1980/81 to something approaching fever pitch among Old Trafford fans who had not had a title to celebrate for thirteen years. Of course, they had no way of knowing that their period in the wilderness was but half over, so the consequent letdown of a return to mid-table mediocrity came as a bitter blow.

By the time Liverpool and United assembled for their third successive Boxing Day get-together, this time at Old Trafford, Sexton's side had mustered a meagre half-dozen League victories and had drawn their previous four home games. The natives were restless and understandably so. For the Merseysiders it was almost a case of business as usual, but not quite. They would finish the day on top of the table – on goals scored, their goal difference being identical to that of Aston Villa – but the all-round assurance of recent seasons had been missing from their play.

This goalless affair, played on a pudding of a pitch at frenetic pace, produced little to suggest that Liverpool wouldn't take the title and even less to hint that United ever would. The hosts were high on commitment but, shorn of long-term injury victim Ray Wilkins, they were woefully low on creativity, leaving Ray Clemence to pass most of his 500th League outing in splendid isolation. Even without the fearsome Souness, absent with an infected shin, Liverpool engineered all the most meaningful openings, Dalglish missing two in the first half and Ray Kennedy going close twice in the second, his best effort being a sharp drive which thudded against a post in the seventy-ninth minute. The Champions seemed no less impregnable after losing Hansen with knee trouble on the hour and when the final whistle sounded a faint but unmistakable groan of discontent rippled around the stadium.

Now Dave Sexton, a lovely, quietly reflective fellow who never relished the media spotlight which had become an integral part of managing Manchester United, found himself trapped in its unwelcome and increasingly hostile glare. As results varied between ho-hum and horrible, speculation about his continued employment at Old Trafford became frenzied yet as the end of term approached, it seemed he was off the danger list. Indeed, after Gordon McQueen's power-headed lone goal at Anfield in mid-April had stretched United's run of straight League victories to five, that hugely experienced and well-connected soccer correspondent Denis Lowe reported in the Daily Telegraph, 'Dave Sexton, a beleaguered manager two months ago, can laugh at his critics.'

The assessment seemed eminently reasonable. Even though Richard Money and Jimmy Case had both rattled the Red Devils' woodwork, and there had been several goal-line clearances, the visitors had held their own on the balance of play. And nothing, not even Bob Paisley's disgusted assertion that his team had begun the game at a stroll, could detract from the visitors' feat in being the second side in ninety-four games to bring down the walls of the Anfield stronghold. True, many spectators had voted with their feet, the attendance of 31,276 being Liverpool's post-war lowest for a meeting with United, but that was down to the Merseysiders having slipped out of the title hunt, just for once, rather than to box-office indifference to the Mancunians.

Yet after the campaign drew to a close with two more victories, suggesting that some sort of corner had been turned, Sexton was sacked. He had paid the price for his team's lack of trophies, but also its perceived dullness. Such a charge as the latter would never be levelled at his successor.

Meanwhile, although Liverpool finished only fifth in the table they did bring home a couple of baubles. There was the League Cup, welcome enough despite being small beer by their usual standards; oh yes, and a little matter of their third European Cup, claimed at the expense of Real Madrid. That took Bob Paisley's haul to nine major trophies, and still counting ...

CHAPTER EIGHT:

HIGH ADVENTURE
1981/2 – 1985/6

Opposite: When Ron Atkinson asked Bill Shankly how much he should give West Bromwich Albion for Bryan Robson in 1981, the retired Liverpool boss replied: 'Whatever it takes, son; just pay the money.' Ten days later Shanks was dead, but Robson would demonstrate the clarity of the great man's judgement for the next decade and more.

OLD Trafford fell under the spell of a Liverpudlian in the summer of 1981. Having been linked with a host of household names, one or two of whom were offered the job of succeeding Dave Sexton, Manchester United installed West Bromwich Albion boss Ron Atkinson as their new manager. Now the rich and famous under-achievers moved to the beat of a different drum, the diffidence and caution of the previous highly professional but rather colourless regime dissolved in a whirl of wisecracks and exuberance.

It's easy to give the wrong impression here. Sure, Big Ron played up to the 'Champagne Charlie' image beloved of the tabloids, but he was a consummate professional where football was concerned. He loved the game, was possessed by it; he preached a gospel of boldness and adventure and his United teams practised it with considerable, if not ultimate, success.

Into this brave new world stepped stars such as Republic of Ireland striker Frank Stapleton from Arsenal, Aston Villa's England international full-back John Gidman, combative midfielder Remi Moses from West Bromwich and, best of all, Bryan Robson, another of Ron's former charges at the Hawthorns.

After an anxious start, in which only one point was garnered from the first three games, the new combination began to gel excitingly and when Atkinson took them to the city of his birth in late October, they were challenging for the First Division leadership. Liverpool, meanwhile, were only four points behind them but having to endure daft whispers that they were bored with domestic competiton, becoming fully motivated only in the European arena.

The full absurdity of such notions would become apparent by season's end, but criticism was fuelled by their deserved demise at the hands of Captain Marvel and company in an Anfield quagmire. The visitors displayed as much resilience as did Sexton's doughty crew, but possessed an extra buoyancy instilled by the man in the flashy suit. Indeed, although the Mancunians' victory came courtesy of a late winner, the *Liverpool Daily Post* described Ron's Red Devils as 'the best Manchester United side to descend on Anfield since the Best-Law-Charlton era'.

Performances justified the compliment. From the start they carried the game to Liverpool, winning the midfield battle and stretching a defence which was, perhaps, still coming to terms with the unexpected summer departure of Ray Clemence to Tottenham. In his place was an acrobatic, if a little eccentric Zimbabwean. Bruce Grobbelaar was fundamentally a fine goalkeeper who would go on to serve the Reds splendidly over many years, but he was a tad less predictable than his magnificent predecessor.

On twenty-five minutes Grobbelaar was at his most agile, springing prodigiously to his right to parry a powerful header from Stapleton, but he couldn't hold it and the ball ran loose for Kevin Moran to poke in from close range. Though Graeme Souness struck a post before the interval, United continued to look the better side by a

comfortable margin until Ronnie Whelan replaced Liverpool marksman David Johnson deep in the second period. Almost immediately the move paid dividends when Moran was adjudged to have nudged his fellow Irishman to the ground and McDermott crashed home a penalty kick.

Now the expected script was for Liverpool to lay siege to their opponents' goal in time-honoured Anfield fashion, but this time the reverse happened, United bounding back with a controlled offensive that was rewarded with only a minute or so to spare. The man of the hour was left-back Arthur Albiston, the 1977 FA Cup Final rookie who was now a regular in the side and on the verge of Scottish international recognition.

He recalls: 'As the end approached we were feeling hard done by because we'd played well and created a lot of chances. When the ball came out to me on the left I concentrated hard on controlling it in the mud. I played a one-two with Frank Stapleton, but even as I bore down on goal I wasn't sure about shooting, that wasn't my forte. Out of the corner of my eye I saw someone come in to tackle me – it turned out to be Graeme Souness – so I let the ball run on a bit and got away from him. When finally I shot, I slipped a bit, not hitting it properly, but it crept into the far corner. I didn't score many goals and have experienced few sweeter feelings on a football pitch than that. What made it even more memorable was that we really deserved the victory that day.'

Stirring stuff but, come April, the same old story of Liverpool domination was taking shape. Under the evergreen, indefatigable Paisley they had revived to such an extent that they were hot title favourites, a position they strengthened immeasurably with a single-goal triumph at Old Trafford. Sometimes, both before and after this encounter, the Merseysiders have been unlucky to leave their rivals' territory empty-handed; this victory made up for a few of those.

In a nutshell, United were the better team and if they had accepted just a small percentage of the opportunities they had fashioned so enterprisingly, they would have won. As it was they began badly when Stapleton's seventh-minute penalty was saved by Grobbelaar, who revealed that he dived the correct way after studying a photograph of Frank's previous spot-kick in the match programme. The most relieved man in the stadium was Phil Thompson, who had handled unnecessarily. 'I must have had a brainstorm. When Bruce saved it I could have kissed him,' gasped the England defender later.

A little later young Scott McGarvey volleyed against Grobbelaar's post, and the affair became more one-sided when Liverpool lost Souness with a recurrence of back trouble. But in the sixty-third minute the occasion was transformed when the visitors' first serious attack yielded a goal, Craig Johnston pouncing on a miscue by Ian Rush to give the wrong-footed Bailey no chance. Later a deflated Ron Atkinson, whose side were now eight points adrift and effectively out of Championship contention, admitted that United had lost patience and had paid dearly for what became an undisciplined cavalry charge.

Liverpool just rolled on, an all-conquering institution the like of which the English game had never known. Each player was an outstanding footballer in his own right, but what made the club exceptional was its continued observance of 'Shanklyism', the collective ideal and the attention to detail. While that situation remained, each new success simply paved the way for more. Thus, having lifted their second successive League Cup and thirteenth title in 1981/2, they claimed their third successive League Cup and fourteenth title in 1982/3.

The Big Two's first clash of that campaign failed to produce a goal, thus negating United's quest for three successive Anfield victories. It was a muscular trial of strength played at the height of a wild autumn storm, the swirling wind rendering controlled passing all but impossible. As Ron Atkinson put it: 'I thought we had the wind behind us in the second half, but after five minutes it was blowing the

other way!' In the circumstances the players excelled, Liverpool having marginally the better of exchanges and Gary Bailey perhaps the most obvious man-of-the-match contender. However, the Reds' versatile Mark Lawrenson, then deployed in midfield but more effective still at the back, ran him close.

Come the return in February, the Merseysiders were already entrenched so firmly at the head of the table that, even with three months of the season left, United had to win to retain the merest hope of catching them. They didn't. Part of Liverpool's greatness was their expertise in plucking points from games in which they were below par, and this was a case in point. Atkinson's men spurned a succession of chances, took a thirty-sixth-minute lead through Arnold Muhren – surely Old Trafford's most skilful footballer since George Best – only to be pegged back by an opportunistic Dalglish strike only four minutes later. That's how it stayed, despite increasingly frantic second-half pressure from United, who thus tasted frustration in yet another Championship quest.

There was a chance of redemption in the League Cup Final but it was not to be *(see Classic Clash Number Eleven on pages 76-7)*. For one of Liverpool's Wembley scorers, Alan Kennedy, netting crucial goals in finals had become an enviable habit. So far he had done so twice in the League Cup, against West Ham in 1981 and now United, and, of far greater import, he had cracked the late winner against Real Madrid in the 1981 European Cup Final. Still to come was the decisive penalty in

Gordon McQueen blocks a shot from his fellow Scot, Kenny Dalglish, at Old Trafford in February 1983. The game ended in a 1-1 draw, with Kenny contributing Liverpool's goal.

League Cup Final
26 March 1983
at Wembley

LIVERPOOL 2

Kennedy 75; Whelan 99

Bruce Grobbelaar, Phil Neal, Alan Kennedy, Mark Lawrenson, Alan Hansen, Ronnie Whelan, Graeme Souness, Kenny Dalglish, Sammy Lee, Ian Rush, Craig Johnston. Sub: David Fairclough for Johnston (83).

MANCHESTER UNITED 1

Whiteside 12

Gary Bailey, Mike Duxbury, Arthur Albiston, Kevin Moran, Gordon McQueen, Remi Moses, Ray Wilkins, Arnold Muhren, Steve Coppell, Norman Whiteside, Frank Stapleton. Sub: Lou Macari for Moran (70).

Half-time: 0-0 After 90 minutes: 1-1
Attendance: 100,000

LIVERPOOL took the League Cup for the third time in succession, but Manchester United left Wembley with their pride intact after a catalogue of ill fortune had contributed to their downfall in extra-time.

Indeed, the Red Devils led for most of the match thanks to a sumptuous twelfth-minute strike by teenage prodigy Norman Whiteside, and bowed the knee to goals from Alan Kennedy and Ronnie Whelan only after losing both central defenders to injury. In addition, Liverpool goalkeeper Bruce Grobbelaar was extremely lucky to escape with only a booking after he body-checked the already crippled Gordon McQueen near the end of normal time.

Against all that, it should be stressed that the Merseysiders enjoyed massive territorial advantage nearly all afternoon and certainly could not be described as unworthy winners. In fact, Bob Paisley's League leaders started the brighter of the two and it came as

something of a surprise when United went ahead, as Liverpool left-back Alan Kennedy recalls: 'Norman's goal was brilliantly executed but I think we could have defended better. He took a long ball from Gordon McQueen on his chest, then turned Alan Hansen and shot past Bruce with his so-called weaker right foot. Alan might be blamed for being a little too close to his man, allowing him to swivel, but perhaps I might be criticized for not being close enough to offer cover. My problem was that with United having so many quality players, I was watching their other options. Whatever, it came as a devastating blow because we had seemed comfortable up to that point.'

For the remainder of the first half and much of the second, Liverpool attacked relentlessly, Whelan squandering one glorious opening with an inaccurate volley and Ian Rush spurning two opportunities which he would have expected to accept with alacrity.

With seventy minutes gone it was beginning to seem as if the Liverpudlians might be fated not to score when an injury to United stopper Kevin Moran changed the balance of the match. Indeed, their longed-for equalizer arrived only five minutes after the battle-scarred Irishman, surely the League's most stitched footballer, was replaced by Lou Macari.

Kennedy, the scorer, remembers it well. 'Oddly enough, only three or four minutes before the goal, I had the luxury of a dress rehearsal. Graeme Souness played the ball to me about twenty-five yards out and Steve Coppell, my direct opponent, had not closed me down. I hit it reasonably well but it just scraped the top of the

crossbar, and I said to myself that if I got another such chance I would keep my head down to be sure of hitting the target. Then, almost at once, I found myself in exactly the same situation, in space with Coppell not having learned his lesson. This time my shot bounced just in front of Gary Bailey and skidded into the net. I think he was worried about Ian Rush, who was waiting to pounce on any rebound.'

From that moment, Alan says, Liverpool expected to win during the ninety minutes, especially when United's other centre-half, McQueen, suffered such a bad knock that he became little more than a passenger at centre-forward. Ron Atkinson reorganized with striker Frank Stapleton and full-back Mike Duxbury taking the central defensive positions and little Macari slotting in gamely at right-back, but the handicap was vast.

Even so, they might have snatched an astonishing victory during injury time when McQueen limped free in the inside-right position with only Grobbelaar to beat. Kennedy recalls: 'McQueen had an opportunity to score until Bruce up-ended him. It was at a time when referees were clamping down on this sort of foul and he was very fortunate not to get his marching orders. Certainly he would not get off as lightly today.'

However, Grobbelaar was spared, Paisley delivered a matter-of-fact pep talk before extra-time, and Liverpool resumed their quest for the winner in confident mode. When it arrived nine minutes into the first added period, Kennedy was involved once again. 'I had the ball in midfield and saw Ronnie Whelan was free. I thought about a one-two, although I

knew if I gave it to Ronnie I probably wouldn't get it back. I tried it anyway and to give him his due he tried to reach me but the ball rebounded to him from a defender. From there the orthodox thing would have been for him to look for another pass but he just glanced up and curled a superb shot beyond Bailey from outside the corner of the box. It was a wonderful piece of opportunism and typical of Ronnie. He practised those shots a lot and knew instinctively when to try them.'

In the time that remained, Liverpool had enough chances to have routed United but, in the circumstances, that would have been unduly hard.

Afterwards United's most eye-catching performer, the precocious Whiteside, was well-nigh inconsolable. His manager said, 'Norman is emotionally and physically drained and he is entitled to be like that because he played like a hero. Make no mistake, he will be back at Wembley many, many times.' Atkinson added that the whole team was down. 'But we have had a little chat and we want to come back here in six weeks time for the FA Cup.' As it turned out, as Brighton discovered to their cost, Big Ron was spot on. And for the record, one of the scorers who put them to the sword in a replayed Final was ... Norman Whiteside.

Yet another bauble for the Anfield trophy cabinet. Liverpool assemble for the ritual team photograph after seeing off a gallant challenge from United at Wembley. Back row (left to right): Mark Lawrenson, David Fairclough, Alan Hansen, Ronnie Whelan, Ian Rush, Bruce Grobbelaar, Bob Paisley. Front row: Craig Johnston, Kenny Dalglish, Phil Neal, Graeme Souness, Sammy Lee, Alan Kennedy.

Ian Rush, the most rampant British predator of his day, splits United central defenders Gordon McQueen (left) and Kevin Moran during the 1983 Charity Shield encounter. The Mancunians triumphed by two Bryan Robson goals to nil.

the shoot-out against AS Roma three years later.

Alan is a delightfully modest fellow, but he cannot conceal a smidgin of justifiable pride at his record. 'My early hero was Bobby Charlton, which made me want to shoot whenever I could. I can remember him hitting some fantastic efforts past both Tommy Lawrence and Ray Clemence. There was something inside me that wanted me to be like Bobby – apart from the haircut, of course!'

Aside from his goal, Alan's lasting memory of the 1983 final was yet another chapter in his ongoing duel with Steve Coppell. 'My greatest concern at Wembley was keeping Steve quiet. He was one of the finest wingers I have ever played against. He was quick, he could deliver an excellent cross and he didn't mind whether he beat you on the inside or the outside. He had a sharp football brain, too, and was always willing to chase back. It was a huge loss to United and England when he was forced to retire, well before his time, because of injury.'

The 1982/3 season wasn't all bad news for United, who made up for their Wembley reverse against Liverpool by winning the FA Cup in a replayed final against Brighton. After two seasons at Old Trafford, Ron Atkinson had needed the impetus of a trophy, and now his buccaneering team seemed admirably equipped to make a sustained assault on the Merseysiders' superiority in 1983/4.

When that challenge came, Bob Paisley was no longer at the Anfield helm to meet it. After establishing himself as by far and away the most successful manager in the history of English football, the unassuming, almost diffident sixty-four-year-old north-easterner had decided to retire at the top. Bob had never oozed charisma like Bill Shankly or courted controversy like Brian Clough; he wasn't revered like Matt Busby or loved like Joe Mercer; but when it came to the pragmatic business of filling trophy cabinets with silverware, he put the lot of them in the shade. After a barren first campaign, he led Liverpool to six League Championships, three European Cups, one UEFA Cup and three League Cups, all in the space of eight years. Before that, of course, he had made a mammoth if characteristically unobtrusive contribution to the triumphant Shankly reign.

Though his departure did not cause quite as many tremors as Shankly's before him, it was clear his loss to the club would be inestimable. Never had there been a cannier tactician, more meticulous planner or shrewder judge of a player. Thus when it was announced that, once again, Liverpool were going to promote from within, giving long-time coach Joe Fagan charge of the team, there were observers who scoffed. As we shall see, the affable Fagan's reaction to succeeding two legends was not merely to equal their achievements in any one season, but to outdo them!

In the circumstances, then, it was mildly astonishing that within two months of taking command, Joe had presided over three defeats by Manchester United. In all honesty, the first of this trilogy was pretty irrelevant, a testimonial game at Windsor Park, Belfast, for Harry Drennan, the outgoing secretary of the Irish FA. If nothing else, though, the encounter on neutral soil provided royal entertainment for the hordes of Ulstermen who followed both sets of English Reds. At half-time Liverpool were 3-1 up only for United, lifted by Ron Atkinson's six second-half substitutions, to force a dramatic 4-3 victory thanks to two late goals from veteran Lou Macari.

The next encounter was to contest the Charity Shield, another appetiser albeit rather more prestigious. Certainly the game was more keenly fought by the two teams widely supposed to be the main contenders for the 1983/4 title and Atkinson could be genuinely encouraged by the Red Devils' 2-0 triumph. Liverpool's opulent passing had taken the eye early on, but after Dalglish's twentieth-minute shot had struck the woodwork the Mancunians took control. Both goals came from a rampant Bryan Robson, rounding Grobbelaar after being put through delightfully by Wilkins on twenty-three minutes and forcing home in a goalmouth scramble on the hour.

Before the match there had been persuasive rumours that Atkinson was on the verge of transferring Wilkins to Arsenal, but the schemer's impressive Wembley display prompted his fellow midfielder Robson to remark, 'If I were the manager I wouldn't sell Ray at any price.' In fact, Wilkins saw out that season at Old Trafford before joining AC Milan, then returning to English football with Queen's Park Rangers to produce arguably the finest form of his career. Alan Kennedy recalls the Charity Shield clash and discounts the theory that the friendly didn't matter. 'We saw it as an important part of our preparation and a lot of fans paid good money to watch. United were far better than us that day and deserved to win. I can remember Robson beating me for the second goal, showing total determination. He was tough, a real gladiator, and he could score goals, too, as he showed at Wembley. When he and Graeme Souness met the very ground would shake.'

After the two pipe-openers, United and Liverpool got down to the real thing at Old Trafford in late September, with the Mancunians desperate to wipe out the two-point advantage their visitors had already established. So they did, turning on an exhilarating display of sustained attack which should have yielded more than a lone goal from Stapleton after fifty-two minutes. At least it was a memorable one, though, created by newcomer Arthur Graham, who skinned Hansen on the right before crossing for Stapleton to dispatch a firm half-volley from ten yards. Graham, who had cost only £45,000 from Leeds and who would not be the last bargain United would pick up at Elland Road, was standing in for Coppell so effectively that it seemed he might prove an adequate medium-term replacement if, as seemed depressingly likely, the Englishman's career was going to be halted by injury.

Joe Fagan's reaction to the setback was utterly refreshing. He told reporters:

FA Cup semi-final replay
17 April 1985
at Maine Road

MANCHESTER UNITED 2

Robson 46; Hughes 57

Gary Bailey, John Gidman, Arthur Albiston, Norman Whiteside, Paul McGrath, Graeme Hogg, Bryan Robson, Gordon Strachan, Mark Hughes, Frank Stapleton, Jesper Olsen.

LIVERPOOL 1

McGrath og 38

Bruce Grobbelaar, Phil Neal, Jim Beglin, Mark Lawrenson, Steve Nicol, Alan Hansen, Kenny Dalglish, Ronnie Whelan, Paul Walsh, Kevin MacDonald, John Wark. Sub: Gary Gillespie for Dalglish (79).

Half-time: 0-1 Attendance: 45,775

LIVERPOOL had been lucky and they were honest enough to admit it. After Ronnie Whelan and Paul Walsh had scored late goals in both normal time and extra-time to steal a draw against Manchester United in their FA Cup semi-final at Goodison Park, the Reds' relieved boss Joe Fagan admitted, 'We were outplayed and we got away with it.'

Or as Mark Lawrenson put it, 'Just like playing Monopoly – we got out of jail twice!'

But, having been granted their unexpected reprieve, would the Merseysiders be able to capitalize in the replay at Maine Road? The answer was negative. Although United did not reprise their dominance of the first encounter, once again they were the better team by a substantial margin, a circumstance emphasized by their confident comeback after going a goal behind.

Still smarting from the effect of their opponents' Houdini act of four days earlier, the Mancunians tore into action, putting the Liverpool goal under sustained early pressure. It seemed Frank Stapleton would give them a seventeenth-minute lead when he blasted the ball towards a gaping net, only for Phil Neal to contrive a near-miraculous block.

As if fortified by that escape, the Merseysiders steadied and after thirty-eight minutes they went ahead, albeit fortuitously and against the run of play, when

Paul McGrath rose to clear a cross from Steve Nicol but succeeded only in nodding it into his own net. Had Nicol not squandered a splendid chance to plump up a two-goal cushion only two minutes later, events might have taken a radically different course, but the Scot screwed his shot wide with only Gary Bailey to beat and United survived.

The game's defining moment came only a minute after the break, and it was Captain Marvel who provided it. Bryan Robson picked up a loose ball in the centre circle, galloped unstoppably down the middle of the field and unleashed an explosive twenty-five-yard left-footer which Bruce Grobbelaar managed to touch but could not keep out.

Now United had the scent of victory once more, and this time they were not to be denied. They buzzed forward relentlessly and after fifty-seven minutes Gordon Strachan held the ball up intelligently, then paralysed the Liverpool offside trap with a perfect through-ball to the marauding Mark Hughes. 'Sparky' shook off the challenge of Mark Lawrenson and raced on before beating Grobbelaar with a firm drive from the edge of the box.

Having allowed Fagan's boys to wriggle off the hook twice already, United were not going to do so again. Liverpool's attempt at a grandstand finish, throwing Lawrenson and Alan Hansen forward, was met with resolution and the world would have to wait another four years for the first all-Merseyside FA Cup Final.

As Ron Atkinson put it afterwards, 'It was a match for men and we had to fight for every ball. Robson's goal was a magnificent effort and it came at the best possible moment for us. What a man he is!'

'Why make excuses? While I'm disappointed to lose for the first time in the League, we were beaten by a magnificent goal. I give Graham and Stapleton full credit rather than blame my own defenders.' The only anxiety clouding United's clear sky on a crisp autumn afternoon was their perennial lack of ruthlessness in front of goal. Too often their failure to make safe a game they had controlled had cost them dearly in the past, and it would continue to be a flaw for the foreseeable future.

Meanwhile Liverpool, complete with goal machine Ian Rush, were progressing with ominous consistency and when the clubs' paths crossed again in January they were three points clear of second-placed United. Anfield was engulfed in filthy weather for a rugged, sometimes unsavoury encounter largely dominated by the 'Pool but, ironically, not won by them because of the precise failing which tended to inflict their rivals, namely serial profligacy among their forwards. To be fair, Gary Bailey made many wonderful saves, but nevertheless Liverpool created enough openings to have triumphed by a street.

They had taken the lead after thirty-two minutes, when a Souness shot was cleared off the line by Albiston, only for Johnston to knock in the rebound from six yards. By then an injury to McQueen had occasioned wholesale reorganization in the United defence and as half-time approached the odds on a home victory were short. These were lengthened a minute after the break when Dalglish, on whom Liverpool relied hugely for attacking guile, suffered a depressed fracture of the cheekbone when he was elbowed by Kevin Moran. It was an accident – the Irishman was a formidable but wholly scrupulous opponent – but it contributed to the already tetchy atmosphere which became downright ill-tempered.

For the irate Kop, the afternoon got worse. With only two minutes remaining, Ray Wilkins crossed, United substitute Garth Crooks – on loan from Spurs and never to find an Old Trafford niche – won a messy challenge with Alan Kennedy and the ball ran to Norman Whiteside. The Ulsterman, whose customary muscular exertion that day had underlined his pantomine-villain status among Liverpool fans, drove home the equalizer.

At that moment, it seemed a catastrophe to Kopites, but by season's end it simply didn't matter. Not only had the Merseysiders claimed their third successive Championship and fourth League Cup in a row, they had lifted their fourth European Cup – while United finished empty-handed yet again. Joe Fagan, that wise, humble and benevolent man, took the unprecedented treble triumph as calmly as he had the September defeat at Old Trafford. He did not deserve what lay in wait for him and for Liverpool FC at the Heysel Stadium in Brussels just one year hence.

Before then, though, came a new season, one in which the Reds' domestic dominance would be assaulted from within their own city. But while Everton emerged as the indisputable team of the moment, the biannual confrontations with Manchester United continued with undiluted ferocity.

As was his wont, Ron Atkinson had been a heavy summer spender, recruiting midfielder Gordon Strachan from Aberdeen, winger Jesper Olsen from Ajax and striker Alan Brazil from Spurs in a bid to clinch the First Division title, the seemingly endless quest for which had become an Old Trafford obsession. But still, while the side was frequently entertaining, it was not quite equal to that particular task.

Liverpool, not surprisingly, were finding it hard to match the standards they had set during the previous campaign so, for a change, the clubs were a little way off the First Division's summit when the battle between them was resumed in Manchester in September. Though buffeted periodically by unseasonal sleet, the players served up an exciting contest which should have been tilted irreversibly United's way by the interval. They had gone ahead from the spot on twenty minutes after Alan Kennedy had felled Strachan as the Scottish sprite danced past him. Gordon, who had netted forty-six penalties in fifty-one attempts for Aberdeen, now obliged for his new employers.

Opposite: Phil Neal's appeal for offside falls on deaf ears as Mark Hughes leaves Mark Lawrenson trailing and lashes United's deserved winner.

With Strachan and Olsen prominent on the flanks, further heavy pressure ensued from the Red Devils until, two minutes from half-time, came the turning point of the game. Bryan Robson unleashed a savage drive which was bound unerringly for the top corner of the net until Bruce Grobbelaar launched himself from a standing start to claw the ball to safety. Robbo stood dumbfounded – later he described the Zimbabwean's feat as 'the greatest save I've ever seen' – and the visitors seemed to be infused with new belief. In the second period, with Hansen and Lawrenson at their regal best, Liverpool held firm in the face of prolonged flurries of United attacking, then rallied spiritedly to snatch an equalizer, and a point, after seventy-three minutes. The goal was extremely lucky: Hogg attempted to clear a Nicol cross only to see the ball rebound off Walsh into the net. But the response bore testimony to the Merseysiders' traditional resilience. Shankly would have approved.

However, the founding father of the modern Liverpool would have been considerably less impressed to discover that when the Reds lost to United at Anfield on the last day of March, it was their fifth home defeat of the season. He would have blanched, too, at the unwelcome statistic that the Mancunians had won three and drawn two of their last five League encounters at Liverpool HQ. This latest indignity came courtesy of a textbook Stapleton header from a deep Whiteside cross thirteen minutes from the end. Lest Shanks' shade should become too pale, though, it should be pointed out that his former club would finish the season as title runners-up while United trailed in a disappointing fourth.

The match, in which Liverpool enjoyed lengthy spells of territorial domination, is remembered by Alan Kennedy as an unwelcome landmark in his distinguished career. 'I went for a ball at the far post with Mark Hughes, who was just beginning to make a name for himself. He was a very strong lad and we fell heavily together. When Ronnie Moran came on to pick up the pieces he thought the main problem was with my head – nothing different there! But my real difficulty was an excruciating pain in my ankle. I couldn't walk and it turned out to be stress fractures of the tib and fib. I missed a lot of games and Jim Beglin became established in my place, so it was the beginning of the end for me at Anfield.'

Alan had seven years of glory to look back on, though, and the Scouse-Mancunian saga looms large among his memories. 'When I think of Man U v Liverpool I think of massive crowds with 10,000 lockouts. There was always the difficulty of getting tickets for family and friends; the demand was so great there was never enough. The Stretford End was awesome, much like the Kop, but it wasn't intimidating because when you're out there you blot everything out but the game. Then there was their pitch, which was so big. You had to toil really hard and try to make the ball do the work.

'There was always an extra edge when we played them, the fans were so intense about the result. United had a fine side in the early 1980s, but while they tended to win games against us, we always finished higher in the League table. It seemed that Ron Atkinson was brilliant at motivating them for really big occasions, and none were bigger than us against them. Ron liked his characters and strong players, but he always made sure his sides had attacking style, too. And, while everyone knows United's stars, they had some wonderful footballers who never got the recognition they deserved, people like Arthur Albiston and Mike Duxbury.'

The fracture meant that Alan was absent when Liverpool and United were thrown together in the semi-final of that season's FA Cup, a see-saw struggle which ran to two matches and in which both teams came from behind to revive their hopes. In the first meeting at Goodison Park, the Mancunians ruled the roost and led twice only to let the Merseysiders gain parity near the end of both normal and extra-time, though it should be pointed out that both United goals were aided by substantial deflections.

Bryan Robson was titanic in midfield as his side created, and wasted, a plethora of chances. It was appropriate that when a goal finally arrived on seventy minutes that this most inspirational of skippers should take the credit, despite his fierce drive glancing off Mark Hughes on its way past Bruce Grobbelaar. Ronnie Whelan pulled Liverpool out of the fire with a sweetly curled twenty-yarder after eighty-seven minutes, but United were unbowed and when Stapleton scored via Lawrenson's backside nine minutes into extra-time it seemed inconceivable that they would relax their stranglehold a second time. But, with only seconds left, Bailey could only parry a Rush header from a Dalglish cross and the unchallenged Walsh bundled home from close range. In terms of the previous action it was nothing less than daylight robbery, but the Anfielders were nothing if not resilient and Ron Atkinson was left to lament the fact that the referee failed to see a linesman's flag raised for offside shortly before Dalglish had delivered. As he put it ruefully, 'A whistle then, and we were at Wembley!'

In the event United triumphed in the replay *(see Classic Clash Number Twelve on page 80)* and went on to beat Everton in the final, thanks to a breathtaking goal from Merseyside's bete noir, Norman Whiteside. In an echo of 1977, they prevented a famous treble, Howard Kendall's Toffees having already collected the League title and the European Cup Winners' Cup. But Atkinson's team had contributed royally to the football of the mid-1980s and were overdue a trophy.

If only that had been the final act of the season. But eleven days later Liverpool met Juventus in the European Cup Final and the football world was plunged into trauma. On a lovely evening in Brussels, thirty-nine people were crushed to death when followers of the English club flattened a wall while attempting to invade the Italian section of the crowd. For once the term 'tragedy' was appropriate to a sporting occasion.

Many people, including Liverpool boss Joe Fagan, would never see football in the same light again. Due to retire after the match, he did so a broken man, uncomprehending of the madness which had overtaken the game to which he had dedicated his working life. For the record, the contest which followed the carnage was won by Juventus, but in such dire circumstances, who could care?

The practical result of the Heysel disaster was the banning of English clubs from European competition for five years, with the Liverpool sentence extending for an extra term. Though the scars would never recede, life went on for English football and for Liverpool, who appointed Kenny Dalglish as player-manager. At the time it was seen as a rash gamble, placing the fate of one of the world's leading clubs in the hands of a man with no management experience. Nine months later, having led the Reds to their first League and FA Cup double, the taciturn Scot had supplied the complete answer.

His fans called him Barney Rubble but Alan Kennedy was no cartoon cut-out, as the men he marked during a medal-studded Anfield sojourn would testify with feeling.

Craig Johnston's neat downward header beats United keeper Gary Bailey, with defender Arthur Albiston unable to prevent the ball crossing the line. The Red Devils hit back to claim a 1-1 draw at Old Trafford in October 1985, but thereafter their status as runaway First Division leaders was rapidly eroded.

During the early months of 1985/6, such an outcome seemed roughly as likely as Kopites and Stretford Enders sitting down together for a quiet discussion about global warming or the debt burden of the Third World. United had got off to the best start in their history, winning their first ten games and were still unbeaten when Liverpool, their thirteenth League opponents, visited in mid-October. With Robson, Whiteside, Hughes and the versatile Paul McGrath all in outstanding form, they had established a ten-point lead at the top of the First Division and the pundits said the Championship was all over bar the shouting.

But those fans who had suffered through the Red Devils' seemingly interminable title drought were fearful of premature celebrations, and wisely so. The Merseysiders' visit produced a typically taut 1-1 draw, which was probably the fairest result although Dalglish's opinion that his side had done enough to win was not outrageous. United were deprived of their touchstone, Robson, and the influential Strachan through injury, and they seemed strangely lethargic. Liverpool, making light of the absence of strikers Rush and Walsh, shaded a goalless first half and after man-of-the-match Johnston had opened the scoring with a neat header just eighteen seconds into the second period, they began to move with the assurance of likely victors. However, the splendid McGrath – playing in midfield on this occasion but an even more accomplished footballer in central defence – equalized unexpectedly from an Albiston cross after sixty-four minutes and the tenor of the game changed. Now United attacked relentlessly and nearly stole the points when Hansen headed against his own bar in the dying seconds.

Justice was done, though, and now serious questions about the Mancunians' Championship pedigree began to be aired. The uncertainty intensified as their debilitating injury crisis continued to mount and their once-handsome lead was whittled away so dramatically that by their late-November League Cup meeting at Anfield they were a mere two points better off than their hosts.

The impression that the tide was flowing remorselessly against United intensified as their sprightly first-half performance, which had yielded a goal by McGrath, was nullified by two goals in a minute by Liverpool's Jan Molby on the hour. The first was a classic, the Danish playmaker surging from near halfway before beating Bailey with a venomous shot from sixteen yards; the second was a precisely placed penalty, contentiously awarded for handball against Moran. Thus the formidable power and the incongruous delicacy of Molby were showcased back to back, the Reds were through to a quarter-final, and a telling psychological blow had been struck against the Old Trafford cause.

As winter wore on, United's position continued to erode. Although rumours were denied strenuously at the time, negotiations were going on for the end-of-season transfer of their young marksman and emerging folk hero, Mark Hughes, to Barcelona. He was confused by the situation, his form collapsed and the fans were outraged that the club should jeopardize their title chances in this way.

Meanwhile, results continued to be patchy and when United arrived at Anfield in February, they were already a point behind Everton and knew that defeat would see Liverpool leapfrog above them, too. In fact, for several minutes after setting foot on Merseyside, football was the last thing on Mancunian minds – they were attacked by morons with aerosol cans as they disembarked from their coach. Eyes burning and spluttering for breath, they sought sanctuary and fresh air on the pitch, hardly ideal preparation for the trial of strength which lay ahead. There was no lasting damage, however – except to football's public image – and it was to Atkinson's vast credit that he declared that the experience did not affect his men's subsequent display.

In fact, United fared better than had seemed probable. For the first quarter of an hour they dictated the play and climaxed this period with a goal when Colin Gibson and Hughes sliced through the Reds' rearguard with a slick one-two, Grobbelaar fumbled Gibson's shot and the former Aston Villa utility man followed up to force the ball home from a narrow angle. After that, though, Liverpool gradually wrested control and were well worth their equalizer, stabbed home by John Wark from close range after Sammy Lee had hit a post four minutes before the interval. During a second half in which United debutant Johnny Sivebaek, the Danish utility man, seemed forlornly disorientated, Dalglish's team was the more convincing by a street, but failed to convert opportunities into goals.

By a short head and two long arms, Bruce Grobbelaar beats Mark Hughes to the ball at Old Trafford in October 1985.

The visitors' point put them level with Everton at the top, but their autumn impetus was long gone and soon the title race was an all-Merseyside affair. In the end Liverpool pipped their local rivals, then beat them in the FA Cup Final to claim the double, about the only honour to have eluded them since the Shankly revolution. Indeed, they might have become the first club to lift the domestic treble, but for a surprising defeat by Queen's Park Rangers in the semi-final of the League Cup.

In all honesty, better Liverpool teams than this – both before and since – have achieved less, which can only enhance the achievement of Kenny Dalglish. From that moment, whatever else came to pass, he would be numbered among the outstanding managers the English name has known.

CHAPTER NINE:

WHEN ALEX MET KENNY 1986/7 – 1991/2

A hurricane of change began to howl through Old Trafford in the late autumn of 1986. The demoralizing anti-climax of the previous campaign and the dismal start to the new term led to Ron Atkinson's dismissal in early November. His record of two FA Cup triumphs and First Division finishes of third, third, fourth and fourth would have prompted most clubs to offer the flamboyant manager an open-ended contract, but to United, casting ever-more-envious eyes on Anfield, his record was tantamount to failure. They wanted the Championship, and nothing less would do.

Into Ron's place strode Aberdeen manager Alex Ferguson, the man who had smashed the duopoly of Rangers and Celtic north of the border, an extremely bristly broom prepared to sweep until Old Trafford was 'clean'. It meant an end of the so-called United drinking club and certain players were told to change their social habits or go. It meant a radically enhanced youth system, which was to form the basis of the Red Devils' fabulous achievements during the next decade. It meant, as Ferguson recognized from day one, overhauling Liverpool.

That process began more auspiciously than the Mancunians had dared to hope, with a 1-0 Boxing Day victory at Anfield making it seven years to the day since they had lost a League game at the home of the Reds. Yet the omens had been ominous: Kenny Dalglish's men were looking to pressurize table-toppers Arsenal while United were uncomfortably close to the relegation scrap, their squad so straitened by injuries that Bryan Robson, that most influential of midfielders, was pressed into emergency central-defensive duty.

For once, too, the two protagonists had more on their minds than garnering points. Following the aerosol attack on Ron Atkinson and company at Anfield in February, the clubs had launched a peace campaign to create a more wholesome relationship between opposing supporters. To this end, Bob Paisley, no less, travelled to the game on the United team coach, the players warmed up on the pitch together, and even kicked a bagful of free footballs into the crowd. The Kop reacted, uncharitably but predictably, by booting the Mancunians' goodwill tokens straight back, and it must be reported that the spirit of togetherness among the players didn't last far beyond the first whistle.

Yet for all the inevitable heat generated by this fixture, there was plenty of neat football on display. What was surprising, though, was that most of it was furnished by United, with Liverpool resorting frequently to uncharacteristic and fruitless long-ball tactics and Robson proving unworried by either the pace of Rush or the guile of Dalglish.

However, it was beginning to appear that the visitors' reward would be no more than a point when they produced a goal after seventy-eight minutes, the despised Whiteside clubbing savagely past Grobbelaar from twenty yards following a long Robson free-kick. The fact that United's eighteen-year-old goalkeeper Gary Walsh, playing only his third senior game, had to make no notable saves until after his side had gone ahead, speaks volumes. Afterwards Dalglish reacted with admirable candour: 'In the first half we were

With that familiar glint in his eye, Alex Ferguson appears ready for his next verbal joust.

totally disorganized, and that really is my fault,' he said.

The way the remainder of the season panned out left United fans happier than their Liverpool counterparts. Fergie led the Red Devils to mid-table safety and in April completed a double over the Anfielders which effectively sabotaged their remaining hopes of retaining their title. The game was a scrappy, tight affair which might have been decided in the seventieth minute when Liverpool marksman Paul Walsh was through on goal, only for his namesake, Gary, to save with his legs. As it was, at about that juncture, Alex Ferguson got lucky. He had decided to take off striker Peter Davenport and the number ten sign was duly brandished from the bench, but then Arthur Albiston signalled that he was struggling and was substituted instead. So Birkenhead-born Davenport remained on the field and, just ninety seconds from the end, he plundered the winner, sweeping home from twenty yards after Hansen had bungled a clearance.

That left Everton six points clear at the top and on their way to their second title in three years, despite losing the Merseyside derby a week later. As ever Ian Rush was severe on the Toffees, scoring twice on this occasion, though come the summer

John Barnes, one of the outstanding footballers of the late 1980s and early 1990s, who just might have ended up at Old Trafford rather than Anfield if Alex Ferguson had received a more positive report on the Jamaican-born Watford star from his scouts. When the extent of John's ability emerged, Alex was not amused . . .

he would leave Liverpool for Juventus having failed to find the net against United in fifteen outings.

The 1987 close-season held immense significance to both Dalglish and Ferguson. Kenny had inherited a splendid side from Joe Fagan and won the double with it; but during the subsequent term the standard had slipped and now he was faced with major reconstruction work upon which his managerial expertise would be judged. Alex, understandably, had made no keynote signings while assessing the existing staff during his first six months at Old Trafford, but now it had become clear that heavy expenditure was essential.

The quality of their respective major acquisitions was impeccable. Liverpool purchased a whole new attack, paying Newcastle £1.9 million for Peter Beardsley, writing Watford a £900,000 cheque for John Barnes and taking the criminally underrated John Aldridge from Oxford for £700,000; then, a few weeks later, Dalglish returned to the Manor Ground to pay £825,000 for Aldridge's fellow Republic of Ireland international, midfielder Ray Houghton. The outcome was one of the most lavishly entertaining sides this country has ever seen. They won the Championship in majestic style and seemed certain to complete an unprecedented League and FA Cup 'double double' until that particular script was ripped up at Wembley by the Wimbledon 'Crazy Gang'.

Meanwhile, despite being comprehensively overshadowed, United could be reasonably satisfied, too, especially bearing in mind that Ferguson's starting point in attempting to assemble a title-worthy side was a long way behind that of Dalglish. Alex paid Celtic £850,000 for the free-scoring Brian McClair, who responded by becoming the first Red Devil since George Best to net twenty times in one League campaign, while England defender Viv Anderson, who mirrored Ferguson's own fanatically competitive nature, was recruited from Arsenal for £250,000; then, midway through the campaign, centre-half Steve Bruce arrived from Norwich for £700,000. McClair and Bruce would turn out to be phenomenal long-term bargains and although Anderson's contribution would be minimized by injury, his acquisition seemed canny at the time. Now Alex had joined battle in earnest, but although his team appeared to make rapid strides in 1987/8, there would be harrowing setbacks before Manchester United attained the supremacy he craved.

There was no shortage of encouraging signs for the Red Devils when Liverpool visited in November 1987. The runaway League leaders were forced on the defensive for the bulk of the afternoon, yet they escaped with a 1-1 draw, courtesy of United's ineptitude in front of goal. After twenty-one minutes of fruitless domination, the hosts were undone by a world-class defender demonstrating the skills of a schemer. Alan Hansen took possession on halfway, near the right touchline; he swayed one way and then another to shake off the attentions of McClair, then chipped an unerring pass to Steve McMahon, who was running into the right side of the Manchester penalty area. Without breaking stride, the England man hooked a perfect first-time cross on to the head of the unmarked John Aldridge, who netted with consummate ease from eight yards. All United's huffing and puffing had come to naught, while the Champions had picked off a goal which oozed class. To their credit, the Mancunians were unfazed by the setback, resuming their barrage until Whiteside swivelled on a loose ball to rifle in from close range after forty-nine minutes.

They could not pierce the Merseysiders' armour again, though, and a visibly frustrated Ferguson grated afterwards, 'Liverpool can think themselves lucky to have got a point.' The inimitably dry Dalglish response was: 'It's not our problem if United can't hit the target when they create chances!' It was not to be the final spirited exchange of words between two Scots whose apparent antagonism actually masks a deep mutual respect.

Indeed, their most famous contretemps followed towards the end of that season

Division One
4 April 1988
at Anfield

LIVERPOOL 3

Beardsley 38; Gillespie 41; McMahon 46

Bruce Grobbelaar, Gary Gillespie, Gary Ablett, Steve Nicol, Nigel Spackman, Alan Hansen, Peter Beardsley, John Aldridge, Ray Houghton, John Barnes, Steve McMahon. Sub: Craig Johnston for Aldridge (78).

MANCHESTER UNITED 3

Robson 2, 65; Strachan 77

Chris Turner, Viv Anderson, Clayton Blackmore, Steve Bruce, Paul McGrath, Mike Duxbury, Bryan Robson, Gordon Strachan, Brian McClair, Peter Davenport, Colin Gibson. Subs: Jesper Olsen for Blackmore (54), Norman Whiteside for Duxbury (54).

Half-time: 2-1 Attendance: 43,497

TWO contrasting images from this pulsating encounter will endure long after the six goals and see-saw sequence of events have faded from the memory. The first is of the strapping Norman Whiteside, called on as a substitute when United were 3-1 down, instantly reducing Liverpool's own midfield enforcer Steve McMahon to so much rubble with one implacable challenge. The second, more savoury picture is of cheeky little Gordon Strachan pretending to puff on a cigar in front of the irate Kop after completing the ten-man Mancunians' unlikely comeback from 3-1 down to all-square.

The first man to rain on the Merseysiders' Easter parade was Bryan Robson, who gave his side a shock second-minute lead after being set up cleverly by Peter Davenport. Unmarked in front of goal, he could hardly miss.

Appalled at being hit by that early sucker punch, the Reds responded in true Championship manner, assuming territorial superiority which brought an equalizer in the thirty-eighth minute when Peter Beardsley controlled a cross from Ray Houghton and deposited it emphatically in the corner of Chris Turner's net.

Three minutes later Beardsley turned provider when his far post cross was knocked back by John Barnes for Gary Gillespie to head into goal, thus making amends for the sloppy pass which had facilitated United's early strike.

Just over a minute into the second half, the issue appeared to be settled beyond any reasonable doubt when McMahon dispatched a piledriver of stunning velocity from twenty-five yards. Thus Alex Ferguson was a desperate man when he sent on Whiteside and Jesper Olsen after fifty-four minutes, and even more so when Colin Gibson was sent off for a second bookable offence, a scything trip on the speeding Steve Nicol, on the hour mark.

Whiteside, though, was in his element. After dealing summarily with McMahon he meted out similar treatment to Ronnie Whelan and Liverpool's midfield grip loosened perceptibly.

The tide took a major turn after sixty-five minutes when a speculative shot from Robson was deflected beyond Bruce Grobbelaar by Alan Hansen. Suddenly the ten men of United were asking the most pertinent questions. Not surprisingly their quest for parity left them stretched at the back – it took a fine diving save from Turner to keep out a John Aldridge header – but they played as if they believed they could force the equalizer, and after seventy-seven minutes they did.

Much of the credit should go to Davenport, whose exquisitely timed pass to Strachan caught Hansen and company square, but it was the Scot who delightedly milked the applause after calmly stroking the ball past Grobbelaar to make it 3-3. There was still time for Brian McClair to threaten a winner, but the ball was cleared and Kopites were spared collective apoplexy. For them, the sight of a grinning Whiteside strolling off the pitch at the end was torment enough.

Norman Whiteside, whose introduction as a 54th-minute substitute had a considerable impact . . .

in the wake of a tempestuous 3-3 draw at Anfield *(see Classic Clash Number Thirteen on page 90)*. United had performed a minor miracle in coming from 3-1 behind against the Champions-elect, especially having had a man sent off, but still Fergie was not content. Having just complained lengthily at a press conference about the difficulty he perceived in visiting teams getting favourable refereeing decisions at Anfield, he was buttonholed in a corridor by a radio journalist just as Dalglish was walking by, his six-week-old daughter in his arms. Getting the gist of another Ferguson outburst, Kenny told the interviewer he'd get more sense from the baby than from the United boss. It would seem that the younger man was merely teasing his fellow Glaswegian but the incensed Alex continued to hold forth colourfully. At that point Dalglish turned to go, pausing only to observe, presumably in reference to Ferguson's choice of words, 'The baby's a bit young for that.'

For the 1988/9 season, both camps were reinforced by the return of former favourites, neither Liverpool's Ian Rush nor United's Mark Hughes having exactly prospered in foreign climes. In due course, both Welshmen were to make nonsense of the old adage about never going back.

For the Mancunians, it was to prove a disappointing campaign, lifted by only the occasional highlight, principally the rousing turn-of-the-year triumph over Liverpool. The Merseysiders, once again, did well on the field, losing the League title to Arsenal only at the very last gasp, and winning the FA Cup in the first all-Merseyside final. But for the second time in five years, the Anfield club was visited by stark calamity when ninety-six of their fans perished at Hillsborough, where they had gathered on 15 April 1989 to watch an FA Cup semi-final against Nottingham Forest. For many people in the city and beyond, football would never be of consequence again.

At one point, after Alex Ferguson had sent a contingent of his club's supporters to pay their respects at Anfield, it seemed that the tragedy might act as a catalyst to improve relations between the most extreme factions of Liverpool and United supporters. But as Kenny Dalglish was to note with profound sadness, it wasn't long before normal hostilities were resumed. The obnoxious chants about Munich, Shankly and the rest were soon back in the respective repertoires; vitriol and spite continued to spew forth unabated; hate was not dead.

To return to the game: back in September United had headed west and been comprehensively outclassed. Indeed, but for the magnificence of Scottish international goalkeeper Jim Leighton, signed the previous spring from Aberdeen, the scoreline might have been embarrassing. As it was the tally was limited to a single penalty, given when the brilliant Barnes might or might not have been upended unfairly by Bruce, and converted by Molby. Apart from that Leighton was unbeatable, the excellence of his display being acknowledged by an embrace from his opposite number, Grobbelaar, at the final whistle. Sadly, incomprehensibly, Jim was destined for a dramatic decline in form during 1989/90 and his Old Trafford career would end with his humiliating omission from an FA Cup Final replay.

For now it was the team as a whole which was struggling and, as a succession of senior players fell prey to injury, the manager put his faith in youth. Thus the media, in a rather wan reference to the Busby Babes, gave flight to 'Fergie's Fledglings', four of whom were on parade when Liverpool checked in at Old Trafford on New Year's Day.

One of them, the skinny but skilful midfielder Russell Beardsmore, was the star of the show as United came from behind to triumph in joyous style *(see Classic Clash Number Fourteen on page 93)*, and he was hailed as one of the most exciting prospects to emerge from the Manchester area in years. For a while he lived up to his billing, contributing some impressive performances both in central midfield and operating wide. He was chosen by Bob Paisley as the outstanding young player of the month and he won England Under-21 recognition. Yet still Russell didn't cement his future as a Red Devil. Why?

'I started the next season in the squad but the team didn't do well and a lot of expensive new players arrived. After that I was always struggling to get in and I might have lost a bit of confidence. When the competition got hotter still I knew I had to get away. I came close to signing for Kenny Dalglish at Blackburn, where I went on loan, but opted to have another go with United instead. That might have been a mistake! But I've got no complaints. Eventually I joined Bournemouth where I've been very happy.'

For one of Beardsmore's team-mates, Ralph Milne, the overturning of Liverpool was a high-water mark, too. 'From a personal point of view I was happy with the way I played against quality opposition, and it seemed as though we might on the verge of mounting a challenge to the leading clubs. Certainly the fans thought so. They were celebrating for ages after the game had finished. But what took the edge off it for us was that we had to play Middlesbrough only twenty hours later. I don't know what joker worked out that fixture. We lost 1-0 and a lot of the impetus we had gained against Liverpool was gone.'

During that anti-climactic season and the next, Ralph was much maligned by United fans searching for a scapegoat, but still he cherishes his Manchester experience. 'Everybody thinks they might have done better at some time in their life, but I have no regrets. It was marvellous to play for such a great club alongside wonderful players.' And for those who continue to wonder why Ferguson bought the little-known Milne from Bristol City in the first place, let them consider this. Earlier in his career he had been a mainstay of Dundee United's Scottish Championship-winning side, and he remains their leading scorer in European competition, with no fewer than fifteen goals in thirty-nine appearances. So the pedigree was there.

The post-Liverpool letdown at Ayresome Park highlighted a syndrome which had long galled the Old Trafford faithful. In their last nineteen League meetings with the all-conquering Merseysiders, United had lost only twice and frequently looked the better team. Yet when trophy time came around, almost invariably it was Liverpool who needed to send out for the polish. Why, if the Red Devils could be so 'up' for specific matches, could they not remain on that plane throughout a season? It was an endlessly perplexing conundrum which would not be put aside until much later in Alex Ferguson's reign.

The 1989/90 season began with the paralysing pall of Hillsborough hovering above it. Thanks to the dignity, strength and compassion he had exhibited throughout the ongoing ordeal, Kenny Dalglish had emerged as a figure of enormous stature, a man who had risen magnificently to an horrific event. Just how much it cost him to turn his thoughts towards another campaign only he and his family can know, but clearly he made a pretty fair fist of it because, come springtime, Liverpool were Champions again.

Alex Ferguson, on the other hand, endured a winter of simmering discontent which he had seemed unlikely to survive with his job intact. Yet he held on through the darkest days of his working life and emerged in May clutching the FA Cup. After that, although the transformation was not instant, Manchester United were on the road to supplanting Liverpool as the dominant force in English football.

At the end of 1988/9 Fergie had taken stock and realized that his squad was not good enough. Thus, at gigantic expense, he bought what was effectively half a new team: central defender Gary Pallister, midfielders Paul Ince, Neil Webb and Mike Phelan, and forward Danny Wallace. Yet an influx of stars did not a successful side make, and the Red Devils were at a depressingly low ebb when they visited Anfield on the Saturday morning before Christmas.

It wasn't merely poor results that upset the fans, it was that the football was dull, and had been so, bar a handful of memorable instances, since Ferguson's arrival. Inevitably, pressure on the manager from media and supporters had mounted

Division One
1 January 1989
at Old Trafford

MANCHESTER UNITED 3

McClair 71; Hughes 75;
Beardsmore 77

Jim Leighton, Lee Martin, Lee Sharpe,
Steve Bruce, Russell Beardsmore,
Mal Donaghy, Bryan Robson, Gordon
Strachan, Brian McClair, Mark Hughes,
Ralph Milne.
Subs: Mark Robins for Strachan (33),
Paul McGrath for Martin (66).

LIVERPOOL 1

Barnes 70

Mike Hooper, Gary Ablett, Steve
Staunton, Steve Nicol, Ronnie Whelan,
David Burrows, Peter Beardsley,
John Aldridge, Ray Houghton, John
Barnes, Steve McMahon.
Sub: Jan Molby for Staunton (78).

Half-time: 0-0 Attendance: 44,745

F EW United victories have
ever been more rapturously
received. Though all it meant, in
realistic terms, was that the
Red Devils edged a tad closer to
the First Division's leading
group, to fans sickened by
Liverpool's serial successes the
manner of it was sweet beyond
their fondest imaginings.

For seventy minutes United
had been the more positive
side, pushing forward
relentlessly only to be denied
repeatedly by goalkeeper Mike
Hooper, but as the game moved
into its last quarter a hint of
desperation began to set in.
Was all that enterprise to
count for nothing?

Then came utter dismay. Peter
Beardsley passed to John Barnes,
who cut inside Mal Donaghy from
the left flank and dispatched an
exquisite dipping cross-shot
beyond the reach of Jim Leighton.
The away supporters warbled
merrily; to them it was the classic
scam – keep cool under pressure

and then hit the enemy when
they're least expecting it.

Old Trafford shuddered, as if
preparing for a communal vomit,
but the sick bags proved
unnecessary. Suddenly, as if
stung by Barnes' inspirational
intervention, United struck back
to swamp Liverpool with a
coruscating spell of three goals
in six minutes. At the heart of it
all was local boy Russell
Beardsmore, one of the so-called
Fledglings, who began the
sequence by dancing past two
defenders on the right flank and
crossing towards Brian McClair
some eight yards out from goal.
The ball was dropping slightly
behind him, but the Scot
adjusted smartly and gave
Hooper no chance with an
acrobatic scissors kick.

Four minutes later the scrawny
but effervescent twenty-year-old
gulled another opponent and
slipped the ball to Mark Hughes.
'Sparky', hero of the masses,
made the most of a lucky rebound
off Steve Nicol, charged into the
box and drove in a savage shot to
which poor Hooper got a hand but
could not repel. Finally, amidst
scenes of mounting euphoria, Lee
Sharpe – the only Fledgling who
would go on to carve out a
productive long-term niche at Old
Trafford – reached the left byline
and crossed; Bryan Robson
deflected the ball high in the air
and it dropped to the unmarked
Beardsmore, who netted in
textbook style with his instep
from eight yards.

Russell remembers it well.
'The atmosphere was incredible
but it didn't really get to me.
There's a lack of fear when
you're young, and playing against
Liverpool was just part of the
job. I was lucky in that our fans
love to see a local come through
the ranks, especially one who

Russell Beardsmore, who
gave the performance of
his life to inspire United's
rousing comeback.

can take the ball past defenders,
as I did from time to time. They
always gave me a boost,
especially after this game, which
brought me to national
prominence.'

Another midfielder-cum-winger
who recalls that New Year's Day
as the highlight of a brief Old
Trafford sojourn is the diminutive
Scot, Ralph Milne. 'I'd played a lot
of football around the world but I'd
never witnessed anything like the
passion in the ground that day. It
was wonderful – I even won a
tackle against Steve McMahon!'

Caught on the hop?
Gary Pallister attempts to
block the headlong
progress of John Barnes
during the lacklustre
Charity Shield meeting
between Liverpool and
United in 1990.

inexorably, yet he seemed upbeat before kick-off, offering the opinion that his team might be at their most dangerous having lost three in a row.

So it proved with United having the better of the first half and sharing the honours in the second. Still, though, like an old gramophone record stuck in a groove that no one in the vicinity of Old Trafford wanted to hear any more, there was the same old story of chance after chance going begging. When the goalless contest was over, Dalglish had the grace to declare, 'We were lucky to get a point.' Ferguson, meanwhile, could say against most pre-match expectations, 'We're a wee bit disappointed with a draw.'

Liverpool's problem – if a team which still stood only a point behind League leaders Arsenal could be said to have a problem – seemed to be a lack of empathy between centre-backs Alan Hansen and Glenn Hysen. Both cut elegant, stately figures, unflappable and cultured in possession, but each of them would have benefited from a speedier partner. As for United's scoring difficulties, there seemed nothing intrinsically wrong with marksmen Hughes and McClair; it was just that everyone in a white shirt appeared to want to walk the ball into the net instead of shooting.

Three months later at Old Trafford, as Liverpool claimed their first League victory on United soil in eight years, the teams' respective performances bore not the slightest resemblance to their Anfield displays. Though the 2-1 scoreline did not begin to reflect the gulf between the two, this was arguably the Merseysiders' most comprehensive triumph over their old foes since the war. Inspired by John Barnes, who had missed the Anfield clash through injury, they outclassed the Mancunians in every department. The England winger – monitored by United during his Watford days but rejected as inconsistent, a decision which had a bearing on Fergie's revamping of his scouting system – appeared to shred his opponents' defence almost at will and looked a world-class footballer at the peak of his powers. He opened the scoring after fifteen minutes, running forty yards with the ball after being fed neatly by Beardsley, then dispatching a cool shot under Leighton's despairing dive. Thereafter Liverpool did as they liked, the only surprise being that Ian Rush failed to hit the target for the first time against the Red Devils. However, he did earn the penalty from which Barnes doubled the tally after fifty-four minutes, and would surely have registered subsequently himself had John not opted to go for his hat-trick instead of passing to the better-placed Welshman.

Even United's eightieth-minute reply came courtesy of a Liverpool player when Ronnie Whelan, perhaps guilty of complacency, placed what would have been an exquisite lob, in other circumstances, over the head of Bruce Grobbelaar. In fact, the Irishman's lapse almost proved costly as, soon afterwards, Beardsmore crossed, McClair hit a crisp volley and Ronnie was indebted to Bruce for a save later described by Dalglish as 'one of the best you'll ever see'.

Long before the end, travelling Kopites were chortling 'Fergie must stay' at the top of their voices, having been persuaded by the poverty of United's performance that their bitter rivals would not be contenders for honours as long as the Scot remained at their helm. In all honesty, there had been no shortage of long-time Old Trafford habitues who wanted Ferguson out. It has become part of the club's folklore that early elimination from the FA Cup would have sealed his fate and although his chairman, Martin Edwards, has denied this steadfastly, it is inconceivable that the beleaguered boss could have survived further haemorrhaging of popular support. However, United inched their way to Wembley and, a mere two months after the Anfielders had revelled in their derision, Alex held aloft the game's oldest and most famous trophy. After a period of severe trauma, the healing had begun.

With Liverpool having clinched their eighteenth Championship – incredibly their tenth in fifteen years – the Big Two were thrown together to contest the Charity Shield, but the entertainment they produced for a near sell-out crowd was low-key in the extreme. The high spot of the day occurred before kick-off, when the faithful Ronnie Moran, who had served the club man and boy, was given the honour of leading the side out at Wembley. From that moment onwards, the excitement ebbed away.

It was clear that the Merseysiders – shorn by injury of Hansen, Nicol, Molby and Gillespie – were using the game as a fitness-honing exercise, and they strode coolly through the muggy afternoon, the familiar jagged edge of competition conspicuous by its absence from their approach. United, even without Webb and their principal on-the-field motivator, Robson, were more eager for the fray and deserved the lead given to them by Clayton Blackmore almost on the stroke of half-time. Later Barnes equalized from the spot after being tripped by the otherwise immaculate Pallister, but the proceedings had little relevance to the season which would begin in earnest a week later.

When the serious stuff started, Liverpool were duly transformed. They began with four straight wins before entertaining the ever-optimistic United, who had got off to a fairly encouraging if less rarefied start, having dropped two points behind and played a game more. The Red Devils were humbled, mown down 4-0, their heaviest defeat at Anfield for sixty-five years. And yet, as all but the most blinkered of Kopites would admit, the game was not especially one-sided, certainly not in comparison with their heroes' romp at Old Trafford six months earlier.

What Liverpool displayed was a poise and ruthlessness in front of goal which, for a long, long time, had seemed alien to United's nature. While Beardsley, who had been unable to claim a first-team place during a brief stint with the Mancunians in 1982/3, completed a polished hat-trick and Barnes nodded unerringly between the posts following a miscued Nicol volley, the visitors bungled a succession of chances. True they were unlucky when, at 1-0 down, a Webb header looped on to Grobbelaar's bar, but they paid the price for their own profligacy. It should be stressed, too, that the Robson-less Red Devils had no one in their midfield to match McMahon, whose all-round contribution was immense.

For Beardsley, whose third goal eight minutes from time was a particularly delectable lob following an insolently flipped free-kick from Houghton, there was a minor disappointment at the finish when Manchester keeper Sealey expressed his despair by booting the ball into the Kop. Despite appeals by Peter it was not returned, and he went home without his rightful trophy. He had, though, the considerable consolation that, even at that early stage of the campaign, another title medal seemed in the offing.

For United, such a thrashing was hardly ideal preparation for their return to European competition after the lifting of the post-Heysel ban on all English clubs except Liverpool. Ferguson's men were at home to Pecsi Muncas of Hungary in the Cup-Winners' Cup just three days hence, while the Anfielders would have to wait a further year before being received back into the European fold.

The Red Devils made tidy progress in Europe but what their fans craved was revenge over the Merseysiders, and it was delivered in scintillating style at Old Trafford in a Hallowe'en League Cup encounter which took on a distinctly grisly tinge for the unbeaten League leaders. It was nothing new for United to exert fearsome pressure but this time, despite a superb performance from Grobbelaar, the goals went in. Steve Bruce opened the scoring with a penalty after Nicol handled a deep cross from newly-signed full-back Denis Irwin on thirty-seven minutes, but if that was pretty routine fare, what followed only seventeen seconds after Liverpool had re-started the game was anything but. Mark Hughes controlled a bouncing ball on halfway, shrugged off a challenge from Molby, side-stepped Gillespie and reduced Grobbelaar to irrelevance with a thunderous dipping drive from thirty yards. After that, late strikes from Sharpe for United and Houghton for the Merseysiders were only window dressing.

This victory, though deeply satisfying to the Mancunian soul, did nothing to alter the fact that Liverpool remained the pre-eminent power in the land. Yet after winning twelve of their first thirteen League games, they began to stutter, their aura of invincibility evaporating as midwinter advanced. And, though it is easy to make this point in retrospect, Kenny Dalglish began to look ever more strained.

However, the Liverpool boss acted decisively to boost his title chances, paying Coventry £700,000 for Scottish international striker David Speedie, a feisty little fighting cock whom it was felt might do for the Reds what his countryman, Andy Gray, had once done for Everton. His debut would be away to United, whose last whimsical hopes of reviving their own Championship credentials would wither and die without a win.

In the event, Speedie took forty minutes to manage what his new partner, Ian Rush, had been unable to accomplish in twenty-three outings against the Red Devils – he scored a goal. A Bruce penalty, after Hysen had handled, had given the hosts an early lead and they were looking capable of increasing their tally when the newcomer struck, courtesy of John Barnes at his mesmeric best. The Jamaican-born star took possession on the left flank from a haphazard Robson clearance, then swerved past four opponents before delivering a cross at which Sealey flapped ineffectually. It fell to Speedie who rammed it home gleefully from close range. There were no more goals, United were thus consigned yet again to the ranks of also-rans, and Dalglish could take credit for the instant dividend paid by his latest acquisition. Liverpool were right on the tail of the new pacesetters, Arsenal, adrift only on goal difference and with a game in hand.

But a sensation was brewing. Unknown to the watching world, the Reds' manager had been suffering from intense stress, no doubt a delayed reaction to his selfless and deeply humane exertions connected with Hillsborough. Add the mammoth pressure of his job and it was inevitable that he would crack at some point. That point arrived in late February when, on the morning after a tumultuous 4-4 FA Cup tussle with Everton, he announced his resignation, sending shock waves reverberating around the football world. For a long time, many observers refused to take his decision at face value, adding to his trauma, and for that he deserves sympathy.

Thereafter, events moved pretty swiftly. Ronnie Moran held the fort until distinguished Anfield old boy Graeme Souness took over in April, but their joint efforts were not enough to prevent Arsenal from becoming Champions. United, meanwhile, had swallowed their latest League disappointment and made amends by winning the European Cup-Winners' Cup, Mark Hughes supplying both goals against his former employers, Barcelona, on a misty night in Rotterdam. The balance of power between the two north-western giants was beginning to shift perceptibly.

Of course, Souness did not inherit a bad side. True, some of the key members were ageing but only five months before his arrival they had been striding out with awesome assurance, the rest of the First Division firmly in their wake. Now he set about remoulding that side, signing some splendid footballers and others who would turn out to be indifferent, as well as instituting more fundamental and controversial changes. The new broom swept through the Boot Room, making alterations to the training regime which caused consternation among certain senior players. Not surprisingly, the atmosphere at both Anfield and the Melwood training ground became strained and that autumn's results were exceedingly poor by the exacting standards of the past quarter of a century.

All the while, United were increasingly buoyant. The giant Danish goalkeeper Peter Schmeichel was proving to be of the highest calibre, while the attack was newly vibrant thanks to the emergence of Welsh wunderkind Ryan Giggs and the arrival of Ukrainian flyer Andrei Kanchelskis. With the likes of Hughes, McClair and Sharpe already in situ, exciting possibilities were beginning to unfold.

Indeed, come the first meeting with Liverpool in early October, the Red Devils had won eight and drawn two of their ten League games. They were eleven points clear of the mediocre Merseysiders and there was a far more convincing look to them than when they had made a statistically even more impressive start six years earlier.

It turned out to be a typically tempestuous but exasperatingly disjointed goalless draw, with the tenacious David Burrows detailed to man-mark Bryan Robson and the rest of Souness' side very much in negative mode. Indeed, the visitors didn't manage one shot on target all afternoon while Mike Hooper, who had taken the place of Grobbelaar, faced a searching examination of his skills, which he passed with flying colours.

Each side had a man sent off, Liverpool's Ablett departing after sixty-seven minutes for his second bookable offence, United's Hughes following nine minutes later for allegedly attempting to head-butt Burrows. Despite their territorial domination, the home side lacked the subtlety to break down their opponents, who deserved their point for their sheer doggedness and well-organized resistance.

The man-of-the match accolade went to Robson, but by far the most remarkable achievement was that of Liverpool's nineteen-year-old right-back Rob Jones. Plucked from the relative obscurity of Crewe Alexandra only two days earlier, then plunged into the Old Trafford cauldron for one of the biggest games of the season, the boy shone. He quelled the menace of the speedy Giggs, matching him stride for stride, and remained unflappable under constant fire until he was withdrawn, suffering from cramp, after sixty-six minutes. In Rob Jones, grandson of the stalwart post-war Anfield defender Bill Jones, Souness had unearthed a nugget.

The remainder of Liverpool's League season was not to the taste of their fans, many of whom had come to take success for granted, but though the sixth-place finish was the club's lowest for twenty-seven years – an incredible statistic in itself – there was considerable consolation in their FA Cup Final triumph over Sunderland. Given that the injury-plagued Reds were going through a period of transition, and that their manager had undergone heart-bypass surgery in the spring, things might have been worse.

Meanwhile Old Trafford was engulfed in frustration. United had won the League Cup but their dream of regaining the League title after a gap of twenty-five years was in ruins. In the end they had surrendered to Leeds on the last lap, a dire enough circumstance in itself. But what made the wound deep was that the last shred of hope had been destroyed in a 2-0 defeat at Anfield *(see Classic Clash Number Fifteen opposite)*. Somehow a Liverpool combination which had floundered abjectly over the previous month now transformed itself into a team of tigers which devoured their rivals with fierce relish.

In the immediate aftermath, Alex Ferguson was shocked by the strength of the anti-United feeling evinced on that sunny late-April afternoon. A gratuitously nasty obscenity, something far in excess of the expected and acceptable banter, emanated from one Liverpool player while some of the home supporters went to malevolent lengths to rub the Mancunians' faces in the mire. As the morose losers prepared to depart, some of them were asked for autographs and, when they obliged, the signatures were torn up mockingly in front of them.

The United boss was desolate, but he took something positive from the moment. He saw the raw pain on the faces of his footballers and, when the time was right, he would remind them of it. He didn't want them to forget the feeling, so they would move mountains to make sure that it didn't happen again …

Below: Rob Jones, whose debut for Liverpool at Old Trafford was of the fairytale variety.

Opposite: Two Marks, Wright of Liverpool (left) and Hughes of United, contest possession on a day which ended with the Mancunians suffering deep desolation.

Division One

26 April 1992

at Anfield

LIVERPOOL 2

Rush 12; Walters 88

Mike Hooper, Rob Jones, David Burrows, Nicky Tanner, Jan Molby, Mark Wright, Dean Saunders, Ray Houghton, Ian Rush, John Barnes, Michael Thomas.
Subs: Barry Venison for Tanner (22), Mark Walters for Rush (27).

MANCHESTER UNITED 0

Peter Schmeichel, Denis Irwin, Mal Donaghy, Steve Bruce, Gary Pallister, Paul Ince, Bryan Robson, Andrei Kanchelskis, Brian McClair, Mark Hughes, Ryan Giggs.
Sub: Mike Phelan for Pallister (31).

Half-time: 1-0 Attendance: 38,669

IT was the worst footballing moment the Red Devils had known since relegation in 1974 – and Liverpool had played an integral part in precipitating the Manchester misery. After this 2-0 victory ended United's chances of a Championship which had once seemed theirs for the taking, Anfield indulged in an orgy of communal gloating the like of which had rarely, if ever, been witnessed at an English football ground.

It wasn't just the Kop; the denizens of the stands stood as one and chanted in unison 'You'll never win the League' and if the home directors desisted, they were the only Merseysiders who did so.

In fact, the title race was all but ended earlier in the day by the freak own-goal by Brian Gayle which gave Leeds victory over Sheffield United. After that the Mancunians would have needed something akin to a soccer miracle if they were to end a quarter of a century of under-achievement.

Such desperate straits called for extraordinary measures and Alex Ferguson responded by throwing in midfield gladiators Bryan Robson and Paul Ince, neither of them fully fit but just the type of men needed for such a battle. But Liverpool were up for it too, seemingly more than for any other game in their own disappointing League campaign, and from the moment Ian Rush put them ahead on twelve minutes they seemed destined to prevail.

The goal was clinically executed, the Welshman making one of his trademark diagonal runs to meet a cute through-ball from John Barnes before beating Peter Schmeichel with ease. The celebrations were ecstatic, all the more so because it was Rush's first successful strike against United in his twenty-four matches against them.

Now the visitors rallied courageously, and were unlucky not to gain parity when a scorching Ince drive hit the inside of Mike Hooper's post and rebounded to safety midway through the first period. Shortly after that they lost stopper Gary Pallister with a severed foot artery and Dean Saunders (twice) and Barry Venison both missed chances to increase Liverpool's advantage.

Alex Ferguson's half-time chat must have been of the do-or-die variety, as United resumed bristling with attacking intent. Within two minutes, though, they must have got the message that it wasn't going to be their day when Brian McClair headed against the bar from Denis Irwin's free-kick and Andrei Kanchelskis rapped the same patch of woodwork with his follow-up shot.

Thereafter United continued to press forward courageously, but their relaxed hosts, inspired by the promptings of Barnes, created the clearer-cut opportunities and Schmeichel had to be at his best to deny them.

The title finally disappeared in the direction of Elland Road in the eighty-eighth minute when the towering Dane could only turn a shot from Ray Houghton against his bar and Mark Walters swept in the rebound.

Cue an Anfield party which couldn't have been more joyous if Liverpool themselves had been crowned Champions. But 'You'll never win the League', as directed at Manchester United, did not turn out to be the most inspired of footballing prophecies ...

CHAPTER TEN:

SO VERY, VERY SWEET 1992/3 – 1998/9

THE hurt had been deep and it had gone on all summer; meanwhile, some thirty miles along the road, so had the exultation. In the cold light of day it was clear that United's defeat at Anfield had not cost them the title. The damage had already been done. But the stark fact remained that the last rites had been read by Scousers and those thundering choruses of 'You lost the League on Merseyside' just refused to recede from Mancunian minds. It was easy to talk about revenge but what was the point? Sabre rattling had invited ridicule all too often over the past quarter of a century. What was new that would make a scrap of difference?

Well, by the spring of 1993 there were several extremely salient variations on the theme of Liverpool v United rivalry. Firstly, in contrast to tradition, the Anfielders were a palpably creaky combination in whom a transformation would have to be wrought before they could become Championship contenders again; secondly, having come genuinely close last time, United had both the scent and an all-consuming desire; thirdly, there was Cantona.

When the clubs had met at Old Trafford in mid-October *(see Classic Clash Number Sixteen on page 102)*, the 2-2 draw had been a fair result and on the day the disparity between the sides had not appeared vast. However, a close look at the respective squads revealed that United boasted overall man-for-man superiority; all they needed, it would soon transpire, was a catalyst to lift them into the further dimension their talent suggested was possible.

The Frenchman arrived at Old Trafford in November 1992, a £1.2 million windfall from Leeds who appeared unable to accommodate his individualism. At the time, the Red Devils were languishing just behind the leading group and most fans, if they were honest, would say they anticipated another title blight, but salvation was at hand. When Eric made his entrance, there were twenty-five Premier League games remaining; United lost only two of them and for one of the defeats, at Oldham, the Gallic newcomer was absent.

The full extent of the bargain Alex Ferguson had picked up from his chum, Howard Wilkinson, was becoming head-turningly apparent come early March, when the Mancunians visited Liverpool. They arrived at an Anfield locked in a situation which was all the more chilling for its unfamiliarity. The fact was that, while United were jousting with Aston Villa and Norwich City for the Championship, the Reds were far from certain of avoiding relegation. A Doomsday scenario was not out of the question.

If the Scouse legions were fearful, they might have been reassured by the first half-hour of the match, during which their team was on top. Indeed, had Paul Parker's sliced clearance not cannoned to safety off his own crossbar and had Schmeichel not made a stupendous save from Don Hutchison's low shot, the outcome might have been different. But as Liverpool themselves had demonstrated to the rest down the years, 'ifs' count for nothing.

As the interval approached, United grew stronger and went ahead when a sloppy

And they say the game
has no characters these
days . . . Peter Schmeichel
greets Bruce Grobbelaar
at Old Trafford in October
1992.

clearance by Paul Stewart resulted in Hughes netting with a powerful header from Giggs' clever cross. During the break Graeme Souness sought to gee up Ian Rush, whom he had dropped, saying, 'Get out there and prove me wrong.' Within five minutes the Welshman had done so, spectacularly, allowing a dinked through-ball from young Jamie Redknapp to bounce before lashing it home from eighteen yards, despite being surrounded by defenders. Later Alex Ferguson referred to it as no more than a quarter-chance; by any standards, it was a great hit.

It might have been a crucial turning point, but now United were playing with the sort of collective belief which had used to characterize Liverpool, and five minutes later they were ahead again when keeper David James misjudged a Sharpe corner, Pallister flicked on and McClair was left with a simple header. After that the visitors reigned supreme, though it took a late reflex block from Schmeichel to deny Rush an equalizer. Ferguson's reaction? 'I didn't see it. I'd fainted!' The result meant United now led the table, while Souness' men were only three points clear of the relegation zone. Graeme was frank. 'I'm not enjoying this experience. I'd rather be at the other end.'

The only blot on the Manchester copybook – and that deposited by a tiny minority of puerile 'fans' – was the interruption to the pre-match minute's silence for Hillsborough victim Tony Bland. To their credit, there was no shortage of United followers who remonstrated with the miscreants, but it was a sad comment on the values of both camps that Anfield was sober in communal mourning one moment, then awash with customary venom the next.

The rest of that season will be bathed forever in a rosy glow for disciples of the Red Devils. They went on to win the Championship, their first for twenty-six years, and there was a feeling of a burden being lifted, that more good days were just around the corner.

Anfield was witnessing the other side of the coin. Recovery to finish sixth in the table could not disguise the truth that Souness was mightily unpopular with many supporters, partly because they didn't like his team, but also over his dealings with the *Sun* newspaper, reviled on Merseyside over its coverage of Hillsborough. The board decided to sack him, then changed their mind; Roy Evans, his eventual successor,

FA Premier League
18 October 1992
at Old Trafford

MANCHESTER UNITED 2

Hughes 78, 90

Peter Schmeichel, Paul Parker, Steve Bruce, Gary Pallister, Denis Irwin, Darren Ferguson, Paul Ince, Andrei Kanchelskis, Brian McClair, Mark Hughes, Ryan Giggs. Sub: Clayton Blackmore for Kanchelskis (66).

LIVERPOOL 2

Hutchison 23; Rush 44

Bruce Grobbelaar, Mike Marsh, Steve Nicol, Torben Piechnik, David Burrows, Jamie Redknapp, Jan Molby, Don Hutchison, Steve McManaman, Ian Rush, Ronny Rosenthal. Subs: Michael Thomas for Redknapp (72), Nicky Tanner for Molby (82).

Half-time: 0-2   Attendance: 33,243

THE spoils were shared but emotions in the opposing camps contrasted vividly after an afternoon of compelling drama at Old Trafford. For more than three-quarters of the contest, the Red Devils strove frenetically but displayed barely a shred of inspiration against a Liverpool side which was beginning to hint that manager Graeme Souness was presiding over a genuine Anfield renaissance.

With only twelve minutes and a thirty-mile westbound jaunt separating the travelling Kopites from a joyous Sunday tea, their team led deservedly by two goals and United looked a despairingly long way from title aspirants. Enter Mark Hughes to transform the day with a brace of late strikes, both brilliant, both destructive, but deliciously different in their execution.

Before the start the hosts had introduced Hank Marvin to the crowd. They then spent the ensuing hour or so in pursuit of shadows. Indeed, the immediate impression was that the sides' relative League standings – United near the top and Liverpool, astonishingly, not far off the foot – were hugely misleading. The visitors pushed forward with brisk enterprise, their passing crisper and more precise than that of a home side equipped with boundless commitment but limited finesse.

It was entirely on merit when Souness's men went ahead after twenty-three minutes, albeit thanks to Don Hutchison's low left-footer being deflected past Peter Schmeichel by Steve Bruce's heel. Now United might have been expected to raise their game, but it was the green-shirted Reds who continued in the ascendancy and it was no surprise when they doubled their lead shortly before the interval, Ian Rush stabbing home from eight yards with customary economy. It was his 287th Liverpool strike, taking him past the club record for all competitions held by Roger Hunt.

More importantly, it seemed likely to secure a victory which might prove the turning point in the Merseysiders' campaign. United exerted boundless effort but no breakthrough appeared imminent when substitute Clayton Blackmore picked up a loose ball just inside his opponents' territory in the seventy-eighth minute. Displaying the vision which had once suggested that he would become an outstanding midfield general, he floated a delightful chip towards his long-time chum, Mark Hughes, on the edge of the Liverpool box. A quick glance having told him that Bruce Grobbelaar had left his line, 'Sparky' produced the deftest of first-time stun-volleys, over the head of the stranded custodian and into the empty net.

Suddenly there was hope for the home cause, and the balance of power changed hands. At last United pressed forward with cohesion, but as the ninety-minute point passed, it seemed that the visitors would prevail.

Then came the final act of high drama. A raking pass from Paul Parker was nodded on by Brian McClair to Ryan Giggs, who hit an instant, wickedly curving cross towards the near post. The marauding Hughes launched himself horizontally to put a header of unstoppable velocity past Grobbelaar.

was appointed as his assistant; it was a messy and potentially debilitating situation.

The 1993/4 campaign saw the pendulum swing ever more emphatically in the direction of Old Trafford, though the turn of the year brought a hiccup in their headlong progress towards another title, Liverpool pinning them back to 3-3 after being 3-0 down *(see Classic Clash Number Seventeen on page 104).* That was only papering over the Anfield cracks, however, and in February Souness cheated the axe by resigning, the worldly, sometimes headstrong high-flier being replaced by the popular Boot Room graduate, Roy Evans, a Merseysider whose only employer had been Liverpool FC.

One of Roy's early tasks was to take his struggling side to Old Trafford, where a crisis of confidence appeared to be mounting. Once sixteen points clear of the pack, United were now just three ahead of Kenny Dalglish's Blackburn, hardly the ideal circumstances under which to greet the Merseysiders, no matter how preoccupied they might be with their own problems. Having lost four away games in succession, Evans opted for the cautious approach, going for a five-man midfield and leaving precociously gifted rookie marksman Robbie Fowler on the bench.

In terms of the play, it worked. Three days earlier United had lost the League Cup Final to Aston Villa, thus relinquishing hopes of becoming the first club to claim the domestic treble. Now they were tense, knowing that defeat would deal a stinging psychological blow to their remaining aspirations, and the visitors took advantage. Where United's engine coughed fitfully, with Cantona peripheral in his last outing before a five-match suspension, Liverpool's purred with a smooth assurance harking back to more successful days, with Barnes, Redknapp and the new wizard of the dribble, Steve McManaman, all prominent.

Yet the game's only goal fell to United on thirty-seven minutes, when Lee Sharpe's inswinging corner was met with a near-post glancing header by the inexplicably ill-policed Paul Ince. Even then, the Champions did not convince and were outrageously fortunate not to concede a sixty-ninth-minute penalty, when Michael Thomas appeared to be wrestled to the ground by Andrei Kanchelskis. Referee Keith Hackett, who had been close to the incident, signalled for a spot-kick, only to reverse his decision after consulting with a linesman who had viewed the fall from a considerably greater distance. His version was that the Ukrainian had been retaliating to an earlier foul and the home side breathed again.

Precisely how valuable that victory turned out to be was emphasized by United's defeat at Blackburn three days later. But just when the Red Devils' whole campaign seemed in danger of turning to ashes, Alex Ferguson, that master of us-against-the-world kidology, turned the situation around and the Old Trafford club lifted the League and FA Cup double for the first time in their history. Meanwhile at Anfield, which seemed a much more cheerful place with Evans in charge, they were glad to see the back of a troubled term.

When Liverpool began 1994/5 at a gallop, it seemed that a counter-revolution had been successfully effected. Graeme Souness was gone and Shanklyism was prospering under Evans; a team packed with enchantingly talented young stars such as McManaman, Redknapp and Fowler was winning games with attractive football and two of the League's most accomplished central defenders, John Scales and Phil Babb, had just been acquired. So it was with justifiable confidence that the Merseysiders took themselves to Old Trafford in mid-September, and they were slightly unfortunate to finish up on the wrong end of a 2-0 scoreline.

For the first hour, with McManaman teasing the United rearguard in general and out-of-position David May in particular – the former Blackburn man was far more comfortable in the centre than at full-back, where he found himself on this day – the visitors were the more potent force. Barnes and Molby oozed class in midfield and Redknapp was robbed of a famous goal when his twenty-five yarder struck

Opposite: The diving header by Mark Hughes which salvaged a point for United was deeply satisfying for the Welshman, who was not renowned for scoring at close range. Don Hutchison makes the unavailing challenge.

FA Premier League
4 January 1994
at Anfield

LIVERPOOL 3

Clough 25, 38; Ruddock 79

Bruce Grobbelaar, Rob Jones, Julian Dicks, Jamie Redknapp, Mark Wright, Neil Ruddock, Nigel Clough, John Barnes, Ian Rush, Steve McManaman, Robbie Fowler. Sub: Stig Inge Bjornebye for McManaman (78).

MANCHESTER UNITED 3

Bruce 9; Giggs 20; Irwin 24

Peter Schmeichel, Paul Parker, Denis Irwin, Steve Bruce, Gary Pallister, Roy Keane, Paul Ince, Andrei Kanchelskis, Brian McClair, Eric Cantona, Ryan Giggs.

Half-time: 2-3 Attendance: 42,795

IT was the kind of comeback Melchester Rovers might have managed when Roy Race was in his all-conquering prime. But Liverpool? They had no price when Manchester United's dashing men in black silenced a bewildered Anfield with three goals in the opening twenty-four minutes. Yet somehow the valiant Reds, dredging up hitherto unsuspected reserves of pride and passion when they needed them most, hauled themselves back on level terms in what was arguably the most enthralling encounter in the Premiership's brief history.

Astonishingly enough, in view of the blitz which was about to erupt about their heads, it was Liverpool who mounted a furious barrage of attacks in the opening minutes, and Robbie Fowler might have done better than shoot wildly over the bar when well placed.

Soon after that the flow of the game was abruptly reversed when Eric Cantona floated a perfect centre from the left and Steve Bruce expertly glanced the ball just inside Bruce Grobbelaar's left-hand post. Now United slipped smoothly into their intimidating top gear and their pressure paid after twenty minutes when Jamie Redknapp sold Mark Wright short with a dreadful pass. Ryan Giggs eluded the defender's desperate lunge and caught Grobbelaar off his line with a sublimely curled left-foot chip from twenty yards.

Four minutes later and the Merseysiders were facing a Doomsday scenario. Neil Ruddock committed an unnecessary foul on the edge of the 'D' and United were so sure of Denis Irwin's ability to convert that they didn't even place a man in the box. Duly the Irishman obliged with an unstoppable curver, and even though most of the match had yet to be played, the result no longer seemed in doubt.

Enter Nigel Clough. Within a minute he had reduced the arrears with a sweetly-struck snapshot from twenty-five yards, then seven minutes before the interval he repeated the trick from eighteen yards after an uncharacteristic mix-up between Bruce and Roy Keane. Game on.

Thereafter the action ebbed and flowed in dramatic fashion, with plenty of scoring opportunities created, most of them by United for whom Giggs was particularly profligate. It should be noted here that Grobbelaar, later to be accused of not trying his best (an allegation he denied vehemently) made several marvellous saves.

Thirteen minutes from the end, as Liverpool wound themselves up for a final series of assaults, Graeme Souness threw on that sweetest of crossers, Stig Inge Bjornebye, and reaped an almost immediate dividend. Ruddock, rampaging in the centre-forward position, played the ball to the Norwegian on the left flank; Stig responded with an exquisite dispatch onto Razor's ample forehead and the Manchester net bulged. It was 3-3 and Liverpool deserved parity for their sheer spirit.

There were some near things as the final whistle approached but no more goals, leaving Graeme Souness to pay tribute to his braves and quip: 'At least, after that, there can be nothing wrong with my heart!' As for Alex Ferguson, he spoke of a once-in-a-lifetime game. But what was his frame of mind when Liverpool's third went in? 'I was bloody raging,' he admitted.

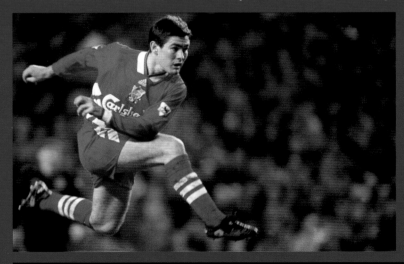

Schmeichel's crossbar in the forty-eighth minute. But the outcome was to hinge on two substitutions. After sixty minutes Alex Ferguson replaced Hughes, who was not fully fit, with McClair, and suddenly United began to create chances. Ten minutes later, the massively influential but admittedly tiring Molby was replaced with Babb, who was asked to make his debut in an unfamiliar midfield role. Where earlier they had flowed, now Liverpool looked edgy and almost at once United took the lead, Kanchelskis capitalizing on a weak Scales header which had been intended to reach his own goalkeeper. Then, only two minutes later, McClair played a slick one-two with Cantona and put the issue beyond all doubt.

For Eric it was a largely frustrating afternoon. Maybe seeking to take advantage of the Frenchman's known volatility, maybe merely having a joke, Neil Ruddock persisted in goading his opponent by adjusting that trademark upturned collar. The subject of this attention was not amused and largely ineffective, and it was no surprise when he was booked for a wild lunge at his hulking tormentor in the second half. In retrospect, this flash of Gallic tetchiness would appear as a popping cork beside a volcano when compared to the eruption which was coming later in the season.

Liverpool and United would not meet again until mid-March, by which time Alex Ferguson had paid Newcastle the equivalent of £7 million for striker Andy Cole, and Mount Cantona had well and truly blown. His summary manner of silencing a foul-mouthed yob at Selhurst Park in January had removed him from the Premiership equation for the remainder of the season and beyond. One man does not make a team, but there was no doubt at Anfield that the Red Devils were significantly diminished without the attacking options afforded by his unique flair.

In contrast Liverpool were dripping with ideas and had added a steel not always apparent against less exalted opposition to the undoubted craft of Barnes, McManaman and Redknapp. They were worthy 2-0 winners through Redknapp's low fifteen-yard cross-shot after twenty-five minutes and Bruce's own goal, following a McManaman effort near the end. The result did Kenny Dalglish a power of good, leaving his new club, Blackburn, six points clear of United with eight to play. More importantly, it raised the Reds into fourth place, on course for European qualification, and was the ideal morale-booster as they approached their League Cup Final confrontation with Bolton Wanderers.

The Trotters were duly overcome and, with United missing out narrowly on both legs of a second double and with mega-buy Cole not wholly satisfactory, Liverpool fans enjoyed a feel-good summer. Indeed, there was a persuasive case to be made that the Reds were on the verge of a genuine return to power. After all, they had trumped United's Cole manoeuvre by laying out £8.5 million to land the brooding but intoxicatingly talented centre-forward Stan Collymore from Nottingham Forest. If he and Robbie Fowler could meld as a pair and capitalize on all that sweet approach play, then there appeared no limits to what could be achieved, especially with United potentially in disarray. During the close-season Old Trafford had bade farewell to three key players, the ageing but still mightily effective Hughes, the midfield warrior Ince and, the most unwelcome departure, the speed merchant Kanchelskis. In addition, it was impossible at this stage to gauge the future mindset of Cantona who, in any case, would be suspended until October. True, they had a host of fabulous young prospects but as one illustrious ex-Anfielder turned TV pundit put it after the Mancunians' opening-day reverse at Villa Park, 'You win nothing with kids!'

For much of the 1995/6 season it seemed that Alan Hansen had got it right. United's youngsters showed rare verve and resilience to occupy second slot for most of the campaign, but Kevin Keegan's Newcastle compiled such a hefty Premiership lead that it seemed virtually inconceivable that they would lose it. Liverpool, meantime, for all their bountiful ability, remained slightly off the pace, usually third but never threatening to gain the summit. The Merseysiders, especially Robbie

Opposite: Nigel Clough cracks home his second goal and Liverpool fans are thinking, 'What a bargain!'

Fowler, could take enormous credit for their positive display at Old Trafford on the first day of October, when they all but stole the show from the returning Frenchman *[see Classic Clash Number Eighteen, opposite]*, but infinitely more was needed to avert further disappointment come trophy time.

As if turning their brilliance on and off like a tap, the Reds ran white-hot for United's visit a week before Christmas, routing the Mancunians far more conclusively than the 2-0 scoreline suggests. With his side badly missing the fire of the absent Keane and Butt in midfield, where Michael Thomas reigned supreme, Ferguson must have been close to apoplexy during their almost pathetically tepid first-half performance. Liverpool attacked with undiluted ferocity, as if venting their collective spleen at the indignities of recent years. They created an avalanche of opportunities,

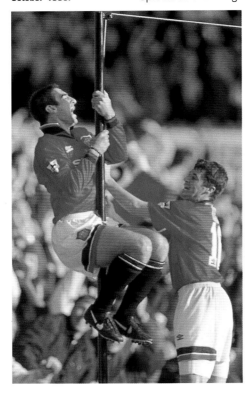

Below: Having driven plenty of others there in his time, Eric Cantona goes up the pole after equalizing against Liverpool from the penalty spot at Old Trafford in October 1995.

and it was due only to the phenomenal Schmeichel that the interval lead was a ludicrously unrepresentative 1-0. When a goal did materialize, in the forty-fourth minute, it was somewhat bizarre, Fowler striking a free-kick from twenty-five yards which the keeper, presumably unsighted, allowed to pass within two yards of him without lifting a finger to stop it.

At the break the Reds might have felt apprehensive at not having made the most of their advantage but, although their opponents displayed considerably more passion after a quiet word from their boss, they continued to be outplayed. Fowler completed his second brace of the season against United in the eighty-seventh minute, when he waltzed past David Beckham and chipped neatly beyond the overworked Schmeichel. Collymore, playing his best game since his transfer, should have far exceeded his partner's tally, making no less than thirteen attempts on goal and losing out on half a dozen one-on-ones with the imposing Dane, but the closest he came was rapping the woodwork just after the hour.

Afterwards, Ferguson delivered a rare public rebuke to his players, admitting that it was difficult to remember a worse performance, and while the result left United seven points adrift of Newcastle, the manner of it suggested that a fightback was out of the question. By late January the margin had stretched to twelve points; the title race was surely as good as run.

But with expectations at their lowest, inspired by Cantona at one end and Schmeichel at the other, Ferguson and his team heaped such pressure on the soar-away Magpies that they fell, rather limply in the end, out of the sky. Thus United claimed their third title in four years just six days in advance of their third consecutive FA Cup Final appearance – and this time their Wembley opponents were Liverpool.

The Merseysiders had finished third in the Premiership table, but there was a widely-held view that with all the talent at their disposal they should have done better, maybe even lifted the crown. The theory was voiced, over and over again in the city itself but also farther afield, that 'New Liverpool' was somehow soft; that Roy Evans was too easy-going; that some of the players were more interested in being style symbols than professional athletes; thus the 'Spice Boys' tag was born.

Opposite: Robbie Fowler may have been upstaged in the publicity stakes, but in realistic terms he was the afternoon's outstanding performer. Here he celebrates, with Ian Rush in attendance.

This impression was given vivid added currency when the team turned up at Wembley arrayed in eye-catching cream suits tailored by Giorgio Armani. The only problem was that every vestige of sharpness disappeared when the real business of the day began *[see Classic Clash Number Nineteen on pages 108-109]*. Liverpool's display was overwhelmingly disappointing, the flop emphasized by the fact that they

FA Premier League
1 October 1995
at Old Trafford

MANCHESTER UNITED 2

Butt 2; Cantona 71 (pen)

Peter Schmeichel, Gary Neville, Phil Neville, Steve Bruce, Gary Pallister, Lee Sharpe, Roy Keane, Nicky Butt, Eric Cantona, Ryan Giggs, Andy Cole. Subs: David Beckham for Butt (45), Paul Scholes for Phil Neville (73).

LIVERPOOL 2

Fowler 35, 54

David James, John Scales, Steve Harkness, Neil Ruddock, Phil Babb, Jason McAteer, Michael Thomas, Jamie Redknapp, Steve McManaman, Ian Rush, Robbie Fowler.

Half-time: 1-1 Attendance: 34,934

IT was French Liberation Day at Old Trafford, which appeared to be staging a religious convention rather than a soccer match. Yet for the all hysteria and hype surrounding the return of 'Dieu' after 248 days in the wilderness, to which he had been banished for placing his boot in the chest of a lout, it was Liverpool who emerged as moral victors.

True, Eric Cantona set up United's opening goal and supplied the equalizer which earned them a point, but in between these celestial interventions the visitors had played the more convincing football and in two-goal Robbie Fowler they had the real man of the match.

After strolling on to the pitch to a cacophony of adulation, the Frenchman lost little time in making his mark. Within sixty-eight seconds, to be precise, he had drifted to the left flank, accepted a pass from Andy Cole and crossed for Nicky Butt to net deftly from close range. From a Liverpool point of view, allowing Cantona so much space amounted to defensive suicide

and the unfortunate culprit was Jason McAteer, who was unused to the wing-back role into which he had been drafted because of injury to Rob Jones.

It could have been the signal for a United beanfeast, but the Merseysiders demonstrated their own considerable mettle by embarking on spells of patient possession and gradually assumed control of the midfield. Steadily the tempo of their attacks mounted as Ian Rush went close and Fowler was denied a penalty after he had been impeded by Steve Bruce, so that when they gained parity after thirty-five minutes it was well merited.

Ironically, the goal came from a feeble miss by Lee Sharpe at the other end, the ball being transferred rapidly to Fowler, who escaped down the left flank before beating Peter Schmeichel at his near post with a savage rising drive from fifteen yards.

After the break, Liverpool continued to be party-poopers and Fowler doubled his tally on fifty-four minutes when he ran on to a through-ball from the influential Michael Thomas, shrugged off a challenge from Gary Neville and

lifted the ball almost insolently over Schmeichel.

Now United, convinced that Neville had been fouled, were stung into retaliation and the play became more even, with young David Beckham, who had replaced Butt for the second half, taking the eye with his neat distribution. Cantona? He was on his best behaviour, strutting through the hectic action with characteristic elan but rarely causing serious alarm to the Liverpool rearguard. Then suddenly, inevitably, he was centre stage, freeing Giggs for a run on goal; the Welshman was pulled back by Jamie Redknapp and referee David Elleray awarded a penalty.

Who would take it? No doubt about that. Up strode Eric to strike the ball perfectly to David James' right and Old Trafford threatened to explode in a communal orgasm of delight. The man himself, who celebrated by climbing the net-pole, had twenty minutes left to complete the fairy tale by contriving a winner. That proved beyond him and the teams finished all-square, which was the very least Liverpool deserved. However, they would hear from Cantona again before the season was out ...

FA Cup Final
11 May 1996
at Wembley

MANCHESTER UNITED 1

Cantona 86

Peter Schmeichel, Phil Neville,
Denis Irwin, David May, Gary Pallister,
David Beckham, Nicky Butt, Roy Keane,
Ryan Giggs, Eric Cantona, Andy Cole.
Subs: Paul Scholes for Cole (64),
Gary Neville for Beckham (89).

LIVERPOOL 0

David James, Rob Jones, John Scales,
Mark Wright, Phil Babb, Jason McAteer,
Jamie Redknapp, John Barnes, Steve
McManaman, Robbie Fowler, Stan
Collymore. Subs: Ian Rush for Collymore
(75), Michael Thomas for Jones (86).

Half-time: 0-0   Attendance: 79,007

'Cantona the Incomparable' proclaimed one headline and why not? His barely credible journey from banished pariah to captain and leading scorer of the League Champions, with the Footballer of the Year accolade thrown in for good measure, would have been more than enough to justify the label even if United had never reached the FA Cup Final. But events at Wembley, which would have invited derision had they been submitted as a comic-strip plot, justified every superlative that went his way.

Consider the scenario. Four minutes from the end, with Cantona and company locked in a goalless stalemate against Liverpool, David Beckham dispatches a teasing, away-swinging corner from the right. David James is lured to stretch for an off-balance punch and the ball strikes Ian Rush before dropping into the path of the predatory Frenchman, who is lurking with intent on the edge of the box. Adjusting his body shape with a balletic backward step, Cantona executes a perfect waist-high volley which arrows through a thicket of rooted defenders to nestle in the Merseysiders' net. In that one sublime sequence, he has clinched not only the Cup and the much-coveted double, but also the hitherto never-achieved 'double double' – and he has done it all against United's bitterest rivals. Incomparable? Oh yes.

In all honesty, a game which was tipped to produce untold spectacle was untidy, a pronounced letdown for everyone but supporters of Manchester United. Alex Ferguson's men, still bubbling after lifting the title six days earlier at Middlesbrough, began by creating a flurry of chances. One of them, a venomous drive from Beckham, was parried spectacularly by the in-form James but the others fell to Andy Cole, who seemed miserably nervy and out of touch despite having contributed a scintillating goal at the Riverside.

Sadly that enterprising opening petered out into an arid midfield battle in which United's enforcers, man-of-the-match Roy Keane and his faithful lieutenant, Nicky Butt, suppressed the Liverpool think-tank, comprising Messrs Barnes, Redknapp and McManaman, so thoroughly that it was nearly half-time before the Merseysiders fashioned a genuine opportunity. When it arrived Redknapp, set up neatly by McManaman and Mark Wright, blazed over when well placed some fifteen yards out. Amazingly for a team so well endowed with attacking options, it was the closest they would come to scoring throughout the whole ninety minutes.

Not that the Mancunians were at their expansive best; far from it. Instead of adopting the swashbuckling approach which many expected of recently-crowned champions, they opted to squeeze the life out of Liverpool by denying them space, dictating the tempo of the game and believing that in the end their own mixture of efficiency and flair would fashion enough chances to win the game.

As the second period progressed, the plan continued to work perfectly. Poor Stan Collymore and Robbie Fowler, the Merseyside strike-force, were so isolated and starved of service that they could manage no more than hopeful, long-distance potshots that were highly unlikely to trouble Peter Schmeichel.

Meanwhile Cantona was playing well within himself, obliging James to pull off an acrobatic, one-handed grab from a technically delightful volley soon after the break, thereafter contenting himself with the occasional artful flick or silky lay-off.

Even though proceedings appeared to be moving inexorably towards extra-time, United remained the smoother, more comfortable combination – particularly after the inventive Paul Scholes had replaced Cole – and it wasn't the fact of their eighty-sixth-minute breakthrough which arrested the senses, merely its fairy-tale manner.

Still, it wasn't quite all over. Immediately after Eric's flight of fancy, Liverpool attacked and there was a split-second when it seemed as if Jason McAteer might force home a close-range equalizer, but the threat was cleared and the game ended with United in cruise control.

As Cantona led the way up the thirty-nine steps to the royal box, the extent of his apparent

reformation since his infamous encounter with a Selhurst Park cretin was pleasingly illustrated. Several imbeciles purporting to be Liverpool fans spat on the Old Trafford skipper and onlookers held their breath. How would he react? Surely not another kung-fu kick which would certainly end his English career? Mais non! Merely a haughty glance of pity as he wiped away the spittle and continued towards his rendezvous with the Duchess of Kent. Later, holding forth to the assembled scribes as was his duty as captain, he said of the incident, 'We understand the differences, the rivalry, between the fans of Manchester United and Liverpool and this is a fact of life. But never mind, on a day like this it does not matter.'

Yet Alex Ferguson, too, had to fend off a would-be assailant, emphasizing the undercurrent of vitriol which continues to exist between extremists at either end of the East Lancs Road. To his credit, the United boss played down the incident, preferring to

concentrate on the football. He conceded that the game had been no showpiece but referring to the 'double double' and his club's record ninth FA Cup triumph, he summed up, 'I can't think of anything better.'

Roy Evans, on the other hand, could think of plenty. He said: 'I hate the fact that United have won the double. I could cry. But you've got to give them credit. The double certainly didn't look on at Christmas but they have put together a stunning run. I'm gutted that we didn't win it and just as disappointed with our performance. We were very edgy and we just didn't play.'

And that was the truth.

Above: Defying belief, as was his wont, Eric Cantona strikes his fabulous late winner.
Left: A study in concentration. Sombre-faced managers Roy Evans and Alex Ferguson lead their teams into the famous old arena.

had let Manchester United, of all clubs, trample over the aspirations of countless fans to whom the outcome was of colossal importance.

For the victors, to win the double double in the space of three years was an achievement which, viewed historically, beggared belief – especially as it could easily have been the treble double. But viewed dispassionately, the feat is less surprising. As the giant clubs grow richer and richer, their squads ever more packed with internationals from all over the globe, the likelihood of smaller fry lifting the major prizes becomes increasingly remote.

After such a crushing experience, Liverpool needed a bright start to the 1996/7 season and they got one, an eight-game unbeaten run taking them to the top of the table by early October. However, their ninth game, which happened to be on a Saturday morning at Old Trafford, brought defeat, albeit undeserved, and their season lost its lustre from that point.

United were the more incisive and ambitious side in the early stages and when Beckham gave them a twenty-third-minute lead, arrowing a low first-time twenty-yarder past James after smart work by Norwegian newcomer Ole Gunnar Solskjaer, they were worth the advantage. But then their outlook changed radically. As if saving themselves for their Champions' League trip to Fenerbahce the following week, they became distressingly passive, back-pedalling furiously and inviting Liverpool to play.

The invitation was accepted with alacrity as the visitors mounted a wondrous display of pinpoint passing and bemusing movement, all orchestrated beautifully by Barnes. It was sumptuous entertainment for purists, but whereas United at their best could push the ball around with equal assurance before counter-attacking with deadly pace, Liverpool's gear changes were less explosive. Pass and move is an admirable policy but not if opponents are allowed precious seconds in which to regroup.

That said, on this occasion the visitors carved enough clear opportunities to take all three points, with McManaman and Patrik Berger being the principal culprits. In the end they took none and the injured Fowler, watching from the stand, must have felt like weeping; meanwhile United absentees Keane and Pallister would have been involuntarily kicking every ball as their colleagues took the strain. Defensively, it must be said, there were some United heroes, notably the sometimes maligned David May, but Cantona was a cipher in attack and he admitted later, 'I am playing some of the worst football of my career. I will try to do better.' Maybe the decision to retire at the end of the season was already taking shape.

Opposite: Once again, David James goes one way and the ball goes another. The much-pilloried Liverpool keeper, who endured another high-profile expose of his indecision, fails to impose himself on Andy Cole.

Undoubtedly, this Liverpool side would play worse and win, but Alex Ferguson would not admit to being impressed, saying that for all their possession the Merseysiders had lacked penetration. An unusually testy Roy Evans begged to differ, pointing out, 'We made six or seven good chances. If that's not penetrative, I don't know what is!'

An intriguing sidelight on the game in such cash-conscious times was that, when Karel Poborsky was replaced by substitute Paul Scholes during the second half, the entire United line-up had cost less than the price of Stan Collymore. Food for thought.

As Liverpool supporters trailed morosely away from the ground, their mood would have been transformed could they have been given a glimpse of their rivals' near future, which encompassed a 5-0 thrashing at Newcastle, a 6-3 humbling at Southampton, the loss of their forty-year-old unbeaten home record in Europe and a defeat on their own turf by Chelsea. In the longer term, though, they would be swallowing bitter gall, reflecting at the end of another trophy-less campaign on a comprehensive reverse at the hands of their foes, this time at Anfield in April *(see Classic Clash Number Twenty, opposite)*.

For United, though, the euphoria of their fourth Championship in five years was tainted slightly by the news of Cantona's departure to seek a new career in the movies. Throughout a gilded period in the club's history, the Frenchman had been their talisman, their touchstone. Would they ever be the same without him?

FA Premier League
19 April 1997
at Anfield

LIVERPOOL 1

Barnes 19

David James, Stig Inge Bjornebye, Bjorn Tore Kvarme, Mark Wright, Steve Harkness, Jason McAteer, Michael Thomas, John Barnes, Jamie Redknapp, Steve McManaman, Robbie Fowler. Subs: Stan Collymore for McAteer (51), Patrik Berger for Barnes (68).

MANCHESTER UNITED 3

Pallister 13, 42; Cole 63

Peter Schmeichel, Gary Neville, Phil Neville, Ronny Johnsen, Gary Pallister, Roy Keane, Nicky Butt, David Beckham, Eric Cantona, Paul Scholes, Andy Cole. Sub: Brian McClair for Scholes (81).

Half-time: 1-2 Attendance: 40,892

OF all the indignities heaped on Liverpool heads during the 1990s by Manchester United, this was perhaps the most humiliating. The game was billed as a Championship decider, which was only a slight exaggeration, yet the Merseysiders succumbed so meekly to Alex Ferguson's men that the Anfield stands were emptying long before the final whistle. United were workmanlike and occasionally thrilling but some way below their free-flowing best, yet they outclassed their hosts comprehensively.

Beginning the day in Premiership pole position, the Mancunians might have been expected to advance cautiously. Instead, obviously unfazed by the mid-morning start dictated by TV schedules, they attacked with sustained cohesion from the off.

The first blow fell after thirteen minutes when David Beckham delivered a raking corner from the right and Gary Pallister shrugged off Mark Wright to net with a thunderous header from eight yards. David James, rooted to his line, was blameless on this occasion, being entitled to expect protection from his defenders.

Six minutes later Liverpool kindled brief hopes of a meaningful revival when a beautiful cross from Jason McAteer found John Barnes unmarked and the ageing playmaker netted with a glancing header which Peter Schmeichel reached but could not keep out. Now the Reds enjoyed their most encouraging spell of the match and had Robbie Fowler not missed an eminently acceptable chance then a different story might have unfolded.

Probably not, though, because United's smoothly confident style gave the inescapable impression that they could go up a gear if the need arose – and so it proved. Four minutes before the interval Ronny Johnsen met a Beckham corner to induce a blindingly brilliant tip-over from the Liverpool goalkeeper. Back to the corner flag went Beckham, over came another low-trajectory missile and there was Pallister again to shrug aside the ineffectual Wright and direct a bullet near-post header past the flailing James.

This time the hapless custodian could be faulted, as he came for the ball but never reached it, but at least he could claim the extenuating circumstance of being under severe pressure from the towering centre-back. There was no such excuse just after the hour when Gary Neville, having delightfully gulled Bjornebye near the right touchline, dispatched a high, hanging centre. Poor James, clearly a bag of nerves, had ample time and space to pluck the ball from the air, but he misjudged the flight calamitously, allowing Andy Cole to nod into an empty net.

The remainder of the match, during which the lead would have doubled but for the profligacy of Cole, was a shameful doddle for the visitors, watched in agonized silence by those home fans with enough stomach to stay until the end. When a dejected Fowler, suspended for the remainder of the season following a recent sending-off against Everton, threw his boots into the Kop on the way to the dressing room, it was an apt symbol of his club's sorry capitulation.

David Beckham is understandably ecstatic after delivering the decisive goal with a scintillating free-kick at Anfield in December 1997.

During the first half of the 1997/8 season, the evidence was that they would. In the course of a richly profitable autumn they built a substantial Premiership lead, so that a win at Anfield in December would maintain their lead at the top as three points over Chelsea, and stretch it to a swingeing twelve over Liverpool who, yet again, had been under-achieving depressingly.

Almost everyone who followed the Reds was immensely fond of Roy Evans, recognizing his decency, integrity and appealing lack of arrogance, but increasingly they doubted his ability to do the job on which their peace of mind depended. There was a feeling that Roy was not the man to control a collection of super-rich young players, some of whom seemed as much intent on projecting their public image as winning games for Liverpool. Then there was the great goalkeeper debate. David James, though possessing enormous natural talent, had proved horrendously unreliable in key encounters during the previous term, and was doing so again. Surely it wasn't asking too much for Evans to have found a suitable replacement, or at least a serviceable understudy while James' fragile confidence was rebuilt? The consensus on the street seemed to be that the Reds had flattered to deceive for too long and that nice-guy Roy should pay, if not with his head then at least by moving sideways into a less demanding role. The board, however, did not agree. Evans soldiered on, and the television image of the beleaguered boss rolling his eyes heavenwards in despair during United's visit summed up his club's predicament.

The match, another Saturday morning affair, was wholly demoralizing from Liverpool's viewpoint. After a scrappy first half in which both sides spurned chances, the Red Devils took over with devastating assurance, the most eloquent testimony to their superiority being their apparent ability to play within themselves, then raise their game at will.

They went ahead shortly after the break, when Bjorn Tore Kvarme was caught dithering by Cole, who robbed him before sidestepping Dominic Matteo and hammering a low drive past James. Ten minutes later Liverpool levelled from the spot through Fowler after Michael Owen had been clattered, and for the next ten they demonstrated enough spirit to raise the Kopites' hopes. But then United won a free-kick on the edge of the Reds' box and David Beckham stepped up to demonstrate his knack of coaxing a football to rise and fall at high velocity over the space of around twenty yards, his superb effort crossing the goal-line via the underside of the crossbar. At that point the Merseysiders sagged; and their marking was abysmal when Teddy Sheringham was allowed to flick on a Giggs corner for Cole to stab in unopposed in the seventy-fourth minute.

The worst was still to come. There were no more goals but United were able to stroll at their ease and their fans were in a merciless frame of mind. Paul Ince, the former United hero whom Evans had recruited from Inter Milan but who missed the match through suspension, was a prime target for personal jibes, but the overall tone was more general and typified by the maliciously barbed 'You used to be a big club'. The home contingent could hardly raise a response and their silence was an accolade to their sworn adversaries. The vast knowledgeable majority of Merseysiders knew an outstanding team when they saw one; they knew they could not complain about the result; their glazed expressions said it all – for the time being, at least, Alex Ferguson had turned United into what Liverpool used to be. In the week that an imposing bronze statue of Bill Shankly had been unveiled at the new Anfield visitors centre, that was a symbolically grave admission. To his eternal credit, though, Roy Evans retained his sense of humour. 'I expect I'll be getting the sack again after this!'

Ferguson, not a man to crow unduly, admitted that the performance had given him 'a special tingle'. However, football being the delightfully unfathomable game that it is, United's awesome form lasted only two months into the New Year. Then, by their standards, they crumbled and Liverpool – for whom eighteen-year-old Michael Owen was looking ever more like the international star he was destined to become just a few months hence – had the satisfaction of delivering a telling blow to the Champions' hopes of retaining their title. United needed a win in this Good Friday teatime fixture

Michael Owen is ready to party after poaching Liverpool's equalizer at Old Trafford in April 1998. United have not heard the last of this young man!

to have any realistic chance of staving off the formidable challenge of Arsene Wenger's revitalized Arsenal and they began as if they were going to get it. In the first minute Giggs burst through on goal, only to be denied by the courage and judgement of American Brad Friedel, the long-awaited replacement for James. Now, for a while, the yellow-shirted Reds looked horribly vulnerable at the back, especially in the centre, and sure enough after eleven minutes they gave way, allowing the unattended Ronny Johnsen to head in from a Beckham corner.

It might have been the signal for United to dominate, but the game began to follow

'I say, Paul, I'm not one to moan, but I think you might have been a trifle over-vigorous with that challenge, old boy.' 'Gosh, Peter, please accept my apologies. Perhaps we can get together later for a glass of shandy and a natter over old times.'
Or something like that . . .

the pattern of the two clubs' previous meeting at Old Trafford, when Liverpool had surged back after going behind. This game was nothing like as one-sided, but the visitors were well worth their thirty-fifth-minute equalizer, chipped impudently and expertly by Owen after Schmeichel and Pallister had left a loose ball to each other.

It's hardly an original thought, but this young man looks set to join the select band of truly great footballing forwards these islands have produced, the likes of Matthews, Finney, Charlton, Best, Greaves, Dalglish and one or two others. To be sure he has an impetuous streak, which got him sent off in this same match and might have cost his side victory, but that will not be a bar to progress; rather that bit of devil will prove a priceless asset.

Michael lost his self-control only five minutes after his goal, lunging artlessly at Johnsen and catching his ankle. It could have crippled the Norwegian and, arguably, was worth a dismissal in its own right. The referee opted to brandish the yellow card and, having been booked for an earlier transgression, the prodigy was off.

Despite being reduced to ten men, with reserve midfielder Danny Murphy operating as an impressively subtle lone front-runner, Liverpool looked the better side for much of the second period until weight of numbers began to wear them down. Then United created a flurry of late chances and when the last of these was fluffed by the generally splendid Scholes, their chances of retaining the title had been drastically reduced.

One of the most tiresome and unedifying but wholly predictable aspects of the afternoon was the constant jeering of Paul Ince in his first serious game at Old Trafford since his departure three years earlier. Was there the slightest hint of recognition, perhaps even affection, proffered to a man whose contributions to earlier Mancunian triumphs was simply enormous? Or, if that was a bit much to expect, perhaps some good-humoured ribbing? No chance. Just gutter obscenities of the most banal nature, and the saddest thing was that nothing else was expected.

At season's end United finished as runners-up, a point behind Arsenal, with Liverpool a further twelve points adrift in third place. 'It cannot go on' came the impassioned cry from Merseyside, and this time the Reds' board took a radical step to ensure that it didn't. Though they didn't part company with the worthy Evans, they shifted him sideways a tad to make room for Gerard Houllier, until recently technical director of the French World Cup winners, who assumed the title of joint-manager. Having taught in Liverpool and stood on the Kop during the 1960s, the personable Houllier had immense affinity for the club and the city, and it was believed that his European experience would mesh ideally with Evans' Boot Room ethos.

There were accusations that the Reds had fudged the issue instead of making a clean break with the old ways, but a sprightly start, in which Owen played a breathtaking part in accruing ten points from a possible twelve, augured well. Then came a worrying stutter, so that their late-September date at Old Trafford came to be seen as an early acid test of the new regime.

Cue anguish. For the sixth successive time on the Manchester ground, Liverpool had masses of possession but failed to win. This time, perhaps, they didn't deserve to, spending far too long meandering through the midfield maze and barely forcing Schmeichel into meaningful action. As for United, they took huge comfort from their 2-0 victory – especially coming in the wake of a three-goal drubbing at Highbury – but their performance was not that of prospective champions.

For the first eighteen minutes, the home team's dominance was total, Liverpool's containment policy verging on absolute passivity. In view of the recent sieve-like quality of the visitors' rearguard, something had to give, but when United's inevitable breakthrough materialized it was bathed in controversy. Goalkeeper Friedel, looking exceedingly nervy following recent uncertain displays, allowed a firmly struck but hardly demanding shot from Solskjaer to squirm under his body for a corner. Over came Beckham's inswinging delivery and, though under no direct pressure, the American punched inconclusively; the ball climbed almost vertically before dropping a few yards to his left, on to the hand of Jason McAteer, who was tussling with Paul Scholes. Referee Stephen Lodge gave a penalty, which seemed harsh, and Denis Irwin netted from the spot with the accurate economy of Cantona in his heyday.

That was the signal for Liverpool to throw off their presumably self-imposed fetters and assume control of midfield, though it was a control which the Mancunians seemed willing to cede, leading, as it did, to practically zero penetration. There was more of the same in the second half, but opportunities at either end were scarce, Solskjaer missing for United, then Berger scuffing weakly at the other end. The German, Riedle, netted after sixty-eight minutes but was correctly flagged offside, and even after the introduction of Fowler, still gaining match fitness after a lengthy lay-off, it seemed unlikely that the match would produce a second goal.

As Liverpool became rather desperate, though, their defence became stretched and the Red Devils took advantage. Andy Cole, currently unsure of his place despite contributing twenty-five goals the previous term, comfortably outpaced Phil Babb on the left and crossed towards Dwight Yorke. United's recent £12.5 million signing from Aston Villa, whose arrival could not have done much for Cole's peace of mind, got a touch which diverted the ball, rather fortuitously, towards Scholes, who was lurking unmarked just inside the box. The pass, intended or not, was going behind the little redhead but he adjusted with characteristic adroitness and belted a blistering, rising, slightly curving drive into Friedel's top right-hand corner with his unfavoured left foot. It was an exquisite execution by a player who doesn't ooze panache in the manner of various contemporaries, but whose technique is second to none. Thereafter United might have doubled their tally, but that would have been dreadfully hard on a

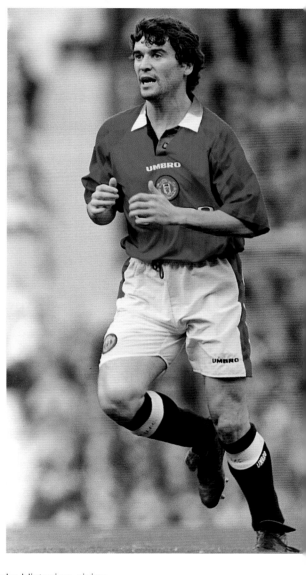

Roy Keane, United's most influential midfield presence since Bryan Robson in his pomp.

Liverpool side which had probed ceaselessly if with precious little invention.

The key to a typically torrid contest, in which four men from each side were booked, was the manner in which deputy central defender Gary Neville snuffed out the threat of Michael Owen. The England right-back, whose early career was spent in the middle until lack of inches prompted a move to the flank, achieved this by standing some two yards off the Merseyside prodigy, thus denying him a start if balls were played in behind the defence. It was a glowing tribute to Neville's own pace, as well as his unflagging concentration, that Owen was practically anonymous. Also outstanding in the United rearguard was Jaap Stam, the £10.5 million Dutch stopper who had encountered a few early problems in adjusting to the English game but was now beginning to look the part.

Ryan Giggs, four title medals to his credit and he's still only 25.

Once the points were in the bag, the home supporters turned their attention to baiting Ince. Before the game, much had been made of a recent TV documentary in which Alex Ferguson had referred to his former midfielder as a 'big-time Charlie'. Accordingly, more acceptably than earlier foul-mouthed offerings, they chorused, 'Charlie, Charlie, what's the score?'

The result, which took United above Liverpool to third place in the fledgling Premiership table, meant that the Merseysiders had not won at Old Trafford since 1990. At the time of writing in the late autumn of 1998 – shortly after poor Roy Evans finally lost his job and Gerard Houllier was placed in sole charge – the tally in all games since the war reads 41 victories to the Mancunians, 27 to the Merseysiders and 35 draws. Curiously, those figures don't even begin to reflect the trophy count during the same era, Liverpool having accumulated 30 to United's 20.

But those are mere statistics. Manchester United against Liverpool is about a maelstrom of far more powerful elements. On the plus side there is high endeavour, artistry, passion and an understandable pride. Against that is ranged the all-too-prevalent image of faces in the crowd, from both sides of the great north-western divide, turning purple with hatred. There is no rightful place for that in sport, or anywhere else in society, though it would be hopelessly unrealistic to expect it to recede.

Clearly the fixture will never gain the family feel of the Everton derby. As one Red put it: 'A father might support Liverpool while his son supports Everton, but after the game they will sit down to tea together. Scousers can forgive Scousers a lot, but Mancs? Never!' Indeed, the chasm widened still further during the autumn of 1998 when Rupert Murdoch, owner of The Sun, launched his epoch-making bid to buy United. The Australian media mogul's flagship paper is still roundly despised by many Merseysiders for its Hillsborough excesses, and any Old Trafford link would serve only to intensify the antithapy.

But let's finish on a positive note. Call to mind the deep friendship and respect shared by Busby and Shankly; remember the deathless deeds of Charlton and Liddell, Best and Dalglish, Beckham and Owen and the rest; then conjure up that overwhelmingly appealing image, mentioned in the opening chapter, of a small Mancunian being befriended on the Kop.

What better way to leave these two proud tribes, playing happily in the sunshine ...

1946/7

Liverpool:
Division One Champions,
FA Cup fourth round.

United:
Division One runners-up,
FA Cup fourth round.

Division One:
11 September 1946,
at Maine Road.

MANCHESTER UNITED 5

Pearson 12, 17, 85;
Rowley 37; Mitten 49

LIVERPOOL 0

Half-time: 3-0

United: Jack Crompton,
Johnny Carey, Billy
McGlen, Jack Warner,
Allenby Chilton, Henry
Cockburn, Jimmy Delaney,
John Hanlon, Jack Rowley,
Charlie Mitten.

Liverpool: Charlie
Ashcroft, Jim Harley,
Barney Ramsden, Phil
Taylor, Laurie Hughes,
Bob Paisley, Berry
Nieuwenhuys, Jack
Balmer, Bill Jones,
Willie Fagan, Bob Priday.

Attendance: 41,657

Division One:
3 May 1947,
at Anfield.

LIVERPOOL 1

Stubbins 12

MANCHESTER UNITED 0

Half-time: 1-0

Liverpool: Cyril Sidlow,
Ray Lambert, Eddie Spicer,
Bill Jones, Laurie Hughes,
Bob Paisley, Stan Polk,
Jack Balmer, Albert
Stubbins, Billy Watkinson,
Billy Liddell.

United: Jack Crompton,
Johnny Carey, John Aston,
Jack Warner, Allenby
Chilton, Billy McGlen,
Jimmy Delaney, John
Hanlon, Ronnie Burke,
Stan Pearson, Jack
Rowley.

Attendance: 48,800

1947/8

United:
Division One runners-up,
FA Cup winners.

Liverpool:
eleventh in Division One,
FA Cup fourth round.

Division One:
27 August 1947,
at Maine Road.

MANCHESTER UNITED 2

Morris 25; Pearson 69

LIVERPOOL 0

Half-time: 1-0

United: Jack Crompton,
Johnny Carey, John Aston,
Jack Warner, Allenby
Chilton, Billy McGlen,
Jimmy Delaney, Johnny
Morris, Jack Rowley,
Stan Pearson,
Charlie Mitten.

Liverpool: Cyril Sidlow,
Jim Harley, Ray Lambert,
Phil Taylor, Laurie Hughes,
Bob Paisley, Billy
Watkinson, Jack Balmer,
Stan Polk, Billy Liddell.

Attendance: 52,385

Division One:
3 September 1947,
at Anfield.

LIVERPOOL 2

Stubbins 48;
Balmer 67 (pen)

MANCHESTER UNITED 2

Mitten 2; Pearson 16

Half-time: 0-2

United: Jack Crompton,
Johnny Carey, John Aston,
Jack Warner, Allenby
Chilton, Billy McGlen,
Jimmy Delaney, Johnny
Morris, Jack Rowley, Stan
Pearson, Charlie Mitten.

Liverpool: Cyril Sidlow,
Bill Jones, Ray Lambert,
Phil Taylor, Laurie Hughes,
Bob Paisley, Billy
Watkinson, Jack Balmer,
Albert Stubbins, Stan
Polk, Billy Liddell.

Attendance: 48,081

FA Cup fourth round:
24 January 1948,
at Goodison Park
(United's home fixture)

MANCHESTER UNITED 3

Rowley 31; Morris 35;
Mitten 36

LIVERPOOL 0

Half-time: 3-0

United: Jack Crompton,
Johnny Carey, John Aston,
John Anderson, Allenby
Chilton, Henry Cockburn,
Jimmy Delaney, Johnny
Morris, Jack Rowley, Stan
Pearson, Charlie Mitten.

Liverpool: Ray Minshull,
Bill Jones, Ray Lambert,
Phil Taylor, Laurie Hughes,
Bob Paisley, Billy Liddell,
Jack Balmer, Albert
Stubbins, Cyril Done,
Bob Priday.

Attendance: 74,721

1948/9

United:
Division One runners-up,
FA Cup semi-finalists.

Liverpool:
twelfth in Division One,
FA Cup fifth round.

Division One:
25 December 1948,
at Maine Road.

MANCHESTER UNITED 0

LIVERPOOL 0

United: Jack Crompton,
Johnny Carey, John Aston,
Henry Cockburn,
Allenby Chilton, Billy
McGlen, Jimmy Delaney,
Stan Pearson, Ronnie
Burke, Jack Rowley,
Charlie Mitten.

Liverpool: Ray Minshull,
Bill Shepherd, Ray
Lambert, Phil Taylor,
Bill Jones, Bob Paisley,
Jimmy Payne, Jack
Balmer, Cyril Done, Tommy
McLeod, Ken Brierley.

Attendance: 47,788

Division One:
27 December 1948,
at Anfield

LIVERPOOL 0

MANCHESTER UNITED 2

Burke; Pearson

Half-time: 0-0

Liverpool: Ray Minshull,
Bill Shepherd, Ray
Lambert, Phil Taylor,
Bill Jones, Bob Paisley,
Jimmy Payne, Jack
Balmer, Cyril Done, Tommy
McLeod, Billy Liddell.

United: Jack Crompton,
Johnny Carey, John Aston,
Henry Cockburn, Allenby
Chilton, Billy McGlen,
Ted Buckle, Stan Pearson,
Ronnie Burke, Jack
Rowley, Charlie Mitten.

Attendance: 53,325

1949/50

United:
fourth in Division One,
FA Cup quarter-finalists.

Liverpool:
eighth in Division One,
FA Cup finalists.

Division One:
7 September 1949,
at Anfield.

LIVERPOOL 1

Stubbins 76

MANCHESTER UNITED 1

Mitten 44

Half-time: 0-1

Liverpool: Cyril Sidlow,
Ray Lambert, Eddie Spicer,
Phil Taylor, Laurie Hughes,
Bob Paisley, Jimmy Payne,
Kevin Baron, Albert
Stubbins, Willie Fagan,
Billy Liddell.

United: Jack Crompton,
Johnny Carey, John Aston,
Tommy Lowrie, Sammy
Lynn, Allenby Chilton,
Jimmy Delaney, Stan
Pearson, Jack Rowley,
Ted Buckle, Charlie Mitten.

Attendance: 51,587

Division One:
15 March 1950,
at Old Trafford

MANCHESTER UNITED 0

LIVERPOOL 0

United: Jack Crompton,
Johnny Carey, John Aston,
Jack Warner, Allenby
Chilton, Henry Cockburn,
Jimmy Delaney, John
Downie, Jack Rowley,
Stan Pearson, Charlie
Mitten.

Liverpool: Cyril Sidlow,
Ray Lambert, Eddie Spicer,
Phil Taylor, Bill Jones,
Bob Paisley, Jimmy Payne,
Kevin Baron, Albert
Stubbins, Frank Christie,
Billy Liddell.

Attendance: 43,456

1950/51

United:
Division One runners-up,
FA Cup quarter-finalists.

Liverpool:
ninth in Division One,
FA Cup third round.

Division One:
23 August 1950,
at Anfield.

LIVERPOOL 2

Liddell 12; Allen og 37

MANCHESTER UNITED 1

Rowley 25

Half-time: 2-1

Liverpool: Cyril Sidlow,
Bill Shepherd, Eddie
Spicer, Bill Jones, Laurie
Hughes, Bob Paisley,
Jimmy Payne, Phil Taylor,
Cyril Done, Jack Balmer,
Billy Liddell.

United: Reg Allen,
Johnny Carey, John Aston,
Eddie McIlvenny,
Allenby Chilton,
Henry Cockburn, Jimmy
Delaney, John Downie,
Jack Rowley, Stan
Pearson, Billy McGlen.

Attendance: 30,211

Division One:
30 August 1950,
at Old Trafford.

MANCHESTER UNITED 1

Downie 24

LIVERPOOL 0

Half-time: 1-0

United: Reg Allen, Johnny Carey, John Aston, Don Gibson, Allenby Chilton, Henry Cockburn, Tommy Bogan, John Downie, Jack Rowley, Stan Pearson, Billy McGlen.

Liverpool: Cyril Sidlow, Bill Shepherd, Eddie Spicer, Bill Jones, Laurie Hughes, Bob Paisley, Jimmy Payne, Phil Taylor, Cyril Done, Willie Fagan, Billy Liddell.

Attendance: 34,835

1951/2

United:
Division One Champions, FA Cup third round.

Liverpool:
eleventh in Division One, FA Cup fifth round.

Division One:
24 November 1951,
at Anfield.

LIVERPOOL 0

MANCHESTER UNITED 0

Liverpool: Charlie Ashcroft, Bill Jones, Ray Lambert, John Heydon, Laurie Hughes, Bob Paisley, Brian Jackson, Kevin Baron, John Smith, Jimmy Payne, Billy Liddell.

United: Jack Crompton, Johnny Carey, Roger Byrne, Jackie Blanchflower, Allenby Chilton, Henry Cockburn, Johnny Berry, Stan Pearson, Jack Rowley, John Downie, Ernie Bond.

Attendance: 42,378

Division One:
12 April 1952,
at Old Trafford.

MANCHESTER UNITED 4

Byrne 30 (pen), 53; Downie 51; Rowley 59

LIVERPOOL 0

Half-time: 1-0

United: Reg Allen, Tommy McNulty, John Aston, Johnny Carey, Allenby Chilton, Jeff Whitefoot, Johnny Berry, John Downie, Jack Rowley, Stan Pearson, Roger Byrne.

Liverpool: Charlie Ashcroft, Ray Lambert, Steve Parr, Bill Jones, John Heydon, Bob Paisley, Brian Jackson, Kevin Baron, John Smith, Jimmy Payne, Billy Liddell.

Attendance: 42,970

1952/3

United:
eighth in Division One, FA Cup fifth round.

Liverpool:
seventeenth in Division One, FA Cup third round.

Division One:
13 December 1952,
at Anfield.

LIVERPOOL 1

Liddell 10

MANCHESTER UNITED 2

Aston 52, Pearson 70

Half-time: 1-0

Liverpool: Charlie Ashcroft, Bill Jones, Ronnie Moran, Phil Taylor, John Heydon, Bob Paisley, Jimmy Payne, Kevin Baron, Albert Stubbins, John Smith, Billy Liddell.

United: Jack Crompton, Bill Foulkes, Roger Byrne, Johnny Carey, Allenby Chilton, Henry Cockburn, Johnny Berry, John Doherty, John Aston, Stan Pearson, David Pegg.

Attendance: 34,450

Division One:
20 April 1953,
at Old Trafford.

MANCHESTER UNITED 3

Pearson 6; Rowley 8; Berry 80

LIVERPOOL 1

Smyth 88

Half-time: 2-0

United: Jack Crompton, John Aston, Roger Byrne, Johnny Carey, Allenby Chilton, Jeff Whitefoot, Johnny Berry, John Downie, Tommy Taylor, Stan Pearson, Jack Rowley.

Liverpool: Charlie Ashcroft, Bill Jones, Ray Lambert, Joe Maloney, Phil Taylor, Brian Williams, Jimmy Payne, Louis Bimpson, Sammy Smyth, Arthur Rowley, Billy Liddell.

Attendance: 20,869

1953/4

United:
fourth in Division One, FA Cup third round.

Liverpool:
twenty-second in Division One (relegated), FA Cup third round.

Division One:
22 August 1953,
at Anfield.

LIVERPOOL 4

Bimpson 20, 54, 58; Jones 44

MANCHESTER UNITED 4

Rowley 9; Byrne (pen) 48; Lewis 60; Taylor 83

Half-time: 2-1

Liverpool: Charlie Ashcroft, Ray Lambert, Eddie Spicer, Phil Taylor, Laurie Hughes, Bob Paisley, Jimmy Payne, Kevin Baron, Louis Bimpson, Bill Jones, Billy Liddell.

United: Jack Crompton, John Aston, Roger Byrne, Don Gibson, Allenby Chilton, Henry Cockburn, Johnny Berry, Jack Rowley, Tommy Taylor, Eddie Lewis, David Pegg.

Attendance: 48,422

Division One:
19 December 1953,
at Old Trafford.

MANCHESTER UNITED 5

Taylor 14, 35; Blanchflower 34, 79; Viollet 45

LIVERPOOL 1

Bimpson 58

Half-time: 4-0

United: Ray Wood, Bill Foulkes, Roger Byrne, Jeff Whitefoot, Allenby Chilton, Duncan Edwards, Johnny Berry, Jackie Blanchflower, Tommy Taylor, Dennis Viollet, Jack Rowley.

Liverpool: Dave Underwood, Ray Lambert, Eddie Spicer, Roy Saunders, Barry Wilkinson, Geoff Twentyman, Brian Jackson, Kevin Baron, Louis Bimpson, Sammy Smyth, Billy Liddell.

Attendance: 26,074

Half-time: 2-1

1959/60

United:
seventh in Division One, FA Cup fifth round.

Liverpool:
third in Division Two, FA Cup fourth round.

FA Cup-Fourth round:
30 January 1960,
at Anfield.

LIVERPOOL 1

Wheeler 36

MANCHESTER UNITED 3

Charlton 13, 44; Bradley 70

Half-time: 1-2

Liverpool: Bert Slater, John Molyneux, Ronnie Moran, Johnny Wheeler, Dick White, Tommy Leishman, Jimmy Melia, Roger Hunt, Dave Hickson, Jimmy Harrower, Alan A'Court.

United: Harry Gregg, Bill Foulkes, Joe Carolan, Maurice Setters, Ronnie Cope, Seamus Brennan, Warren Bradley, Albert Quixall, Dennis Viollet, Bobby Charlton, Albert Scanlon.

Attendance: 56,736

1962/3

Liverpool:
eighth in Division One, FA Cup semi-finalists.

United:
nineteenth in Division One, FA Cup winners.

Division One:
10 November 1962,
at Old Trafford.

MANCHESTER UNITED 3

Herd 39; Quixall (pen) 69; Giles 90

LIVERPOOL 3

St John 51; Melia 85; Moran 89

Half-time: 1-0

United: Harry Gregg, Seamus Brennan, Noel Cantwell, Nobby Stiles, Bill Foulkes, Maurice Setters, Johnny Giles, Albert Quixall, David Herd, Denis Law, Bobby Charlton.

Liverpool: Tommy Lawrence, Gerry Byrne, Ronnie Moran, Gordon Milne, Ron Yeats, Willie Stevenson, Ian Callaghan, Roger Hunt, Ian St John, Jimmy Melia, Alan A'Court.

Attendance: 43,810

Division One:
13 April 1963,
at Anfield.

LIVERPOOL 1

St John 72

MANCHESTER UNITED 0

Half-time: 0-0

Liverpool: Tommy Lawrence, Alan Jones, Ronnie Moran, Gordon Milne, Ron Yeats, Willie Stevenson, Ian Callaghan, Roger Hunt, Ian St John, Alf Arrowsmith, Jimmy Melia.

United: Harry Gregg, Seamus Brennan, Tony Dunne, Pat Crerand, Bill Foulkes, Maurice Setters, Johnny Giles, Nobby Stiles, Albert Quixall, Denis Law, Bobby Charlton.

Attendance: 51,529

1963/4

Liverpool:
Division One Champions,
FA Cup quarter-finalists.

United:
Division One runners-up,
FA Cup semi-finalists,
European Cup-Winners'
Cup third round.

Division One:
23 November 1963,
at Old Trafford.

MANCHESTER UNITED 0
LIVERPOOL 1

Yeats 75

Half-time: 0-0

United: Harry Gregg, Tony
Dunne, Noel Cantwell, Pat
Crerand, Bill Foulkes,
Maurice Setters, Albert
Quixall, Graham Moore,
David Herd, Denis Law,
Bobby Charlton.

Liverpool: Tommy
Lawrence, Phil Ferns,
Ronnie Moran, Gordon
Milne, Ron Yeats, Willie
Stevenson, Ian Callaghan,
Roger Hunt, Ian St John,
Jimmy Melia, Peter
Thompson.

Attendance: 54,654

Division One:
4 April 1964,
at Anfield.

LIVERPOOL 3

Callaghan 6; Arrowsmith
39, 51

MANCHESTER UNITED 0

Half-time: 2-0

Liverpool: Tommy
Lawrence, Gerry Byrne,
Ronnie Moran, Gordon
Milne, Ron Yeats, Willie
Stevenson, Ian Callaghan,
Roger Hunt, Ian St John,
Alf Arrowsmith, Peter
Thompson.

United: Harry Gregg,
Seamus Brennan, Tony
Dunne, Pat Crerand, Bill
Foulkes, Maurice Setters,
George Best, Nobby
Stiles, David Herd, Denis
Law, Bobby Charlton.

Attendance: 52,559

1964/5

United:
Division One Champions,
FA Cup semi-finalists,
Inter-Cities Fairs Cup
semi-finalists.

Liverpool:
seventh in Division One,
FA Cup winners,
European Cup semi-
finalists.

Division One:
31 October 1964,
at Anfield.

LIVERPOOL 0
MANCHESTER UNITED 2

Herd 35; Crerand 60

Half-time: 0-1

Liverpool: Tommy
Lawrence, Chris Lawler,
Gerry Byrne, Gordon
Milne, Ron Yeats, Willie
Stevenson, Ian Callaghan,
Roger Hunt, Ian St John,
Bobby Graham, Peter
Thompson.

United: Pat Dunne,
Seamus Brennan, Tony
Dunne, Pat Crerand, Bill
Foulkes, Nobby Stiles,
John Connelly, Bobby
Charlton, David Herd,
Denis Law, George Best.

Attendance: 52,402

Division One:
24 April 1965,
at Old Trafford.

MANCHESTER UNITED 3

Law 40, 57; Connelly 81

LIVERPOOL 0

Half-time: 1-0

United: Pat Dunne,
Seamus Brennan, Tony
Dunne, Pat Crerand, Bill
Foulkes, Nobby Stiles,
John Connelly, Bobby
Charlton, Noel Cantwell,
Denis Law, George Best.

Liverpool: Tommy
Lawrence, Chris Lawler,
Gerry Byrne, Geoff Strong,
Ron Yeats, Willie
Stevenson, Bobby Graham,
Roger Hunt, Phil Chisnall,
Tommy Smith, Peter
Thompson.

Attendance: 55,772

1965/6

Liverpool:
Division One Champions,
FA Cup third round,
European Cup-Winners'
Cup finalists.

United:
fourth in Division One,
FA Cup semi-finalists,
European Cup semi-finalists.

FA Charity Shield:
14 August 1965,
at Old Trafford.

MANCHESTER UNITED 2

Best 30; Herd 82

LIVERPOOL 2

Stevenson 38; Yeats 86

Half-time: 1-1

United: Pat Dunne, Seamus
Brennan, Tony Dunne, Pat
Crerand, Noel Cantwell,
Nobby Stiles, George Best,
Bobby Charlton, David
Herd, Denis Law, John
Aston. Sub: Willie
Anderson for Law (18).

Liverpool: Tommy
Lawrence, Chris Lawler,
Gerry Byrne, Gordon Milne,
Ron Yeats, Willie
Stevenson, Ian Callaghan,
Roger Hunt, Ian St John,
Tommy Smith, Geoff Strong.

Attendance: 48,502

Division One:
9 October 1965,
at Old Trafford.

MANCHESTER UNITED 2

Best 18; Law 37

LIVERPOOL 0

Half-time: 2-0

United: Pat Dunne,
Seamus Brennan, Tony
Dunne, Pat Crerand, Bill
Foulkes, Nobby Stiles,
John Connelly, George
Best, Bobby Charlton,
Denis Law, John Aston.

Liverpool: Tommy
Lawrence, Chris Lawler,
Roger Byrne, Geoff
Strong, Ron Yeats, Willie
Stevenson, Ian Callaghan,
Roger Hunt, Ian St John,
Tommy Smith, Peter
Thompson.

Attendance: 58,161

Division One:
1 January 1966,
at Anfield.

LIVERPOOL 2

Smith 39; Milne 88

MANCHESTER UNITED 1

Law 2

Half-time: 1-1

Liverpool: Tommy
Lawrence, Chris Lawler,
Gerry Byrne, Gordon
Milne, Ron Yeats, Willie
Stevenson, Ian Callaghan,
Roger Hunt, Ian St John,
Tommy Smith, Peter
Thompson.

United: Harry Gregg, Tony
Dunne, Noel Cantwell, Pat
Crerand, Bill Foulkes,
Nobby Stiles, George Best,
Denis Law, Bobby Charlton,
David Herd, John Connelly.

Attendance: 53,970

1966/7

United:
Division One Champions,
FA Cup fourth round,
League Cup second round.

Liverpool:
fifth in Division One,
FA Cup fifth round,
European Cup second round.

Division One:
10 December 1966,
at Old Trafford.

MANCHESTER UNITED 2

Best 16, 27 (pen)

LIVERPOOL 2

St John 13, 45

Half-time: 2-2

United: Alex Stepney,
Seamus Brennan, Bobby
Noble, Pat Crerand, David
Sadler, Tony Dunne,
George Best, Jim Ryan,
Bobby Charlton, David
Herd, John Aston. Sub:
Willie Anderson for Tony
Dunne (60).

Liverpool: Tommy Lawrence,
Chris Lawler, Gordon Milne,
Tommy Smith, Ron Yeats,
Willie Stevenson, Ian
Callaghan, Roger Hunt, Ian
St John, Geoff Strong, Peter
Thompson.

Attendance: 62,500

Division One:
25 March 1967,
at Anfield.

LIVERPOOL 0
MANCHESTER UNITED 0

Liverpool: Tommy
Lawrence, Chris Lawler,
Emlyn Hughes, Tommy
Smith, Ron Yeats, Willie
Stevenson, Ian Callaghan,
Roger Hunt, Ian St John,
Geoff Strong, Peter
Thompson.

United: Alex Stepney, Tony
Dunne, Bobby Noble, Pat
Crerand, Bill Foulkes,
Nobby Stiles, George
Best, Denis Law, David
Sadler, Bobby Charlton,
John Aston.

Attendance: 53,813

1967/8

United:
Division One runners-up,
FA Cup third round,
European Cup winners.

Liverpool:
third in Division One,
FA Cup quarter-finalists,
League Cup second round,
European Fairs Cup third
round.

Division One:
11 November 1967
at Anfield

LIVERPOOL 1

Hunt 83

MANCHESTER UNITED 2

Best 18, 40

Half-time: 0-2

Liverpool: Tommy
Lawrence, Chris Lawler,
Gerry Byrne, Tommy
Smith, Ron Yeats, Emlyn
Hughes, Ian Callaghan,
Roger Hunt, Tony Hateley,
Ian St John, Peter
Thompson.

United: Alex Stepney, Tony
Dunne, Francis Burns, Pat
Crerand, Bill Foulkes,
David Sadler, John
Fitzpatrick, Brian Kidd,
Bobby Charlton, George
Best, John Aston.

Attendance: 54,515

Division One:
6 April 1968,
at Old Trafford.

MANCHESTER UNITED 1

Best 2

LIVERPOOL 2

Yeats 9; Hunt 17

Half-time: 1-2

United: Alex Stepney, Tony Dunne, Francis Burns, Pat Crerand, David Sadler, John Fitzpatrick, George Best, Alan Gowling, Bobby Charlton, David Herd, John Aston.

Liverpool: Tommy Lawrence, Chris Lawler, Ian Ross, Geoff Strong, Ron Yeats, Emlyn Hughes, Ian Callaghan, Roger Hunt, Tony Hateley, Ian St John, Peter Thompson.

Attendance: 63,059

1968/9

Liverpool:
Division One runners-up, FA Cup fifth round, League Cup fourth round, European Fairs Cup first round.

United:
eleventh in Division One, FA Cup quarter-finalists, European Cup semi-finalists.

Division One:
12 October 1968,
at Anfield.

LIVERPOOL 2

St John 14; Evans 82

MANCHESTER UNITED 0

Half-time: 1-0

Liverpool: Tommy Lawrence, Chris Lawler, Geoff Strong, Tommy Smith, Ron Yeats, Emlyn Hughes, Ian Callaghan, Roger Hunt, Alun Evans, Ian St John, Peter Thompson.

United: Alex Stepney, Seamus Brennan, Frank Kopel, Pat Crerand, Steve James, Nobby Stiles, Jim Ryan, John Fitzpatrick, Bobby Charlton, Alan Gowling, Carlo Sartori.

Attendance: 53,392

Division One:
14 December 1968,
at Old Trafford.

MANCHESTER UNITED 1

Law 53

LIVERPOOL 0

Half-time: 0-0

United: Alex Stepney, Tony Dunne, Francis Burns, Pat Crerand, Steve James, Nobby Stiles, George Best, David Sadler, Bobby Charlton, Denis Law, Carlo Sartori.

Liverpool: Tommy Lawrence, Chris Lawler, Geoff Strong, Tommy Smith, Ron Yeats, Emlyn Hughes, Roger Hunt, Alun Evans, Ian St John, Peter Thompson.

Attendance: 59,000

1969/70

Liverpool:
fifth in Division One, FA Cup quarter-finalists, League Cup third round, European Fairs Cup 2nd round.

United:
eighth in Division One, FA Cup semi-finalists, League Cup semi-finalists.

Division One:
13 September 1969,
at Old Trafford.

MANCHESTER UNITED 1

Morgan 67

LIVERPOOL 0

Half-time: 0-0

United: Alex Stepney, John Fitzpatrick, Tony Dunne, Francis Burns, Ian Ure, David Sadler, Willie Morgan, Brian Kidd, Bobby Charlton, Alan Gowling, George Best.

Liverpool: Tommy Lawrence, Chris Lawler, Geoff Strong, Tommy Smith, Ron Yeats, Emlyn Hughes, Ian Callaghan, Roger Hunt, Bobby Graham, Ian St John, Peter Thompson.

Attendance: 59,387

Division One:
13 December 1969,
at Anfield.

LIVERPOOL 1

Hughes 25

MANCHESTER UNITED 4

Yeats og 20; Ure 59; Morgan 64; Charlton 83

Half-time: 1-1

Liverpool: Tommy Lawrence, Chris Lawler, Peter Wall, Geoff Strong, Ron Yeats, Emlyn Hughes, Ian Callaghan, Ian Ross, Peter Thompson, Ian St John, Bobby Graham. Sub: Roger Hunt for Ross (70).

United: Alex Stepney, Seamus Brennan, Tony Dunne, Francis Burns, Ian Ure, David Sadler, Willie Morgan, George Best, Bobby Charlton, Pat Crerand, John Aston. Sub: Carlo Sartori for Aston (75).

Attendance: 47,682

1970/71

Liverpool:
fifth in Division One, FA Cup finalists, League Cup third round, European Fairs Cup semi-finalists.

United:
eighth in Division One, FA Cup third round, League Cup semi-finalists.

Division One:
5 September 1970,
at Anfield.

LIVERPOOL 1

A Evans 22

MANCHESTER UNITED 1

Kidd 20

Half-time: 1-1

Liverpool: Ray Clemence, Chris Lawler, Roy Evans, Tommy Smith, Larry Lloyd, Emlyn Hughes, Ian Callaghan, Alun Evans, Bobby Graham, John McLaughlin, Peter Thompson.

United: Jimmy Rimmer, Paul Edwards, Tony Dunne, John Fitzpatrick, Ian Ure, David Sadler, Nobby Stiles, Denis Law, Bobby Charlton, Brian Kidd, George Best.

Attendance: 52,542

Division One:
19 April 1971,
at Old Trafford.

MANCHESTER UNITED 0

LIVERPOOL 2

Heighway 20; Edwards og 60

Half-time: 0-1

United: Alex Stepney, Tony Dunne, Francis Burns, Pat Crerand, Paul Edwards, David Sadler, George Best, Alan Gowling, Bobby Charlton, Denis Law, Willie Morgan.

Liverpool: Ray Clemence, Chris Lawler, Ron Yeats, Tommy Smith, Ian Ross, John McLaughlin, Ian Callaghan, Peter Thompson, Steve Heighway, John Toshack, Brian Hall.

Attendance: 44,004

1971/2

Liverpool:
third in Division One, FA Cup fourth round, League Cup fourth round, European Cup-Winners' Cup second round.

United:
eighth in Division One, FA Cup quarter-finalists, League Cup fourth round.

Division One:
25 September 1971,
at Anfield.

LIVERPOOL 2

Graham 8; Hall 25

MANCHESTER UNITED 2

Law 53; Charlton 72

Half-time: 2-0

Liverpool: Ray Clemence, Chris Lawler, Alec Lindsay, Ian Ross, Larry Lloyd, Emlyn Hughes, Kevin Keegan, Brian Hall, Steve Heighway, Bobby Graham, Ian Callaghan.

United: Alex Stepney, Tommy O'Neil, Francis Burns, Alan Gowling, Steve James, David Sadler, Willie Morgan, Brian Kidd, Bobby Charlton, Denis Law, George Best.

Attendance: 55,642

Division One:
3 April 1972,
at Old Trafford.

MANCHESTER UNITED 0

LIVERPOOL 3

Lawler 59; Toshack 61; Hughes 85

Half-time: 0-0

United: Alex Stepney, Tommy O'Neil, Tony Dunne, Martin Buchan, Steve James, Alan Gowling, Willie Morgan, George Best, Bobby Charlton, Denis Law, Ian Moore. Sub: Tony Young for Law (75).

Liverpool: Ray Clemence, Chris Lawler, Alec Lindsay, Tommy Smith, Larry Lloyd, Emlyn Hughes, Kevin Keegan, Brian Hall, Steve Heighway, John Toshack, Ian Callaghan. Sub: Phil Thompson for Toshack (80).

Attendance: 54,000

1972/3

Liverpool:
Division One Champions, FA Cup fourth round, League Cup quarter-finalists, UEFA Cup winners.

United:
eighteenth in Division One, FA Cup third round, League Cup third round.

Division One:
15 August 1972,
at Anfield.

LIVERPOOL 2

Toshack 12; Heighway 20

MANCHESTER UNITED 0

Half-time: 2-0

Liverpool: Ray Clemence, Chris Lawler, Alec Lindsay, Tommy Smith, Larry Lloyd, Emlyn Hughes, Kevin Keegan, Brian Hall, Steve Heighway, John Toshack, Ian Callaghan.

United: Alex Stepney, Tommy O'Neil, Tony Dunne, Tony Young, Steve James, Martin Buchan, Willie Morgan, Brian Kidd, Bobby Charlton, George Best, Ian Moore. Sub: Sammy McIlroy for Kidd (77).

Attendance: 54,778

Division One:
11 November 1972,
at Old Trafford.

MANCHESTER UNITED 2

Davies 44; MacDougall 54

LIVERPOOL 0

Half-time: 1-0

United: Alex Stepney, Tommy O'Neil, Tony Dunne, Willie Morgan, David Sadler, Martin Buchan, George Best, Ted MacDougall, Bobby Charlton, Wyn Davies, Ian Moore. Sub: Sammy McIlroy for Dunne (68).

Liverpool: Ray Clemence, Chris Lawler, Alec Lindsay, Tommy Smith, Larry Lloyd, Emlyn Hughes, Kevin Keegan, Peter Cormack, Steve Heighway, John Toshack, Ian Callaghan. Sub: Phil Thompson for Heighway (80).

Attendance: 53,944

1973/4

Liverpool:
Division One runners-up,
FA Cup winners,
League Cup quarter-finalists,
European Cup second round.

United:
twenty-first in Division One (relegated),
FA Cup fourth round,
League Cup second round.

Division One:
29 September 1973
at Old Trafford

MANCHESTER UNITED 0

LIVERPOOL 0

United: Alex Stepney, Martin Buchan, Tony Young, Brian Greenhoff, Jim Holton, Steve James, Willie Morgan, Trevor Anderson, Lou Macari, Brian Kidd, George Graham. Sub: George Buchan for Graham (75).

Liverpool: Ray Clemence, Chris Lawler, Alec Lindsay, Tommy Smith, Larry Lloyd, Emlyn Hughes, Kevin Keegan, Peter Cormack, Steve Heighway, Brian Hall, Ian Callaghan.

Attendance: 53,882

Division One:
22 December 1973,
at Anfield.

LIVERPOOL 2

Keegan 30 (pen); Heighway 66

MANCHESTER UNITED 0

Half-time: 1-0

Liverpool: Ray Clemence, Tommy Smith, Roy Evans, Phil Thompson, Larry Lloyd, Emlyn Hughes, Kevin Keegan, Peter Cormack, Alan Waddle, Steve Heighway, Ian Callaghan.

United: Alex Stepney, Martin Buchan, Tony Young, Brian Greenhoff, Arnold Sidebottom, Clive Griffiths, Willie Morgan, Lou Macari, Brian Kidd, George Graham, George Best. Sub: Sammy McIlroy for Kidd (45).

Attendance: 40,420

1975/6

Liverpool:
Division One Champions,
FA Cup fourth round,
League Cup third round,
UEFA Cup winners.

United:
third in Division One,
FA Cup finalists,
League Cup fourth round.

Division One:
8 November 1975,
at Anfield.

LIVERPOOL 3

Heighway 12; Toshack 46; Keegan 78

MANCHESTER UNITED 1

Coppell 52

Half-time: 1-0

Liverpool: Ray Clemence, Phil Neal, Joey Jones, Phil Thompson, Brian Hall, Emlyn Hughes, Kevin Keegan, Ray Kennedy, Steve Heighway, John Toshack, Ian Callaghan.

United: Paddy Roche, Jimmy Nicholl, Stewart Houston, Tommy Jackson, Brian Greenhoff, Martin Buchan, Steve Coppell, Sammy McIlroy, Stuart Pearson, Lou Macari, Gerry Daly. Sub: David McCreery for Jackson (64).

Attendance: 49,136

Division One:
18 February 1976,
at Old Trafford.

MANCHESTER UNITED 0

LIVERPOOL 0

United: Alex Stepney, Alex Forsyth, Stewart Houston, Gerry Daly, Brian Greenhoff, Martin Buchan, Steve Coppell, Sammy McIlroy, Stuart Pearson, Lou Macari, Gordon Hill. Sub: David McCreery for McIlroy (70).

Liverpool: Ray Clemence, Tommy Smith, Phil Neal, Phil Thompson, Ray Kennedy, Emlyn Hughes, Kevin Keegan, Jimmy Case, Steve Heighway, John Toshack, Ian Callaghan.

Attendance: 59,709

1976/7

Liverpool:
Division One Champions,
FA Cup finalists,
League Cup second round,
European Cup winners.

United:
sixth in Division One,
FA Cup winners,
League Cup quarter-finalists,
UEFA Cup second round.

Division One:
16 February 1977,
at Old Trafford.

MANCHESTER UNITED 0

LIVERPOOL 0

United: Alex Stepney, Jimmy Nicholl, Stewart Houston, Sammy McIlroy, Brian Greenhoff, Martin Buchan, Steve Coppell, Jimmy Greenhoff, Stuart Pearson, Lou Macari, Gordon Hill.

Liverpool: Ray Clemence, Phil Neal, Joey Jones, Phil Thompson, Ray Kennedy, Emlyn Hughes, Kevin Keegan, Jimmy Case, Steve Heighway, John Toshack, Ian Callaghan.

Attendance: 57,487

Division One:
3 May 1977,
at Anfield.

LIVERPOOL 1

Keegan 15

MANCHESTER UNITED 0

Half-time: 1-0

Liverpool: Ray Clemence, Phil Neal, Joey Jones, Tommy Smith, Ray Kennedy, Emlyn Hughes, Kevin Keegan, Jimmy Case, David Johnson, David Fairclough, Terry McDermott.

United: Alex Stepney, Jimmy Nicholl, Stewart Houston, Sammy McIlroy, Alex Forsyth, Arthur Albiston, Steve Coppell, Jimmy Greenhoff, Stuart Pearson, Lou Macari, Gordon Hill. Sub: David McCreery for Jimmy Greenhoff (65).

Attendance: 53,046

FA Cup Final:
21 May 1977,
at Wembley.

MANCHESTER UNITED 2

Pearson 50; J Greenhoff 55

LIVERPOOL 1

Case 52

Half-time: 0-0

United: Alex Stepney, Jimmy Nicholl, Arthur Albiston, Sammy McIlroy, Brian Greenhoff, Martin Buchan, Steve Coppell, Jimmy Greenhoff, Stuart Pearson, Lou Macari, Gordon Hill. Sub: David McCreery for Hill (82).

Liverpool: Ray Clemence, Phil Neal, Joey Jones, Tommy Smith, Ray Kennedy, Emlyn Hughes, Kevin Keegan, Jimmy Case, Steve Heighway, David Johnson, Terry McDermott. Sub: Ian Callaghan for Johnson (63).

Attendance: 100,000

1977/8

Liverpool:
Division One runners-up,
FA Cup third round,
League Cup finalists,
European Cup winners.

United:
tenth in Division One,
FA Cup fourth round,
League Cup second round,
European Cup-Winners' Cup second round.

FA Charity Shield:
13 August 1977,
at Wembley.

LIVERPOOL 0

MANCHESTER UNITED 0

Liverpool: Ray Clemence, Phil Neal, Joey Jones, Phil Thompson, Ray Kennedy, Emlyn Hughes, Kenny Dalglish, Jimmy Case, David Fairclough, Terry McDermott, Ian Callaghan.

United: Alex Stepney, Jimmy Nicholl, Arthur Albiston, Sammy McIlroy, Brian Greenhoff, Martin Buchan, Steve Coppell, Jimmy Greenhoff, Stuart Pearson, Lou Macari, Gordon Hill. Sub: David McCreery for Jimmy Greenhoff (23).

Attendance: 82,000

Division One:
1 Oct 1977,
at Old Trafford.

MANCHESTER UNITED 2

Macari 62; McIlroy 69

LIVERPOOL 0

Half-time: 0-0

United: Alex Stepney, Jimmy Nicholl, Arthur Albiston, Sammy McIlroy, Brian Greenhoff, Martin Buchan, Chris McGrath, Steve Coppell, Jimmy Greenhoff, Lou Macari, Gordon Hill.

Liverpool: Ray Clemence, Phil Neal, Joey Jones, Tommy Smith, Ray Kennedy, Alan Hansen, Kenny Dalglish, Jimmy Case, David Fairclough, Terry McDermott, Ian Callaghan.

Attendance: 55,089

Division One:
25 February 1978,
at Anfield.

LIVERPOOL 3

Souness 38; R Kennedy
49; Case 84

MANCHESTER UNITED 1

McIlroy 60

Half-time: 1-0

Liverpool: Ray Clemence,
Phil Neal, Tommy Smith,
Phil Thompson, Ray
Kennedy, Emlyn Hughes,
Kenny Dalglish, Graeme
Souness, Steve Heighway,
David Fairclough, Terry
McDermott. Sub: Jimmy
Case for Fairclough (65).

United: Paddy Roche, Jimmy
Nicholl, Arthur Albiston,
Sammy McIlroy, Gordon
McQueen, Stewart Houston,
Steve Coppell, Joe Jordan,
Stuart Pearson, Lou Macari,
Gordon Hill.

Attendance: 49,094

1978/9

Liverpool:
Division One Champions,
FA Cup semi-finalists,
League Cup second round,
European Cup first round.

United:
ninth in Division One,
FA Cup finalists,
League Cup 3rd round.

Division One:
26 December 1978,
at Old Trafford.

MANCHESTER UNITED 0

LIVERPOOL 3

R Kennedy 5; Case 24;
Fairclough 67

Half-time: 0-2

United: Gary Bailey, Brian
Greenhoff, Tom Connell,
Sammy McIlroy, Gordon
McQueen, Martin Buchan,
Steve Coppell, Jimmy
Greenhoff, Andy Ritchie, Lou
Macari, Mickey Thomas.

Liverpool: Ray Clemence,
Phil Neal, Emlyn Hughes,
Phil Thompson, Ray
Kennedy, Alan Hansen,
Kenny Dalglish, Jimmy
Case, David Fairclough,
Terry McDermott, Graeme
Souness.

Attendance: 54,910

FA Cup semi-final:
31 March 1979,
at Maine Road.

MANCHESTER UNITED 2

Jordan 20; B Greenhoff 56

LIVERPOOL 2

Dalglish 18; Hansen 82

Half-time: 1-1

United: Gary Bailey, Jimmy
Nicholl, Arthur Albiston,
Sammy McIlroy, Gordon
McQueen, Martin Buchan,
Steve Coppell, Jimmy
Greenhoff, Joe Jordan,
Brian Greenhoff, Mickey
Thomas.

Liverpool: Ray Clemence,
Phil Neal, Emlyn Hughes,
Phil Thompson, Ray
Kennedy, Alan Hansen,
Kenny Dalglish, David
Johnson, Jimmy Case,
Terry McDermott, Graeme
Souness. Sub: Steve
Heighway for Case (63).

Attendance: 52,524

FA Cup semi-final replay:
4 April 1979,
at Goodison Park.

MANCHESTER UNITED 1

J Greenhoff 78

LIVERPOOL 0

Half-time: 0-0

United: Gary Bailey, Jimmy
Nicholl, Arthur Albiston,
Sammy McIlroy, Gordon
McQueen, Martin Buchan,
Steve Coppell, Jimmy
Greenhoff, Joe Jordan,
Lou Macari, Mickey
Thomas. Sub: Andy Ritchie
for Macari (78).

Liverpool: Ray Clemence,
Phil Neal, Emlyn Hughes,
Phil Thompson, Ray
Kennedy, Alan Hansen,
Kenny Dalglish, David
Johnson, Steve Heighway,
Terry McDermott, Graeme
Souness. Sub: Jimmy Case
for Johnson (82).

Attendance: 53,069

Division One:
14 April 1979,
at Anfield.

LIVERPOOL 2

Dalglish 36; Neal 47

MANCHESTER UNITED 0

Half-time: 1-0

Liverpool: Ray Clemence,
Phil Neal, Alan Kennedy,
Phil Thompson, Ray
Kennedy, Alan Hansen,
Kenny Dalglish, Jimmy
Case, David Johnson,
Terry McDermott, Graeme
Souness.

United: Gary Bailey, Jimmy
Nicholl, Arthur Albiston,
Sammy McIlroy, Brian
Greenhoff, Martin Buchan,
Steve Coppell, Andy
Ritchie, Joe Jordan, Lou
Macari, Mickey Thomas.
Sub: Stewart Houston for
Ritchie (54).

Attendance: 46,608

1979/80

Liverpool:
Division One Champions,
FA Cup semi-finalists,
League Cup semi-finalists,
European Cup first round.

United:
Division One runners-up,
FA Cup third round,
League Cup third round.

Division One:
26 December 1979,
at Anfield.

LIVERPOOL 2

Hansen 15; Johnson 85

MANCHESTER UNITED 0

Half-time: 1-0

Liverpool: Ray Clemence,
Phil Neal, Alan Kennedy,
Phil Thompson, Ray
Kennedy, Alan Hansen,
Kenny Dalglish, Jimmy
Case, David Johnson, Terry
McDermott, Graeme
Souness.

United: Gary Bailey, Jimmy
Nicholl, Stewart Houston,
Sammy McIlroy, Gordon
McQueen, Martin Buchan,
Steve Coppell, Ray Wilkins,
Joe Jordan, Lou Macari,
Mickey Thomas. Sub: Ashley
Grimes for Thomas (77).

Attendance: 51,073

Division One:
5 April 1980,
at Old Trafford.

MANCHESTER UNITED 2

Thomas 20; Greenhoff 65

LIVERPOOL 1

Dalglish 14

Half-time: 1-1

United: Gary Bailey, Jimmy
Nicholl, Arthur Albiston,
Jimmy Greenhoff, Gordon
McQueen, Martin Buchan,
Steve Coppell, Ray
Wilkins, Joe Jordan, Lou
Macari, Mickey Thomas.

Liverpool: Ray Clemence,
Phil Neal, Alan Kennedy,
Phil Thompson, Ray
Kennedy, Alan Hansen,
Kenny Dalglish, Jimmy
Case, David Johnson,
Terry McDermott, Graeme
Souness. Sub: Sammy Lee
for Alan Kennedy (21).

Attendance: 57,342

1980/81

Liverpool:
fifth in Division One,
FA Cup fourth round,
League Cup winners,
European Cup winners.

United:
eighth in Division One,
FA Cup fourth round,
League Cup second round,
UEFA Cup first round.

Division One:
26 December 1980,
at Old Trafford.

MANCHESTER UNITED 0

LIVERPOOL 0

United: Gary Bailey, Jimmy
Nicholl, Arthur Albiston,
Sammy McIlroy, Nikola
Jovanovic, Kevin Moran,
Steve Coppell, Mike
Duxbury, Joe Jordan, Lou
Macari, Mickey Thomas.

Liverpool: Ray Clemence,
Phil Neal, Alan Kennedy,
Colin Irwin, Ray Kennedy,
Alan Hansen, Kenny
Dalglish, Sammy Lee,
David Johnson, Terry
McDermott, Jimmy Case.
Sub: Richard Money for
Hansen (61).

Attendance: 57,049

Division One:
14 April 1981,
at Anfield.

LIVERPOOL 0

MANCHESTER UNITED 1

McQueen 7

Half-time: 0-1

Liverpool: Ray Clemence,
Phil Neal, Richard Money,
Phil Thompson, Ray
Kennedy, Alan Hansen,
Kenny Dalglish, Sammy
Lee, Ian Rush, Terry
McDermott, Jimmy Case.

United: Gary Bailey, Mike
Duxbury, Arthur Albiston,
Kevin Moran, Gordon
McQueen, Martin Buchan,
Steve Coppell, Garry
Birtles, Joe Jordan, Lou
Macari, Ray Wilkins.

Attendance: 31,276

1981/2

Liverpool:
Division One Champions,
FA Cup fifth round,
League Cup winners,
European Cup third round.

United: third in Division
One, FA Cup third round,
League Cup second round.

Division One:
24 October 1981,
at Anfield.

LIVERPOOL 1

McDermott 74 (pen)

MANCHESTER UNITED 2

Moran 25; Albiston 89

Half-time: 0-1

Liverpool: Bruce
Grobbelaar, Phil Neal,
Mark Lawrenson, Phil
Thompson, Ray Kennedy,
Alan Hansen, Kenny
Dalglish, Sammy Lee,
David Johnson, Terry
McDermott, Graeme
Souness. Sub: Ronnie
Whelan for Johnson (69).

United: Gary Bailey, John
Gidman, Arthur Albiston,
Ray Wilkins, Kevin Moran,
Martin Buchan, Bryan
Robson, Garry Birtles,
Frank Stapleton, Remi
Moses, Steve Coppell.

Attendance: 41,438

Division One:
7 April 1982,
at Old Trafford.

MANCHESTER UNITED 0

LIVERPOOL 1

Johnston 63

Half-time: 0-0

United: Gary Bailey, Mike Duxbury, Arthur Albiston, Ray Wilkins, Kevin Moran, Martin Buchan, Bryan Robson, Scott McGarvey, Frank Stapleton, Remi Moses, Steve Coppell. Sub: Ashley Grimes for Buchan (86).

Liverpool: Bruce Grobbelaar, Phil Neal, Alan Kennedy, Mark Lawrenson, Ronnie Whelan, Phil Thompson, Kenny Dalglish, Sammy Lee, Ian Rush, Craig Johnston, Graeme Souness. Sub: Terry McDermott for Souness (46).

Attendance: 48,371

1982/3

Liverpool:
Division One Champions,
FA Cup fifth round,
League Cup winners,
European Cup third round.

United:
third in Division One,
FA Cup winners,
League Cup finalists,
UEFA Cup first round.

Division One:
16 October 1982,
at Anfield.

LIVERPOOL 0

MANCHESTER UNITED 0

Liverpool: Bruce Grobbelaar, Phil Neal, Alan Kennedy, Phil Thompson, Ronnie Whelan, Alan Hansen, Kenny Dalglish, Sammy Lee, Ian Rush, Mark Lawrenson, Graeme Souness.

United: Gary Bailey, Mike Duxbury, Arthur Albiston, Ray Wilkins, Kevin Moran, Gordon McQueen, Bryan Robson, Ashley Grimes, Frank Stapleton, Norman Whiteside, Steve Coppell.

Attendance: 40,853

Division One:
26 February 1983,
at Old Trafford.

MANCHESTER UNITED 1

Muhren 36

LIVERPOOL 1

Dalglish 40

Half-time: 1-1

United: Gary Bailey, Mike Duxbury, Arthur Albiston, Remi Moses, Kevin Moran, Gordon McQueen, Ray Wilkins, Arnold Muhren, Frank Stapleton, Norman Whiteside, Steve Coppell. Sub: Lou Macari for Moran (29).

Liverpool: Bruce Grobbelaar, Phil Neal, Alan Kennedy, Phil Thompson, Ronnie Whelan, Mark Lawrenson, Kenny Dalglish, Sammy Lee, Ian Rush, Craig Johnston, Graeme Souness.

Attendance: 57,397

League Cup Final:
26 March 1983,
at Wembley.

LIVERPOOL 2

Kennedy 75; Whelan 99

MANCHESTER UNITED 1

Whiteside 12

After extra-time

Half-time: 0-1. After 90 minutes: 1-1

Liverpool: Bruce Grobbelaar, Phil Neal, Alan Kennedy, Mark Lawrenson, Ronnie Whelan, Alan Hansen, Kenny Dalglish, Sammy Lee, Ian Rush, Craig Johnston, Graeme Souness. Sub: David Fairclough for Johnston (83).

United: Gary Bailey, Mike Duxbury, Arthur Albiston, Remi Moses, Kevin Moran, Gordon McQueen, Ray Wilkins, Arnold Muhren, Frank Stapleton, Norman Whiteside, Steve Coppell. Sub: Lou Macari for Moran (70).

Attendance: 100,000

1983/4

Liverpool:
Division One Champions,
FA Cup fourth round,
League Cup winners,
European Cup winners.

United:
fourth in Division One,
FA Cup third round,
League Cup fourth round,
European Cup-Winners' Cup semi-finalists.

Friendly
(Billy Drennan Testimonial):
3 August 1983,
at Windsor Park, Belfast.

LIVERPOOL 3

Souness 9; Rush 24, 39

MANCHESTER UNITED 4

Whiteside 38; Moran 66; Macari 84, 89

Half-time: 3-1

Liverpool: Bruce Grobbelaar, Phil Neal, Alan Kennedy, Mark Lawrenson, Alan Hansen, Craig Johnston, Graeme Souness, Sammy Lee, David Hodgson, Kenny Dalglish, Ian Rush.

United: Gary Bailey, Mike Duxbury, Arthur Albiston, Kevin Moran, Gordon McQueen, Bryan Robson, Arnold Muhren, Ray Wilkins, Arthur Graham, Norman Whiteside, Frank Stapleton. Subs: John Gidman for Duxbury (45), Remi Moses for Muhren (45), Ashley Grimes for Wilkins (45), Paul McGrath for McQueen (60), Lou Macari for Whiteside (60), Alan Davies for Graham (66).

Attendance: 30,000

Charity Shield:
20 August 1983,
at Wembley.

MANCHESTER UNITED 2

Robson 23, 60

LIVERPOOL 0

Half-time: 1-0

United: Gary Bailey, Mike Duxbury, Arthur Albiston, Ray Wilkins, Kevin Moran,

Gordon McQueen, Bryan Robson, Arnold Muhren, Frank Stapleton, Norman Whiteside, Arthur Graham. Sub: John Gidman for Muhren (65).

Liverpool: Bruce Grobbelaar, Phil Neal, Alan Kennedy, Mark Lawrenson, Phil Thompson, Alan Hansen, Kenny Dalglish, Sammy Lee, Ian Rush, Michael Robinson, Graeme Souness. Subs: Craig Johnston for Thompson (60), David Hodgson for Robinson (60).

Attendance: 92,000

Division One:
24 September,
at Old Trafford.

MANCHESTER UNITED 1

Stapleton 52

LIVERPOOL 0

Half-time: 0-0

United: Gary Bailey, Mike Duxbury, Arthur Albiston, Ray Wilkins, Kevin Moran, Gordon McQueen, Bryan Robson, Arnold Muhren, Frank Stapleton, Norman Whiteside, Arthur Graham.

Liverpool: Bruce Grobbelaar, Phil Neal, Alan Kennedy, Mark Lawrenson, Craig Johnston, Alan Hansen, Kenny Dalglish, Sammy Lee, Ian Rush, Michael Robinson, Graeme Souness. Sub: Steve Nicol for Neal (77).

Attendance: 56,121

Division One:
2 January 1984,
at Anfield.

LIVERPOOL 1

Johnston 32

MANCHESTER UNITED 1

Whiteside 88

Half-time: 1-0

Liverpool: Bruce Grobbelaar, Phil Neal, Alan Kennedy, Mark Lawrenson, Steve Nicol, Alan Hansen,

Kenny Dalglish, Sammy Lee, Ian Rush, Craig Johnston, Graeme Souness. Sub: David Hodgson for Dalglish (48).

United: Gary Bailey, Mike Duxbury, Arthur Albiston, Ray Wilkins, Kevin Moran, Gordon McQueen, Remi Moses, Arnold Muhren, Frank Stapleton, Norman Whiteside, Arthur Graham. Sub: Garth Crooks for McQueen (21).

Attendance: 45,122

1984/5

Liverpool:
second in Division One,
FA Cup semi-finalists,
League Cup third round,
European Cup finalists.

United:
fourth in Division One,
FA Cup winners,
League Cup third round,
UEFA Cup quarter-finalists.

Division One:
22 September 1984,
at Old Trafford.

MANCHESTER UNITED 1

Strachan 20 (pen)

LIVERPOOL 1

Walsh 73

Half-time: 1-0

United: Gary Bailey, Mike Duxbury, Arthur Albiston, Remi Moses, Kevin Moran, Graeme Hogg, Bryan Robson, Gordon Strachan, Mark Hughes, Norman Whiteside, Jesper Olsen. Sub: Arnold Muhren for Moran (85).

Liverpool: Bruce Grobbelaar, Phil Neal, Alan Kennedy, Mark Lawrenson, Ronnie Whelan, Alan Hansen, Kenny Dalglish, Sammy Lee, Paul Walsh, John Wark, Steve Nicol.

Attendance: 56,638

Division One:
31 March 1985,
at Anfield.

LIVERPOOL 0

MANCHESTER UNITED 1

Stapleton 77

Half-time: 0-0

Liverpool: Bruce Grobbelaar, Phil Neal, Alan Kennedy, Mark Lawrenson, Steve Nicol, Alan Hansen, Kenny Dalglish, Ronnie Whelan, Ian Rush, Kevin MacDonald, John Wark. Sub: Paul Walsh for Kennedy (42).

United: Gary Bailey, John Gidman, Arthur Albiston, Norman Whiteside, Paul McGrath, Graeme Hogg, Bryan Robson, Gordon Strachan, Mark Hughes, Frank Stapleton, Jesper Olsen.

Attendance: 34,886

FA Cup semi-final:
13 April 1985,
at Goodison Park.

MANCHESTER UNITED 2

Robson 70; Stapleton 99

LIVERPOOL 2

Whelan 87; Walsh 120

After extra-time

Half-time: 0-0. After 90 minutes: 1-1

United: Gary Bailey, John Gidman, Arthur Albiston, Norman Whiteside, Paul McGrath, Graeme Hogg, Bryan Robson, Gordon Strachan, Mark Hughes, Frank Stapleton, Jesper Olsen.

Liverpool: Bruce Grobbelaar, Phil Neal, Jim Beglin, Mark Lawrenson, Sammy Lee, Alan Hansen, Kenny Dalglish, Ronnie Whelan, Ian Rush, Kevin MacDonald, John Wark. Sub: Paul Walsh for Wark (58).

Attendance: 51,690

FA Cup semi-final replay:
17 April 1985,
at Maine Road.

MANCHESTER UNITED 2

Robson 46; Hughes 57

LIVERPOOL 1

McGrath og 38

Half-time: 0-1

United: Gary Bailey, John Gidman, Arthur Albiston, Norman Whiteside, Paul McGrath, Graeme Hogg, Bryan Robson, Gordon Strachan, Mark Hughes, Frank Stapleton, Jesper Olsen.

Liverpool: Bruce Grobbelaar, Phil Neal, Jim Beglin, Mark Lawrenson, Steve Nicol, Alan Hansen, Kenny Dalglish, Ronnie Whelan, Paul Walsh, Kevin MacDonald, John Wark. Sub: Gary Gillespie for Dalglish (79).

Attendance: 45,775

1985/6

Liverpool:
Division One Champions, FA Cup winners, League Cup semi-finalists;

United:
fourth in Division One, FA Cup fifth round, League Cup fourth round.

Division One:
19 October 1985,
at Old Trafford.

MANCHESTER UNITED 1

McGrath 64

LIVERPOOL 1

Johnston 46

Half-time: 0-0

United: Gary Bailey, Mike Duxbury, Arthur Albiston, Norman Whiteside, Kevin Moran, Graeme Hogg, Paul McGrath, Remi Moses, Mark Hughes, Frank Stapleton, Jesper Olsen. Sub: Peter Barnes for Moses (69).

Liverpool: Bruce Grobbelaar, Steve Nicol, Jim Beglin, Mark Lawrenson, Ronnie Whelan, Alan Hansen, John Wark, Craig Johnston, Ian Rush, Jan Molby, Steve McMahon. Sub: Kevin MacDonald for Wark (69).

Attendance: 54,492

League Cup fourth round:
26 November 1985,
at Anfield.

LIVERPOOL 2

Molby 59, 60 (pen)

MANCHESTER UNITED 1

McGrath 7

Half-time: 0-1

Liverpool: Bruce Grobbelaar, Steve Nicol, Jim Beglin, Mark Lawrenson, Ronnie Whelan, Alan Hansen, Paul Walsh, Craig Johnston, Ian Rush, Jan Molby, Steve McMahon.

United: Gary Bailey, John Gidman, Clayton Blackmore, Norman Whiteside, Kevin Moran, Graeme Hogg, Paul McGrath, Gordon Strachan, Frank Stapleton, Alan Brazil, Jesper Olsen.

Attendance: 41,291

Division One:
9 February 1986,
at Anfield.

LIVERPOOL 1

Wark 41

MANCHESTER UNITED 1

C Gibson 15

Half-time: 1-1

Liverpool: Bruce Grobbelaar, Sammy Lee, Jim Beglin, Mark Lawrenson, Ronnie Whelan, Alan Hansen, Paul Walsh, Craig Johnston, Ian Rush, Jan Molby, Gary Gillespie. Sub: John Wark for Walsh (30).

United: Chris Turner, John Gidman, Arthur Albiston, Norman Whiteside, Paul McGrath, Kevin Moran, John Sivebaek, Terry Gibson, Mark Hughes, Colin Gibson, Jesper Olsen. Sub: Frank Stapleton for Olsen (77).

Attendance: 35,044

1986/7

Liverpool:
Division One runners-up, FA Cup third round, League Cup finalists.

United:
eleventh in Division One, FA Cup fourth round, League Cup third round.

Division One:
26 December 1986,
at Anfield.

LIVERPOOL 0

MANCHESTER UNITED 1

Whiteside 78

Half-time: 0-0

Liverpool: Bruce Grobbelaar, Gary Gillespie, Jim Beglin, Mark Lawrenson, Ronnie Whelan, Alan Hansen, Kenny Dalglish, Barry Venison, Ian Rush, Jan Molby, Steve McMahon.

United: Gary Walsh, John Sivebaek, Colin Gibson, Norman Whiteside, Kevin Moran, Mike Duxbury, Bryan Robson, Gordon Strachan, Frank Stapleton, Peter Davenport, Jesper Olsen.

Attendance: 40,663

Division One:
20 April 1987,
at Old Trafford.

MANCHESTER UNITED 1

Davenport 89

LIVERPOOL 0

Half-time: 0-0

United: Gary Walsh, John Sivebaek, Arthur Albiston, Remi Moses, Paul McGrath, Kevin Moran, Mike Duxbury, Gordon Strachan, Peter Davenport, Norman Whiteside, Colin Gibson. Sub: Frank Stapleton for Albiston (70).

Liverpool: Bruce Grobbelaar, Gary Gillespie, Barry Venison, Gary Ablett, Ronnie Whelan, Alan Hansen, Paul Walsh, Craig Johnston, Ian Rush, Nigel Spackman, Steve McMahon.

Attendance: 54,103

1987/8

Liverpool:
Division One Champions, FA Cup finalists, League Cup third round.

United:
runners-up in Division One, FA Cup fifth round, League Cup quarter-finalists.

Division One:
15 November 1987,
at Old Trafford.

MANCHESTER UNITED 1

Whiteside 49

LIVERPOOL 1

Aldridge 21

Half-time: 0-1

United: Gary Walsh, Viv Anderson, Colin Gibson, Mike Duxbury, Clayton Blackmore, Kevin Moran, Bryan Robson, Gordon Strachan, Brian McClair, Norman Whiteside, Jesper Olsen. Sub: Peter Davenport for Moran (70).

Liverpool: Bruce Grobbelaar, Gary Gillespie, Mark Lawrenson, Steve Nicol, Ronnie Whelan, Alan Hansen, Peter Beardsley, John Aldridge, Craig Johnston, John Barnes, Steve McMahon.

Attendance: 47,106

Division One:
4 April 1988,
at Anfield.

LIVERPOOL 3

Beardsley 38; Gillespie 41; McMahon 46

MANCHESTER UNITED 3

Robson 2, 65; Strachan 77

Half-time: 2-1

Liverpool: Bruce Grobbelaar, Gary Gillespie, Gary Ablett, Steve Nicol, Nigel Spackman, Alan Hansen, Peter Beardsley, John Aldridge, Ray Houghton, John Barnes, Steve McMahon. Sub: Craig Johnston for Aldridge (78).

United: Chris Turner, Viv Anderson, Clayton Blackmore, Steve Bruce, Paul McGrath, Mike Duxbury, Bryan Robson, Gordon Strachan, Brian McClair, Peter Davenport,

Colin Gibson. Subs: Jesper Olsen for Blackmore (54), Norman Whiteside for Duxbury (54).

Attendance: 43,497

1988/9

Liverpool:
Division One runners-up,
FA Cup winners,
League Cup fourth round.

United:
eleventh in Division One,
FA Cup quarter-finalists,
League Cup third round.

Division One:
3 September 1988,
at Anfield.

LIVERPOOL 1

Molby 38 (pen)

MANCHESTER UNITED 0

Half-time: 1-0

Liverpool: Bruce Grobbelaar, Gary Gillespie, Barry Venison, Steve Nicol, Ronnie Whelan, Jan Molby, Peter Beardsley, John Aldridge, Ray Houghton, John Barnes, Steve McMahon. Subs: Nigel Spackman for McMahon (25), Ian Rush for Aldridge (79).

United: Jim Leighton, Viv Anderson, Clayton Blackmore, Steve Bruce, Paul McGrath, Mike Duxbury, Bryan Robson, Gordon Strachan, Brian McClair, Mark Hughes, Jesper Olsen. Subs: Peter Davenport for Strachan (10), Billy Garton for McGrath (83).

Attendance: 42,026

Division One:
1 January 1989,
at Old Trafford.

MANCHESTER UNITED 3

McClair 71; Hughes 75; Beardsmore 77

LIVERPOOL 1

Barnes 70

Half-time: 0-0

United: Jim Leighton, Lee Martin, Lee Sharpe, Steve Bruce, Russell

Beardsmore, Mal Donaghy, Bryan Robson, Gordon Strachan, Brian McClair, Mark Hughes, Ralph Milne. Subs: Mark Robins for Strachan (33), Paul McGrath for Martin (66).

Liverpool: Mike Hooper, Gary Ablett, Steve Staunton, Steve Nicol, Ronnie Whelan, David Burrows, Peter Beardsley, John Aldridge, Ray Houghton, John Barnes, Steve McMahon. Sub: Jan Molby for Staunton (78).

Attendance: 44,745

1989/90

Liverpool:
Division One Champions,
FA Cup semi-finalists,
League Cup third round.

United:
thirteenth in Division One,
FA Cup winners,
League Cup third round.

Division One:
23 December 1989,
at Anfield.

LIVERPOOL 0

MANCHESTER UNITED 0

Liverpool: Bruce Grobbelaar, Glenn Hysen, Barry Venison, Gary Ablett, Ronnie Whelan, Alan Hansen, Peter Beardsley, Ray Houghton, Ian Rush, Jan Molby, Steve McMahon. Sub: Steve Nicol for Hansen (46).

United: Jim Leighton, Clayton Blackmore, Lee Martin, Steve Bruce, Mike Phelan, Gary Pallister, Bryan Robson, Paul Ince, Brian McClair, Mark Hughes, Danny Wallace. Sub: Lee Sharpe for Wallace (72).

Attendance: 37,426

Division One:
18 March 1990,
at Old Trafford.

MANCHESTER UNITED 1

Whelan og 80

LIVERPOOL 2

Barnes 15, 54 (pen)

Half-time: 0-1

United: Jim Leighton, Viv Anderson, Lee Martin, Steve Bruce, Mike Phelan, Gary Pallister, Clayton Blackmore, Paul Ince, Brian McClair, Mark Hughes, Danny Wallace. Subs: Mike Duxbury for Anderson (57), Russell Beardsmore for Wallace (57).

Liverpool: Bruce Grobbelaar, Glenn Hysen, Barry Venison, Steve Staunton, Ronnie Whelan, Alan Hansen, Peter Beardsley, Ray Houghton, Ian Rush, John Barnes, Steve McMahon.

Attendance: 46,629

1990/91

Liverpool:
Division One runners-up,
FA Cup fifth round,
League Cup third round.

United:
sixth in Division One,
FA Cup fifth round,
League Cup finalists,
European Cup-Winners'
Cup winners.

FA Charity Shield:
18 August 1990,
at Wembley.

LIVERPOOL 1

Barnes 51 (pen)

MANCHESTER UNITED 1

Blackmore 45

Half-time: 0-1

Liverpool: Bruce Grobbelaar, Glenn Hysen, David Burrows, Barry Venison, Ronnie Whelan, Gary Ablett, Peter Beardsley, Ray Houghton, Ian Rush, John Barnes, Steve McMahon. Sub: Ronny Rosenthal for Beardsley (81).

United: Les Sealey, Denis Irwin, Mal Donaghy, Steve Bruce, Mike Phelan, Gary Pallister, Clayton Blackmore, Paul Ince, Brian McClair, Mark Hughes, Danny Wallace. Sub: Mark Robins for Wallace (36).

Attendance: 66,558

Division One:
16 September 1990,
at Anfield.

LIVERPOOL 4

Beardsley 11, 31, 82;
Barnes 44

MANCHESTER UNITED 0

Half-time: 3-0

Liverpool: Bruce Grobbelaar, Glenn Hysen, David Burrows, Steve Nicol, Ronnie Whelan, Gary Gillespie, Peter Beardsley, Ray Houghton, Ian Rush, John Barnes, Steve McMahon.

United: Les Sealey, Denis Irwin, Clayton Blackmore, Steve Bruce, Mike Phelan, Gary Pallister, Neil Webb, Paul Ince, Brian McClair, Mark Hughes, Mark Robins. Subs: Mal Donaghy for Pallister (46), Russell Beardsmore for Ince (80).

Attendance: 35,726

League Cup third round:
31 October 1990,
at Old Trafford.

MANCHESTER UNITED 3

Bruce 37 (pen); Hughes 38; Sharpe 81

LIVERPOOL 1

Houghton 83

Half-time: 2-0

United: Les Sealey, Denis Irwin, Clayton Blackmore, Steve Bruce, Mike Phelan, Gary Pallister, Neil Webb, Paul Ince, Brian McClair, Mark Hughes, Lee Sharpe. Subs: Danny Wallace for Hughes (46), Mal Donaghy for Phelan (86).

Liverpool: Bruce Grobbelaar, Glenn Hysen, David Burrows, Steve Nicol, Steve Staunton, Gary Gillespie, Peter Beardsley, Ray Houghton, Ian Rush, Jan Molby, Steve McMahon. Sub: Ronny Rosenthal for Burrows (73).

Attendance: 42,033

Division One:
3 February 1991,
at Old Trafford.

MANCHESTER UNITED 1

Bruce 26 (pen)

LIVERPOOL 1

Speedie 40

Half-time: 1-1

United: Les Sealey, Denis Irwin, Clayton Blackmore, Steve Bruce, Mike Phelan, Gary Pallister, Bryan Robson, Neil Webb, Brian McClair, Mark Hughes, Lee Sharpe. Subs: Danny Wallace for Webb (51), Lee Martin for Phelan (85).

Liverpool: Bruce Grobbelaar, Glenn Hysen, David Burrows, Steve Nicol, Ronnie Whelan, Gary Ablett, David Speedie, Steve Staunton, Ian Rush, John Barnes, Steve McMahon. Sub: Jan Molby for McMahon (89).

Attendance: 43,690

1991/2

United:
Division One runners-up,
FA Cup fourth round,
League Cup winners,
European Cup-Winners'
Cup second round.

Liverpool:
sixth in Division One,
FA Cup winners,
League Cup fourth round,
UEFA Cup quarter-finalists.

Division One:
6 October 1991,
at Old Trafford.

MANCHESTER UNITED 0

LIVERPOOL 0

United: Peter Schmeichel, Mike Phelan, Denis Irwin, Steve Bruce, Clayton Blackmore, Gary Pallister, Bryan Robson, Paul Ince, Brian McClair, Mark Hughes, Ryan Giggs. Subs: Andrei Kanchelskis for Phelan (44), Mal Donaghy for Ince (88).

Liverpool: Mike Hooper, Gary Ablett, David Burrows, Steve Nicol, Rob Jones, Nicky Tanner, Dean Saunders, Ray Houghton, Ian Rush, Mark Walters, Steve McMahon. Subs: Steve McManaman for

Saunders (46), Mike Marsh for Jones (66).

Attendance: 44,997

Division One:
26 April 1992,
at Anfield.

LIVERPOOL 2

Rush 12; Walters 88

MANCHESTER UNITED 0

Half-time: 1-0

Liverpool: Mike Hooper, Rob Jones, David Burrows, Nicky Tanner, Jan Molby, Mark Wright, Dean Saunders, Ray Houghton, Ian Rush, John Barnes, Michael Thomas. Subs: Barry Venison for Tanner (22), Mark Walters for Rush (27).

United: Peter Schmeichel, Denis Irwin, Mal Donaghy, Steve Bruce, Andrei Kanchelskis, Gary Pallister, Bryan Robson, Paul Ince, Brian McClair, Mark Hughes, Ryan Giggs. Sub: Mike Phelan for Pallister (31).

Attendance: 38,669

1992/3

United:
FA Premier League Champions,
FA Cup fifth round,
League Cup second round,
UEFA Cup first round.

Liverpool:
sixth in FA Premier League,
FA Cup third round,
League Cup fourth round,
European Cup-Winners' Cup second round.

FA Premier League:
18 October 1992,
at Old Trafford.

MANCHESTER UNITED 2

Hughes 78, 90

LIVERPOOL 2

Hutchison 23; Rush 44

Half-time: 0-2

United: Peter Schmeichel, Paul Parker, Denis Irwin,

Steve Bruce, Darren Ferguson, Gary Pallister, Andrei Kanchelskis, Paul Ince, Brian McClair, Mark Hughes, Ryan Giggs. Sub: Clayton Blackmore for Kanchelskis (66).

Liverpool: Bruce Grobbelaar, Mike Marsh, David Burrows, Steve Nicol, Torben Piechnik, Don Hutchison, Steve McManaman, Jamie Redknapp, Ian Rush, Jan Molby, Ronny Rosenthal. Subs: Michael Thomas for Redknapp (72), Nicky Tanner for Molby (82).

Attendance: 33,243

FA Premier League:
6 March 1993,
at Anfield.

LIVERPOOL 1

Rush 50

MANCHESTER UNITED 2

Hughes 42; McClair 56

Half-time: 0-1

Liverpool: David James, Jamie Redknapp, Rob Jones, Steve Nicol, Mark Wright, Stig Inge Bjornebye, Steve McManaman, Don Hutchison, Mark Walters, John Barnes, Paul Stewart. Subs: Ian Rush for Stewart (43), David Burrows for Walters (78).

United: Peter Schmeichel, Paul Parker, Denis Irwin, Steve Bruce, Lee Sharpe, Gary Pallister, Andrei Kanchelskis, Paul Ince, Brian McClair, Mark Hughes, Ryan Giggs.

Attendance: 44,374

1993/4

United:
FA Premiership Champions, FA Cup winners, League Cup finalists,
European Cup second round.

Liverpool:
eighth in FA Premiership,
FA Cup third round,
League Cup fourth round.

FA Premiership:
4 January 1994,
at Anfield.

LIVERPOOL 3

Clough 25, 38; Ruddock 79

MANCHESTER UNITED 3

Bruce 9; Giggs 20; Irwin 24

Half-time: 2-3

Liverpool: Bruce Grobbelaar, Rob Jones, Julian Dicks, Jamie Redknapp, Mark Wright, Neil Ruddock, Nigel Clough, John Barnes, Ian Rush, Steve McManaman, Robbie Fowler. Sub: Stig Inge Bjornebye for McManaman (78).

United: Peter Schmeichel, Paul Parker, Denis Irwin, Steve Bruce, Roy Keane, Gary Pallister, Eric Cantona, Paul Ince, Brian McClair, Andrei Kanchelskis, Ryan Giggs.

Attendance: 42,795

FA Premiership:
30 March 1994,
at Old Trafford.

MANCHESTER UNITED 1

Ince 37

LIVERPOOL 0

Half-time: 1-0

United: Peter Schmeichel, Paul Parker, Denis Irwin, Steve Bruce, Lee Sharpe, Gary Pallister, Eric Cantona, Paul Ince, Roy Keane, Mark Hughes, Andrei Kanchelskis. Sub: Ryan Giggs for Sharpe (66), Bryan Robson for Cantona (73).

Liverpool: David James, Rob Jones, Julian Dicks, Steve Nicol, Ronnie Whelan, Neil Ruddock, Jamie Redknapp, John Barnes, Ian Rush, Steve McManaman, Michael Thomas. Sub: Robbie Fowler for Thomas (81).

Attendance: 44,751

1994/5

United:
FA Premiership runners-up,
FA Cup finalists,
League Cup third round,
European Champions League first stage.

Liverpool:
fourth in FA Premiership,
FA Cup quarter-finalists,
League Cup winners.

FA Premiership:
17 September 1994,
at Old Trafford.

MANCHESTER UNITED 2

Kanchelskis 72; McClair 74

LIVERPOOL 0

Half-time: 0-0

United: Peter Schmeichel, David May, Denis Irwin, Steve Bruce, Lee Sharpe, Gary Pallister, Andrei Kanchelskis, Paul Ince, Eric Cantona, Mark Hughes, Ryan Giggs. Sub: Brian McClair for Hughes (60).

Liverpool: David James, Rob Jones, Stig Inge Bjornebye, John Scales, Neil Ruddock, Jan Molby, Jamie Redknapp, Steve McManaman, Ian Rush, John Barnes, Robbie Fowler. Sub: Phil Babb for Molby (70).

Attendance: 43,740

FA Premiership:
19 March 1995,
at Anfield.

LIVERPOOL 2

Redknapp 25, Bruce og 86

MANCHESTER UNITED 0

Half-time: 1-0

Liverpool: David James, John Scales, Stig Inge Bjornebye, Neil Ruddock, Mark Wright, Phil Babb, Steve McManaman, Jamie Redknapp, Ian Rush, John Barnes, Robbie Fowler. Subs: Michael Thomas for Barnes (61), Mark Walters for Rush (88).

United: Peter Schmeichel, Roy Keane, Denis Irwin, Steve Bruce, Lee Sharpe, Gary Pallister, Andrei Kanchelskis, Paul Ince,

Brian McClair, Mark Hughes, Ryan Giggs. Subs: Andy Cole for Sharpe (45), Nicky Butt for Keane (84).

Attendance: 38,906

1995/6

United:
FA Premiership Champions,
FA Cup winners,
League Cup second round,
UEFA Cup first round.

Liverpool:
third in FA Premiership,
FA Cup finalists,
League Cup fourth round,
UEFA Cup second round.

FA Premiership:
1 October 1995,
at Old Trafford.

MANCHESTER UNITED 2

Butt 2; Cantona 71 (pen)

LIVERPOOL 2

Fowler 35, 54

Half-time: 1-1

United: Peter Schmeichel, Gary Neville, Phil Neville, Steve Bruce, Lee Sharpe, Gary Pallister, Eric Cantona, Nicky Butt, Andy Cole, Roy Keane, Ryan Giggs. Subs: David Beckham for Butt (45), Paul Scholes for Phil Neville (73).

Liverpool: David James, John Scales, Steve Harkness, Jason McAteer, Neil Ruddock, Phil Babb, Michael Thomas, Jamie Redknapp, Ian Rush, Robbie Fowler, Steve McManaman.

Attendance: 34,934

FA Premiership:
17 December 1995,
at Anfield.

LIVERPOOL 2

Fowler 44, 87

MANCHESTER UNITED 0

Half-time: 1-0

Liverpool: David James, Rob Jones, Steve Harkness, Jason McAteer, Mark Wright, John Scales, Michael Thomas,

Stan Collymore, Robbie Fowler, John Barnes, Steve McManaman.

United: Peter Schmeichel, Gary Neville, Denis Irwin, Steve Bruce, Lee Sharpe, David May, Eric Cantona, David Beckham, Brian McClair, Andy Cole, Ryan Giggs. Sub: Paul Scholes for Cole (53).

Attendance: 40,546

FA Cup Final:
11 May 1996,
at Wembley.

MANCHESTER UNITED 1
Cantona 86
LIVERPOOL 0
Half-time: 0-0

United: Peter Schmeichel, Phil Neville, Denis Irwin, David May, David Beckham, Gary Pallister, Eric Cantona, Nicky Butt, Andy Cole, Roy Keane, Ryan Giggs. Subs: Paul Scholes for Cole (64), Gary Neville for Beckham (89).

Liverpool: David James, Rob Jones, John Scales, Jason McAteer, Mark Wright, Phil Babb, Jamie Redknapp, Stan Collymore, Robbie Fowler, John Barnes, Steve McManaman. Subs: Ian Rush for Collymore (75), Michael Thomas for Jones (86).

Attendance: 79,007

1996/7

United:
FA Premiership Champions, FA Cup fourth round, League Cup fourth round, European Cup semi-finalists;

Liverpool:
fourth in FA Premiership, FA Cup fourth round, League Cup quarter-finalists, European Cup-Winners' Cup semi-finalists.

FA Premiership:
12 October 1996,
at Old Trafford.

MANCHESTER UNITED 1
Beckham 23
LIVERPOOL 0
Half-time: 1-0

United: Peter Schmeichel, Gary Neville, Denis Irwin, David May, Karel Poborsky, Ronny Johnsen, Eric Cantona, Nicky Butt, Ole Gunnar Solskjaer, David Beckham, Jordi Cruyff. Subs: Paul Scholes for Poborsky (55), Ryan Giggs for Solskjaer (81).

Liverpool: David James, Stig Inge Bjornebye, John Scales, Jason McAteer, Dominic Matteo, Phil Babb, Steve McManaman, Stan Collymore, Michael Thomas, John Barnes, Patrik Berger. Sub: Jamie Redknapp for Scales (81).

Attendance: 55,128

FA Premiership:
19 April 1997,
at Anfield.

LIVERPOOL 1
Barnes 19
MANCHESTER UNITED 3
Pallister 13, 42; Cole 63
Half-time: 1-2

Liverpool: David James, Stig Inge Bjornebye, Bjorn Tore Kvarme, Jason McAteer, Mark Wright, Steve Harkness, Steve McManaman, Michael Thomas, Robbie Fowler, John Barnes, Jamie Redknapp. Subs: Stan Collymore for McAteer (51), Patrik Berger for Barnes (68).

United: Peter Schmeichel, Gary Neville, Phil Neville, Ronny Johnsen, Gary Pallister, Roy Keane, Nicky Butt, Eric Cantona, David Beckham, Andy Cole, Paul Scholes. Sub: Brian McClair for Scholes (81).

Attendance: 40,892

1997/8

United:
FA Premiership runners-up, FA Cup fifth round, League Cup third round, European Cup quarter-finalists.

Liverpool:
third in FA Premiership, FA Cup third round, League Cup semi-finalists, UEFA Cup second round.

FA Premiership:
6 December 1997,
at Anfield.

LIVERPOOL 1
Fowler 60 (pen)
MANCHESTER UNITED 3
Cole 51, 74; Beckham 70
Half-time: 0-0

Liverpool: David James, Jason McAteer, Stig Inge Bjornebye, Bjorn Tore Kvarme, Dominic Matteo, Steve McManaman, Jamie Redknapp, Jamie Carragher, Oyvind Leonhardsen, Michael Owen, Robbie Fowler. Subs: Patrik Berger for Kvarme (61), Karlheinz Riedle for Bjornebye (72).

United: Peter Schmeichel, Gary Neville, Gary Pallister, Henning Berg, Phil Neville, David Beckham, Nicky Butt, Ronny Johnsen, Ryan Giggs, Teddy Sheringham, Andy Cole.

Attendance: 41,027

FA Premiership:
10 April 1998,
at Old Trafford.

MANCHESTER UNITED 1
Johnsen 11
LIVERPOOL 1
Owen 35
Half-time: 1-1

United: Peter Schmeichel, Gary Neville, Gary Pallister, Ronny Johnsen, Denis Irwin, Phil Neville, David Beckham, Paul Scholes, Nicky Butt, Ryan Giggs, Andy Cole. Subs: Ben

Thornley for Giggs (39), David May for Johnsen (43), Teddy Sheringham for P Neville (66).

Liverpool: Brad Friedel, Rob Jones, Dominic Matteo, Phil Babb, Steve Harkness, Steve McManaman, Paul Ince, Jamie Redknapp, Oyvind Leonhardsen, Danny Murphy, Michael Owen. Sub: Patrik Berger for Murphy (74).

Attendance: 55, 171

1998/9

FA Premiership:
24 September 1998,
at Old Trafford.

MANCHESTER UNITED 2
Irwin 18 (pen); Scholes 79
LIVERPOOL 0
Half-time: 1-0

United: Peter Schmeichel, Phil Neville, Jaap Stam, Gary Neville, Denis Irwin, David Beckham, Roy Keane, Paul Scholes, Ryan Giggs, Dwight Yorke, Ole Gunnar Solskjaer. Subs: Andy Cole for Solskjaer (69), Nicky Butt for Scholes (88).

Liverpool: Brad Friedel, Jason McAteer, Jamie Carragher, Phil Babb, Stig Inge Bjornebye, Steve McManaman, Paul Ince, Jamie Redknapp, Patrik Berger, Michael Owen, Karlheinz Riedle. Sub: Robbie Fowler for Riedle (74).

Attendance: 55,181

League matches except where indicated

Man Utd 5 Liverpool 0
(11 Sept 1946)

Liverpool 1 Man Utd 0
(3 May 1947)

Man Utd 2 Liverpool 0
(27 Aug 1947)

Liverpool 2 Man Utd 2
(3 Sept 1947)

Man Utd 3 Liverpool 0
(24 Jan 1948, FA Cup)

Man Utd 0 Liverpool 0
(25 Dec 1948)

Liverpool 0 Man Utd 2
(27 Dec 1948)

Liverpool 1 Man Utd 1
(7 Sept 1949)

Man Utd 0 Liverpool 0
(15 March 1950)

Liverpool 2 Man Utd 1
(23 Aug 1950)

Man Utd 1 Liverpool 0
(30 Aug 1950)

Liverpool 0 Man Utd 0
(24 Nov 1951)

Man Utd 4 Liverpool 0
(12 April 1952)

Liverpool 1 Man Utd 2
(13 Dec 1952)

Man Utd 3 Liverpool 1
(20 April 1953)

Liverpool 4 Man Utd 4
(22 Aug 1953)

Man Utd 5 Liverpool 1
(19 Dec 1953)

Liverpool relegated.

Liverpool 1 Man Utd 3 (30 Jan 1960, FA Cup)

Man Utd 3 Liverpool 3 (10 Nov 1962)

Liverpool 1 Man Utd 0
(13 April 1963)

Man Utd 0 Liverpool 1
(23 Nov 1963)

Liverpool 3 Man Utd 0
(4 April 1964)

Liverpool 0 Man Utd 2
(31 Oct 1964)

Man Utd 3 Liverpool 0
(24 April 1965)

Man Utd 2 Liverpool 2
(14 Aug 1965,
Charity Shield)

Man Utd 2 Liverpool 0
(9 Oct 1965)

Liverpool 2 Man Utd 1
(1 Jan 1966)

Man Utd 2 Liverpool 2
(10 Dec 1966)

Liverpool 0 Man Utd 0
(25 March 1967)

Liverpool 1 Man Utd 2
(11 Nov 1967)

Man Utd 1 Liverpool 2
(6 April 1968)

Liverpool 2 Man Utd 0
(12 Oct 1968)

Man Utd 1 Liverpool 0
(14 Dec 1968)

Man Utd 1 Liverpool 0
(13 Sept 1969)

Liverpool 1 Man Utd 4
(13 Dec 1969)

Liverpool 1 Man Utd 1
(5 Sept 1970)

Man Utd 0 Liverpool 2
(19 April 1971)

Liverpool 2 Man Utd 2
(25 Sept 1971)

Man Utd 0 Liverpool 3
(3 April 1972)

Liverpool 2 Man Utd 0
(15 Aug 1972)

Man Utd 2 Liverpool 0
(11 Nov 1972)

Man Utd 0 Liverpool 0
(29 Sept 1973)

Liverpool 2 Man Utd 0
(22 Dec 1973)

Man Utd relegated.

Liverpool 3 Man Utd 1
(8 Nov 1975)

Man Utd 0 Liverpool 0
(18 Feb 1976)

Man Utd 0 Liverpool 0
(16 Feb 1977)

Liverpool 1 Man Utd 0
(3 May 1977)

Man Utd 2 Liverpool 1
(21 May 1977,
FA Cup Final)

Man Utd 0 Liverpool 0
(13 Aug 1977,
Charity Shield)

Man Utd 2 Liverpool 0
(1 Oct 1977)

Liverpool 3 Man Utd 1
(25 Feb 1978)

Man Utd 0 Liverpool 3
(26 Dec 1978)

Man Utd 2 Liverpool 2
(31 March 1979,
FA Cup SF)

Man Utd 1 Liverpool 0
(4 April 1979,
FA Cup SF replay)

Liverpool 2 Man Utd 0
(14 April 1979)

Liverpool 2 Man Utd 0
(26 Dec 1979)

Man Utd 2 Liverpool 1
(5 April 1980)

Man Utd 0 Liverpool 0
(26 Dec 1980)

Liverpool 0 Man Utd 1
(14 April 1981)

Liverpool 1 Man Utd 2
(24 Oct 1981)

Man Utd 0 Liverpool 1
(7 April 1982)

Liverpool 0 Man Utd 0
(16 Oct 1982)

Man Utd 1 Liverpool 1
(26 Feb 1983)

Liverpool 2 Man Utd 1
(26 March 1983,
League Cup Final)

Man Utd 4 Liverpool 3
(3 Aug 1983,
Testimonial in Belfast)

Man Utd 2 Liverpool 0
(20 Aug 1983,
Charity Shield)

Man Utd 1 Liverpool 0
(24 Sept 1983)

Liverpool 1 Man Utd 1
(2 Jan 1984)

Man Utd 1 Liverpool 1
(22 Sept 1984)

Liverpool 0 Man Utd 1
(31 March 1985)

Man Utd 2 Liverpool 2
(13 April 1985, FA Cup SF)

Man Utd 2 Liverpool 1
(17 April 1985, FA Cup
SF replay)

Man Utd 1 Liverpool 1
(19 Oct 1985)

Liverpool 2 Man Utd 1
(26 Nov 1985,
League Cup)

Liverpool 1 Man Utd 1
(9 Feb 1986)

Liverpool 0 Man Utd 1
(26 Dec 1986)

Man Utd 1 Liverpool 0
(20 April 1987)

Man Utd 1 Liverpool 1
(15 Nov 1987)

Liverpool 3 Man Utd 3
(4 April 1988)

Liverpool 1 Man Utd 0
(3 Sept 1988)

Man Utd 3 Liverpool 1
(1 Jan 1989)

Liverpool 0 Man Utd 0
(23 Dec 1989)

Man Utd 1 Liverpool 2
(18 March 1990)

Man Utd 1 Liverpool 1
(18 Aug 1990,
Charity Shield)

Liverpool 4 Man Utd 0
(16 Sept 1990)

Man Utd 3 Liverpool 1
(31 Oct 1990, League Cup)

Man Utd 1 Liverpool 1
(3 Feb 1991)

Man Utd 0 Liverpool 0
(6 Oct 1991)

Liverpool 2 Man Utd 0
(26 April 1992)

Man Utd 2 Liverpool 2
(18 Oct 1992)

Liverpool 1 Man Utd 2
(6 March 1993)

Liverpool 3 Man Utd 3
(4 Jan 1994)

Man Utd 1 Liverpool 0
(30 March 1994)

Man Utd 2 Liverpool 0
(17 Sept 1994)

Liverpool 2 Man Utd 0
(19 March 1995)

Man Utd 2 Liverpool 2
(1 Oct 1995)

Liverpool 2 Man Utd 0
(17 Dec 1995)

Man Utd 1 Liverpool 0
(11 May 1996,
FA Cup Final)

Man Utd 1 Liverpool 0
(12 Oct 1996)

Liverpool 1 Man Utd 3
(19 April 1997)

Liverpool 1 Man Utd 3
(6 Dec 1997)

Man Utd 1 Liverpool 1
(10 April 1998)

Man Utd 2 Liverpool 0
(24 Sept 1998)

Man Utd: 41 wins
Liverpool: 27 wins
Draws: 35